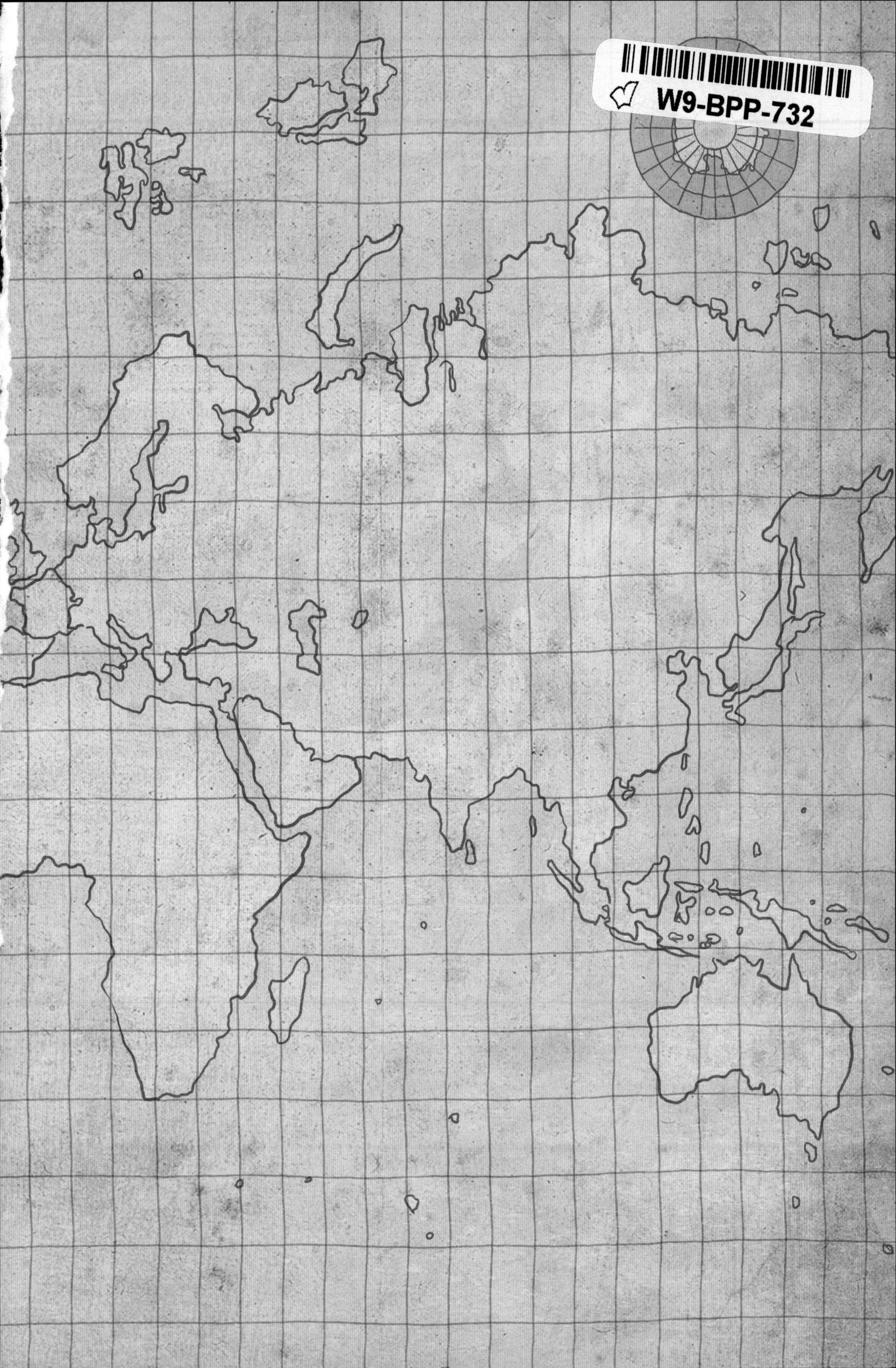

Luciana Cimino   Sergio Algozzino
NELLIE BLY

Translated by Laura Garofalo

Abrams ComicArts • New York

I would like to express my thanks to Luciana, who pulled me into Nellie's world, and to Simona who held me in high esteem: it is a great honor for me to visually launch this series.

Sergio

My thanks to Tonino, for his passion; to Rosanna, for her perseverance; to Giuseppe, for his ravenous curiosity. I would also like to express my thanks to Sergio, who has given life to the Nellie I had in mind; to Simona and Massimiliano, for believing in this story; and to Elena, a wonderful friend who has brought us together. Finally, of course, my gratitude to David Randall, the most remarkable teacher.

Luciana

Originally published in Italian in 2019 by Tunué
ABRAMS EDITION:
Editor: Charlotte Greenbaum
Designer: Megan Kelchner
Managing Editor: Mary O'Mara
Production Manager: Alison Gervais

Cataloging-in-Publication Data has been applied for and may be obtained from the Library of Congress.

ISBN 978-1-4197-5017-5
ebook ISBN 978-1-64700-101-8

Printed and bound in China
10 9 8 7 6 5 4 3 2 1

Abrams ComicArts books are available at special discounts when purchased in quantity for premiums and promotions as well as fundraising or educational use. Special editions can also be created to specification. For details, contact specialsales@abramsbooks.com or the address below.

Abrams ComicArts® is a registered trademark of Harry N. Abrams, Inc.

ABRAMS The Art of Books
195 Broadway, New York, NY 10007
abramsbooks.com

INTRODUCTION

by *David Randall*

There are many remarkable things about Nellie Bly, but perhaps most extraordinary is how modern she seems. She was born in 1864, when social convention limited women's ambitions and achievements to producing children, running the household, and domestic slavery. It is no coincidence that throughout the Victorian period, women's clothes—their crinolines and corsets, their bustles and bodices—were designed to limit, rather than liberate, movement. A woman's life, as well as her waist, was constricted.

So it took a woman of rare character and determination to break free of this restraint and live the life her talents warranted. Few did this as successfully as the daughter of a rural judge from Pennsylvania named Elizabeth Jane Cochran, better known to us by her professional name, Nellie Bly. At a time when most of her contemporaries were obliged to obey their husband's every word and whim and women were banned from virtually every occupation except being a teacher or a servant, Nellie became one of the few female journalists of her time. She defied the chauvinism of editors to become a news reporter; carried out two investigations that made her the most celebrated journalist in America; married, took over her husband's business, and expanded it into one of the country's leading companies; pioneered welfare schemes for her workers;

and then, after an embezzler ruined the firm, she rebuilt her life as a columnist helping people in trouble. No young woman of today could possibly have a better role model than this versatile and resourceful journalist born more than 150 years ago.

Appropriately enough, what triggered Nellie's career was a newspaper column in early 1885 that urged young women to forget any idea of working for a living and instead be "little angels of the home." A few days later the editor received a letter disputing this and describing the lack of opportunities for women. It was simply signed "Lonely Orphan Girl." The editor was more enlightened than his columnist and liked the argumentative tone of the letter. So he placed an announcement in his paper appealing for "Lonely Orphan Girl" to come forward. And so it was that twenty-year-old Miss Cochran came to his office. He asked for articles, which she supplied, and was soon hired as the first woman on his staff. She was an immediate hit with readers, and duly moved to New York to try to break into the big time.

However, once again she found doors and minds closed to the thought of a woman reporter, until, after much frustration, she tricked her way into the offices of the *New York World* and demanded the editor listen to her ideas. He accepted one of them, and so Nellie embarked on one of the most extraordinary pieces of investigative reporting in journalism history: she feigned madness to get herself locked up in an asylum for mentally ill women where she had heard great cruelties were inflicted on the patients. In the ten days she spent there she saw beatings, inmates forced to sit in silence on hard benches in a freezing room for fourteen hours at a time, inmates who had their heads forced under cold water if they dared speak, as well as rancid food and constant torment by the staff. Liberated by a colleague, she emerged to write her report, which was a sensation. The city government gave an extra $1 million to care for the mentally ill, her story was turned into a book, and Nellie was given

what she wanted most: the offer of a job as a reporter at the *World*. She began a series of undercover investigations—posing variously as a servant in search of work, an unmarried mother, a lonely heart looking for a husband, and more—none of which, to this day, have ever been outdone. Then came the second major project, which would seal her reputation as the preeminent reporter in America. Nellie set out to travel around the world in fewer than eighty days, then thought to be impossible. She did it in seventy-two days, six hours, eleven minutes, and fourteen seconds—and became an instant celebrity. Her picture was everywhere, Nellie Bly dolls appeared in shops, a song was written about her, and her journey was even turned into a board game.

In 1895, at the age of thirty-one, in the strangest move of her whole life, she married a businessman thirty-eight years her senior. Four years later she took over the running of his companies, turning a loss-making business into one that made the equivalent of millions in profit. She invented new steel-making processes and transformed the pay and conditions of the workers, but trusted the finances to a Major Edward Gilman. Unfortunately, he was a fraud who stole all the profits, and in 1912 Nellie's businesses went bust. At the age of forty-eight, she was left with virtually nothing. So she returned to journalism, reporting for top New York papers before starting her next great project: a column where she investigated, and tried to solve, the problems of ordinary readers. She found jobs for the unemployed, homes for unwanted babies, started a self-help group for lonely mothers, and did much more. Soon she had a small army of secretaries working with her as she acted as a sort of journalistic fairy godmother. Sadly, she drove herself too hard and, in 1922, she developed pneumonia and passed away less than a month later.

A few years ago, I wrote a book called *Tredici giornalisti quasi perfetti* about the best reporters who've ever lived. Nellie was obviously included. She was a brilliant reporter, but, more than that, she never accepted the restrictions that life and circumstance imposed on her, but always rose above them. The book you now have, with words by Luciana Cimino and illustrations by Sergio Algozzino, is a wonderful evocation of Nellie's character and spirit. I hope it inspires young women to be as Nellie was: forever the author of her own destiny.

David Randall is a British journalist and author. He studied history at Clare College, Cambridge, and worked in national newspapers for more than thirty years as an editor and writer, chiefly for *The Observer* and *The Independent*. His books, published in more than fifteen languages, include *The Universal Journalist* and *Great Reporters*. He is married with four sons, has four grandchildren, and lives in London.

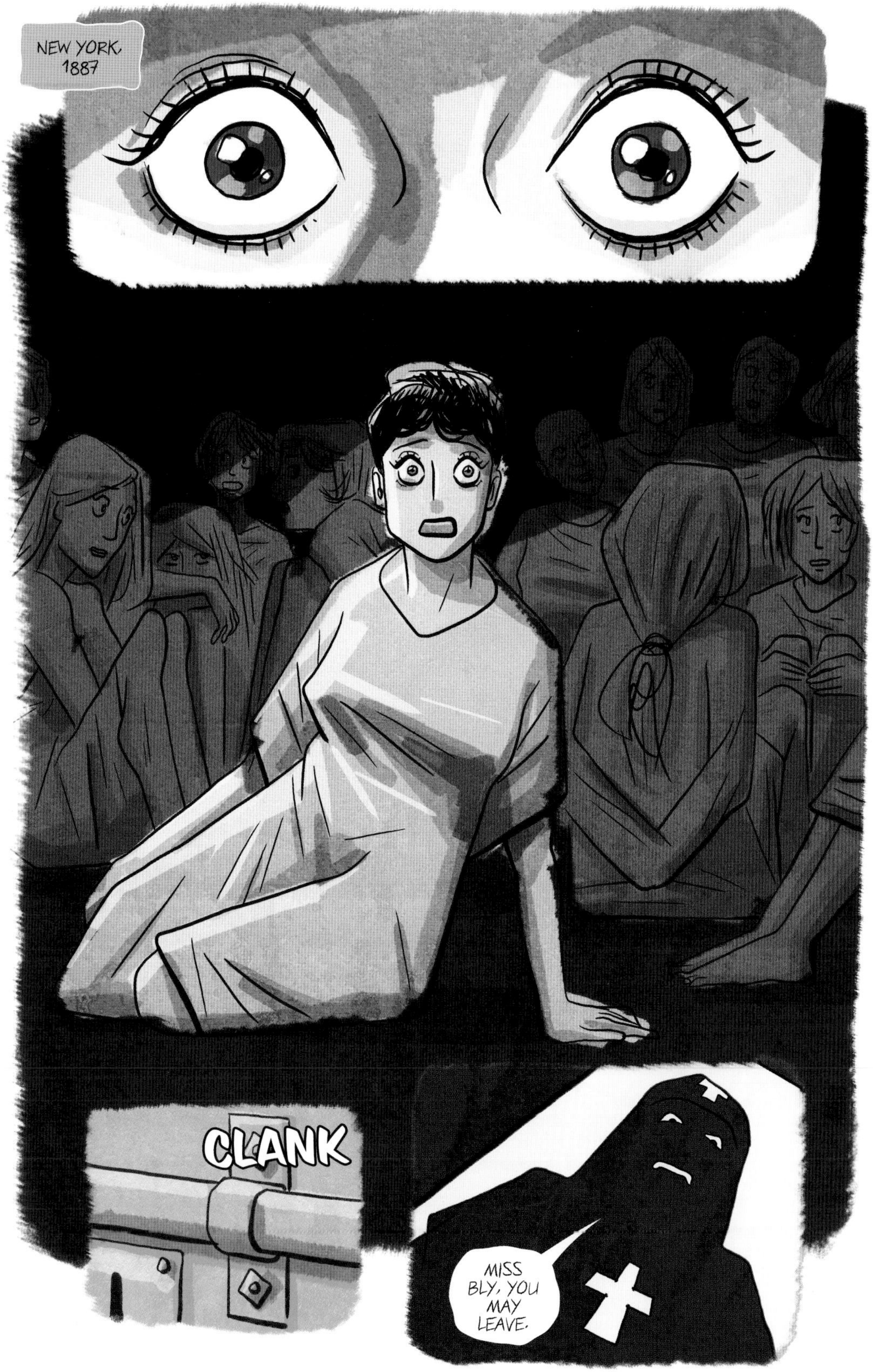
NEW YORK, 1887
CLANK
MISS BLY, YOU MAY LEAVE.

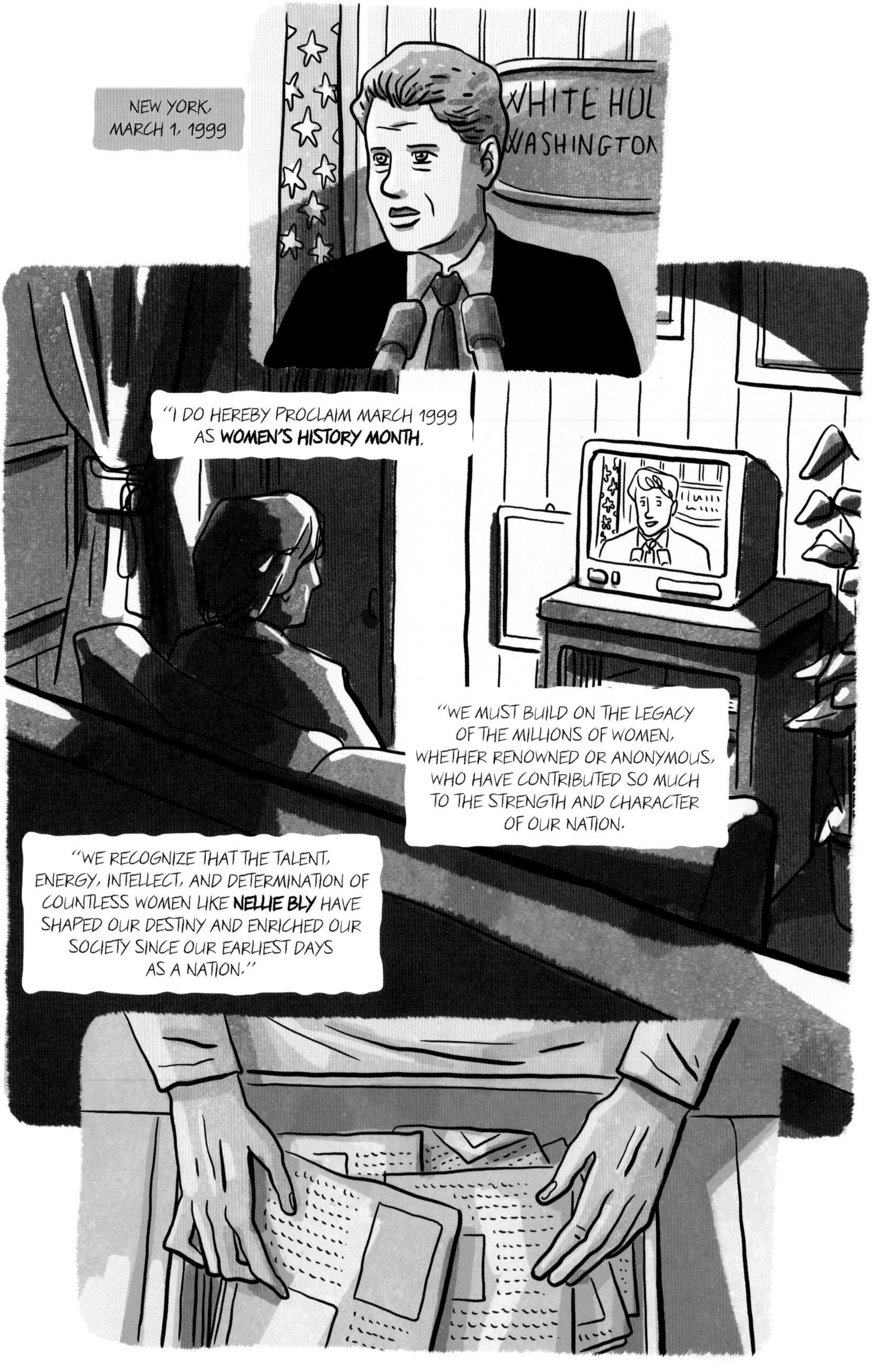
NEW YORK, MARCH 1, 1999
WHITE HOU
WASHINGTON
"I DO HEREBY PROCLAIM MARCH 1999 AS **WOMEN'S HISTORY MONTH**.
"WE MUST BUILD ON THE LEGACY OF THE MILLIONS OF WOMEN, WHETHER RENOWNED OR ANONYMOUS, WHO HAVE CONTRIBUTED SO MUCH TO THE STRENGTH AND CHARACTER OF OUR NATION.
"WE RECOGNIZE THAT THE TALENT, ENERGY, INTELLECT, AND DETERMINATION OF COUNTLESS WOMEN LIKE **NELLIE BLY** HAVE SHAPED OUR DESTINY AND ENRICHED OUR SOCIETY SINCE OUR EARLIEST DAYS AS A NATION."

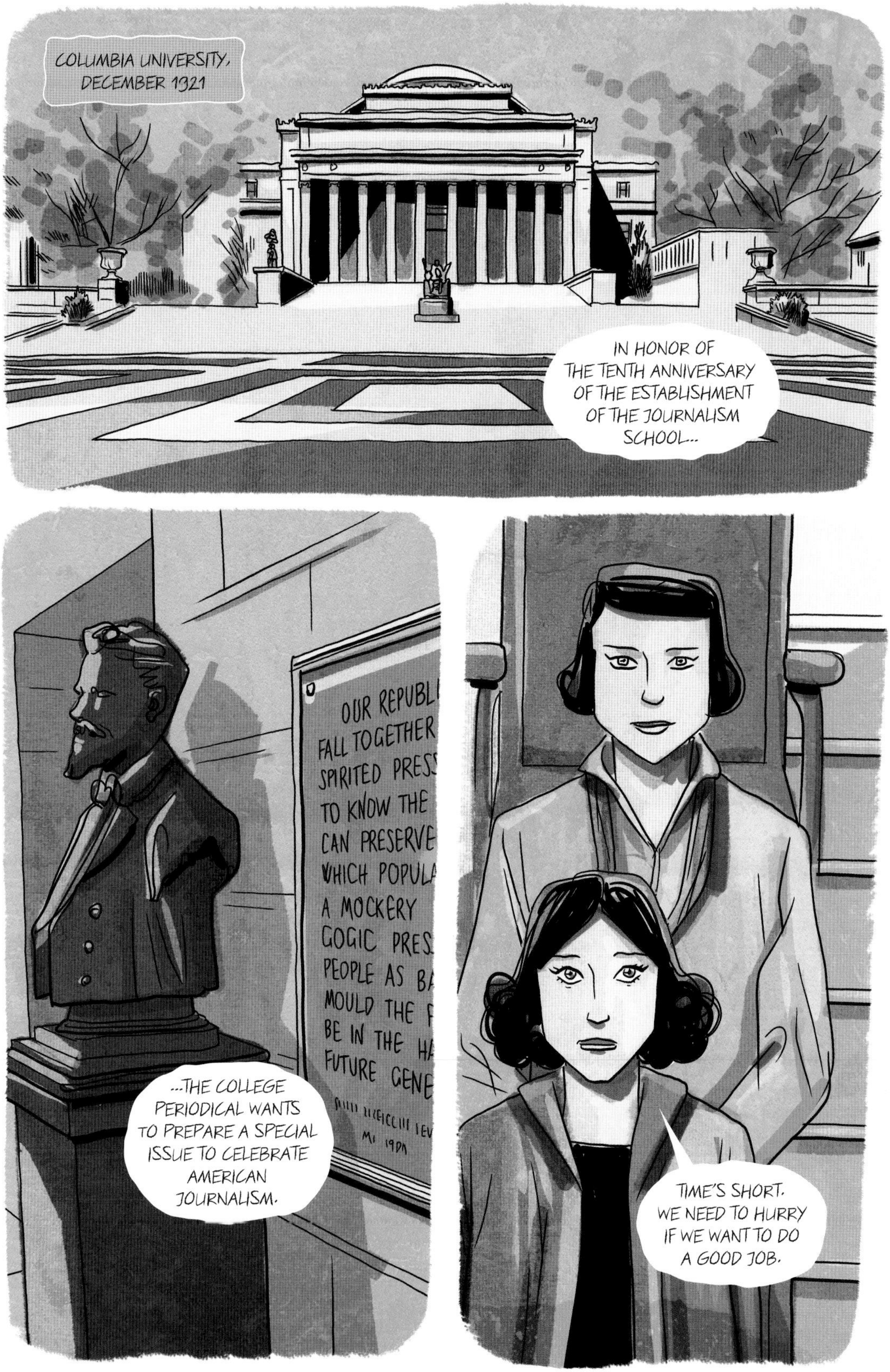
COLUMBIA UNIVERSITY, DECEMBER 1921
IN HONOR OF THE TENTH ANNIVERSARY OF THE ESTABLISHMENT OF THE JOURNALISM SCHOOL...
OUR REPUBL
FALL TOGETHER
SPIRITED PRESS
TO KNOW THE
CAN PRESERVE
WHICH POPULA
A MOCKERY
GOGIC PRESS
PEOPLE AS BA
MOULD THE
BE IN THE HA
FUTURE GENE
...THE COLLEGE PERIODICAL WANTS TO PREPARE A SPECIAL ISSUE TO CELEBRATE AMERICAN JOURNALISM.
TIME'S SHORT. WE NEED TO HURRY IF WE WANT TO DO A GOOD JOB.

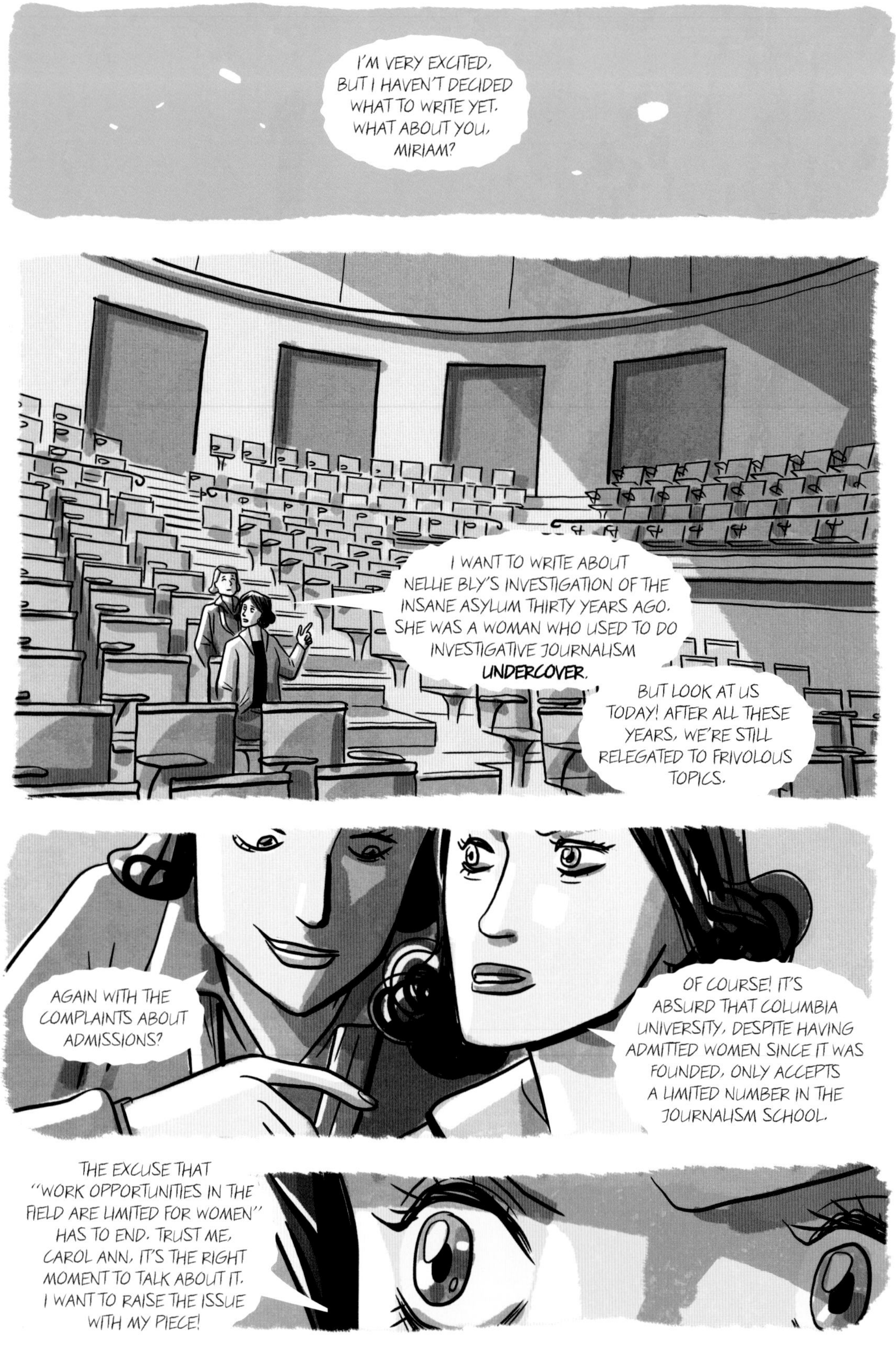
I'M VERY EXCITED, BUT I HAVEN'T DECIDED WHAT TO WRITE YET. WHAT ABOUT YOU, MIRIAM?
I WANT TO WRITE ABOUT NELLIE BLY'S INVESTIGATION OF THE INSANE ASYLUM THIRTY YEARS AGO. SHE WAS A WOMAN WHO USED TO DO INVESTIGATIVE JOURNALISM **UNDERCOVER**.
BUT LOOK AT US TODAY! AFTER ALL THESE YEARS, WE'RE STILL RELEGATED TO FRIVOLOUS TOPICS.
AGAIN WITH THE COMPLAINTS ABOUT ADMISSIONS?
OF COURSE! IT'S ABSURD THAT COLUMBIA UNIVERSITY, DESPITE HAVING ADMITTED WOMEN SINCE IT WAS FOUNDED, ONLY ACCEPTS A LIMITED NUMBER IN THE JOURNALISM SCHOOL.
THE EXCUSE THAT "WORK OPPORTUNITIES IN THE FIELD ARE LIMITED FOR WOMEN" HAS TO END. TRUST ME, CAROL ANN, IT'S THE RIGHT MOMENT TO TALK ABOUT IT. I WANT TO RAISE THE ISSUE WITH MY PIECE!

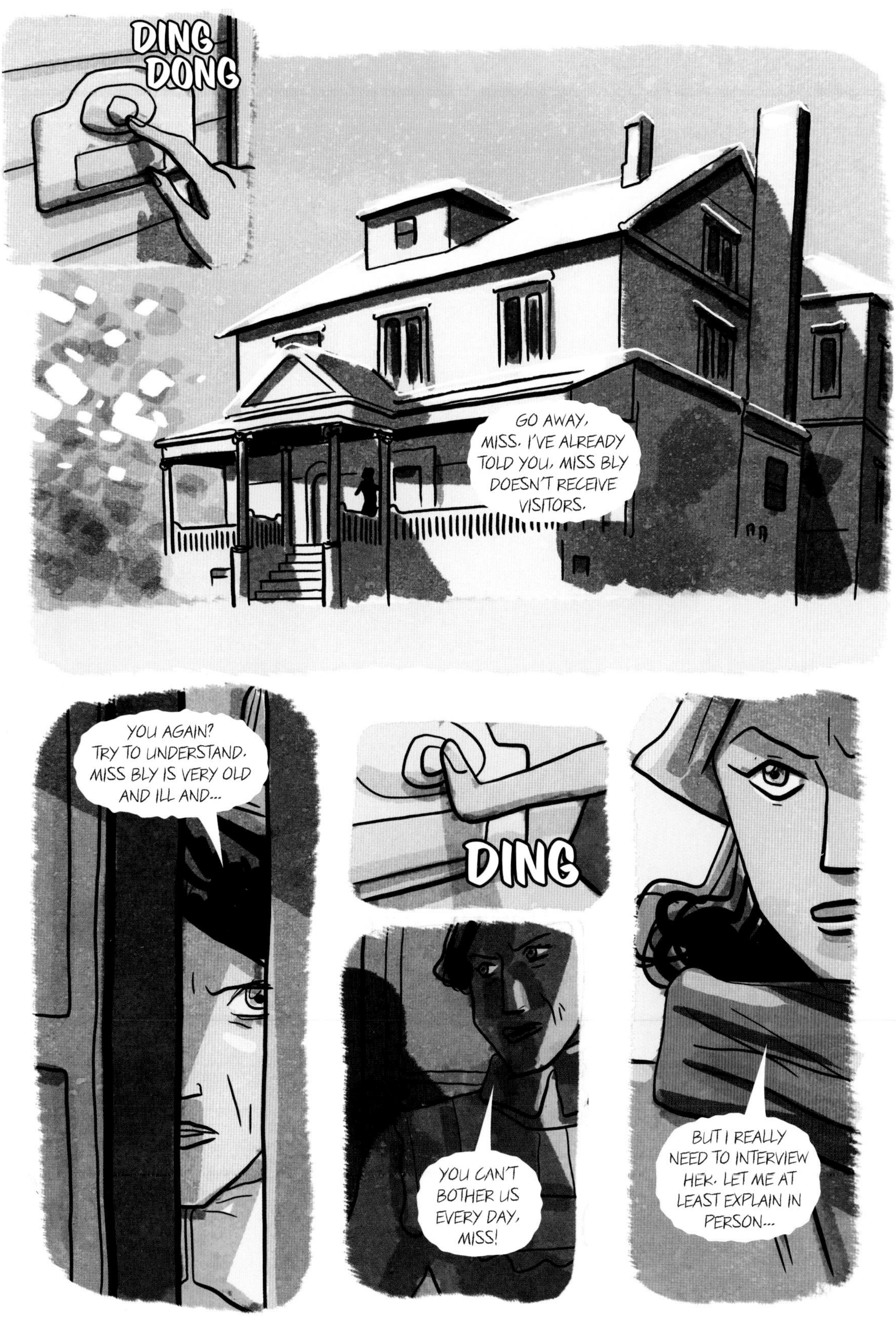
DING DONG
GO AWAY, MISS. I'VE ALREADY TOLD YOU, MISS BLY DOESN'T RECEIVE VISITORS.
YOU AGAIN? TRY TO UNDERSTAND. MISS BLY IS VERY OLD AND ILL AND...
DING
YOU CAN'T BOTHER US EVERY DAY, MISS!
BUT I REALLY NEED TO INTERVIEW HER. LET ME AT LEAST EXPLAIN IN PERSON...

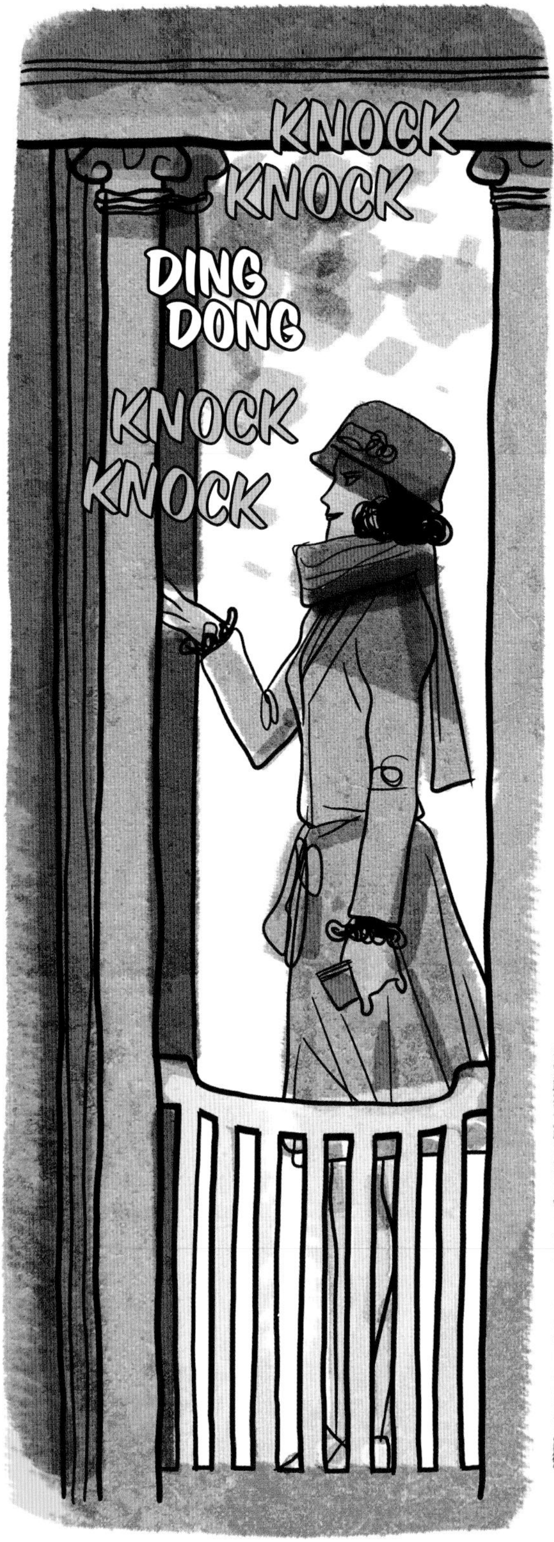
KNOCK
KNOCK
DING
DONG
KNOCK
KNOCK

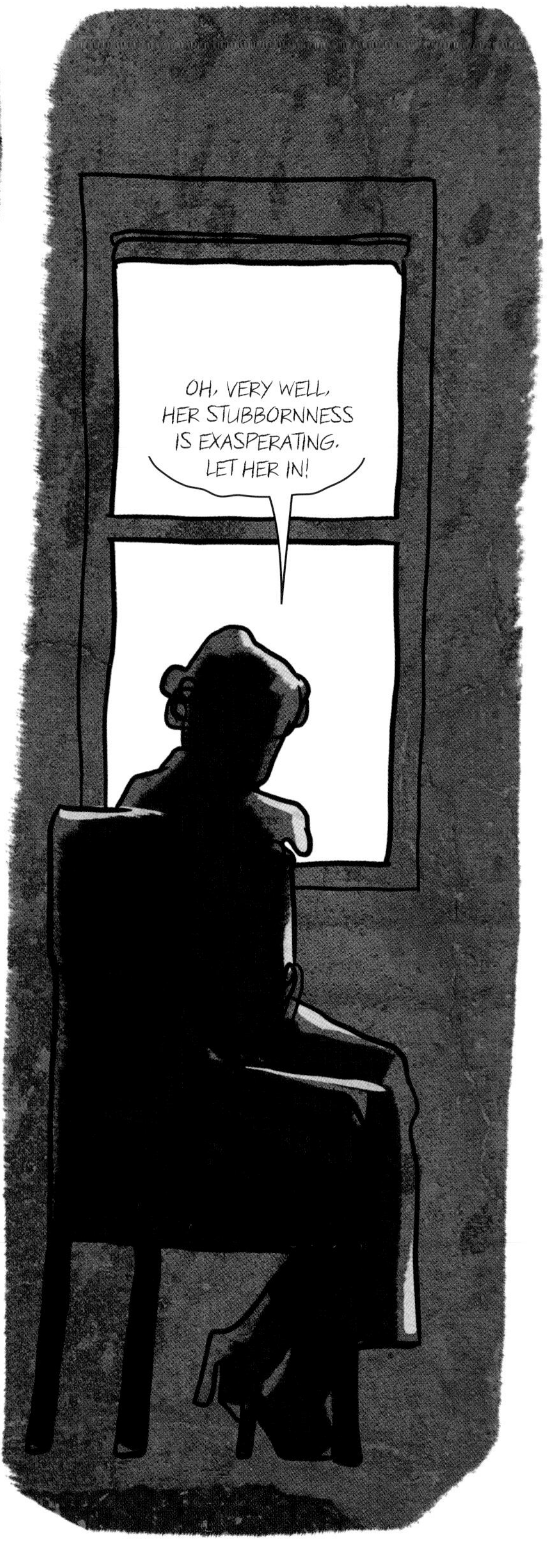
OH, VERY WELL, HER STUBBORNNESS IS EXASPERATING. LET HER IN!

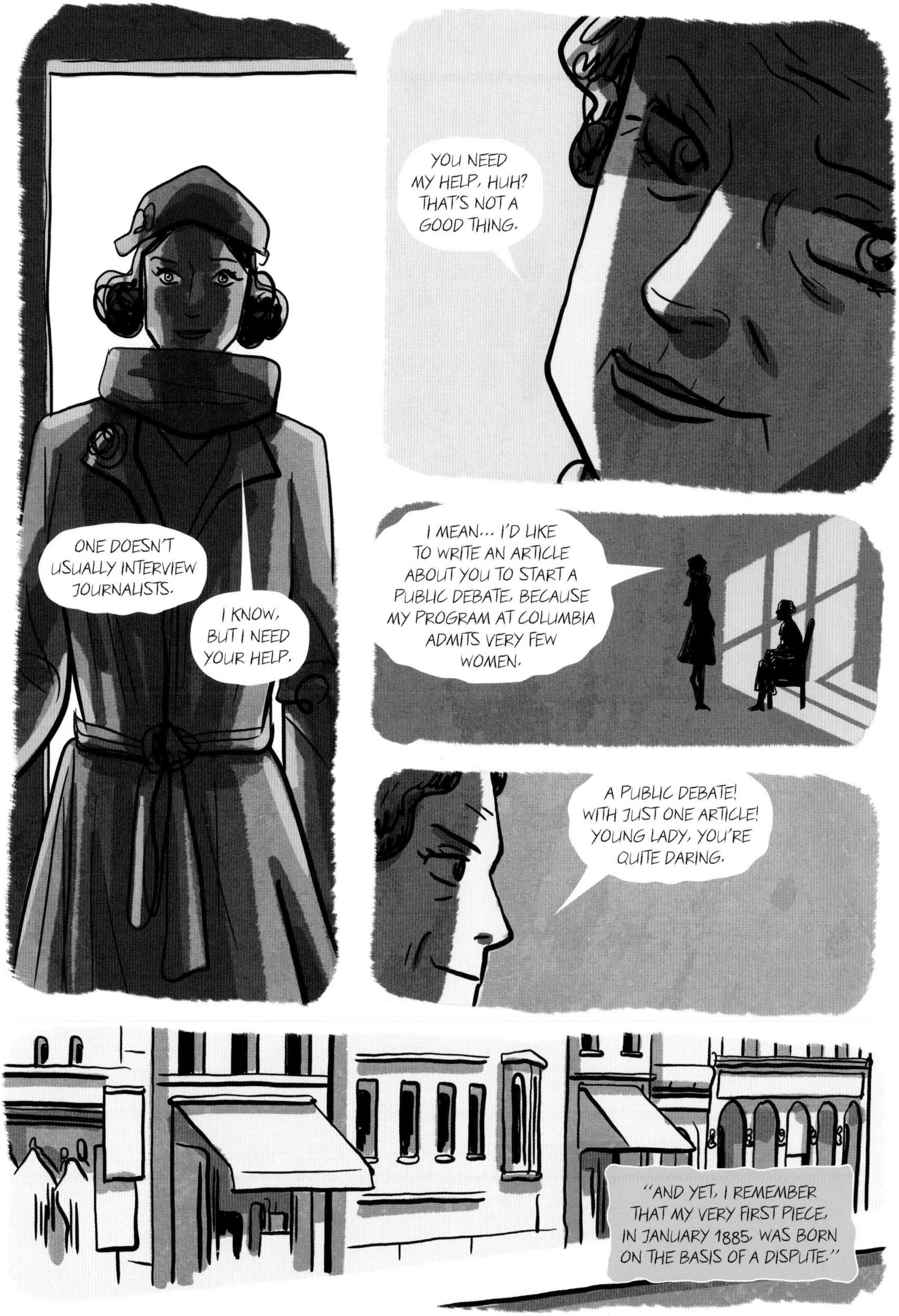
ONE DOESN'T USUALLY INTERVIEW JOURNALISTS.
I KNOW, BUT I NEED YOUR HELP.
YOU NEED MY HELP, HUH? THAT'S NOT A GOOD THING.
I MEAN... I'D LIKE TO WRITE AN ARTICLE ABOUT YOU TO START A PUBLIC DEBATE, BECAUSE MY PROGRAM AT COLUMBIA ADMITS VERY FEW WOMEN.
A PUBLIC DEBATE! WITH JUST ONE ARTICLE! YOUNG LADY, YOU'RE QUITE DARING.
"AND YET, I REMEMBER THAT MY VERY FIRST PIECE, IN JANUARY 1885, WAS BORN ON THE BASIS OF A DISPUTE."

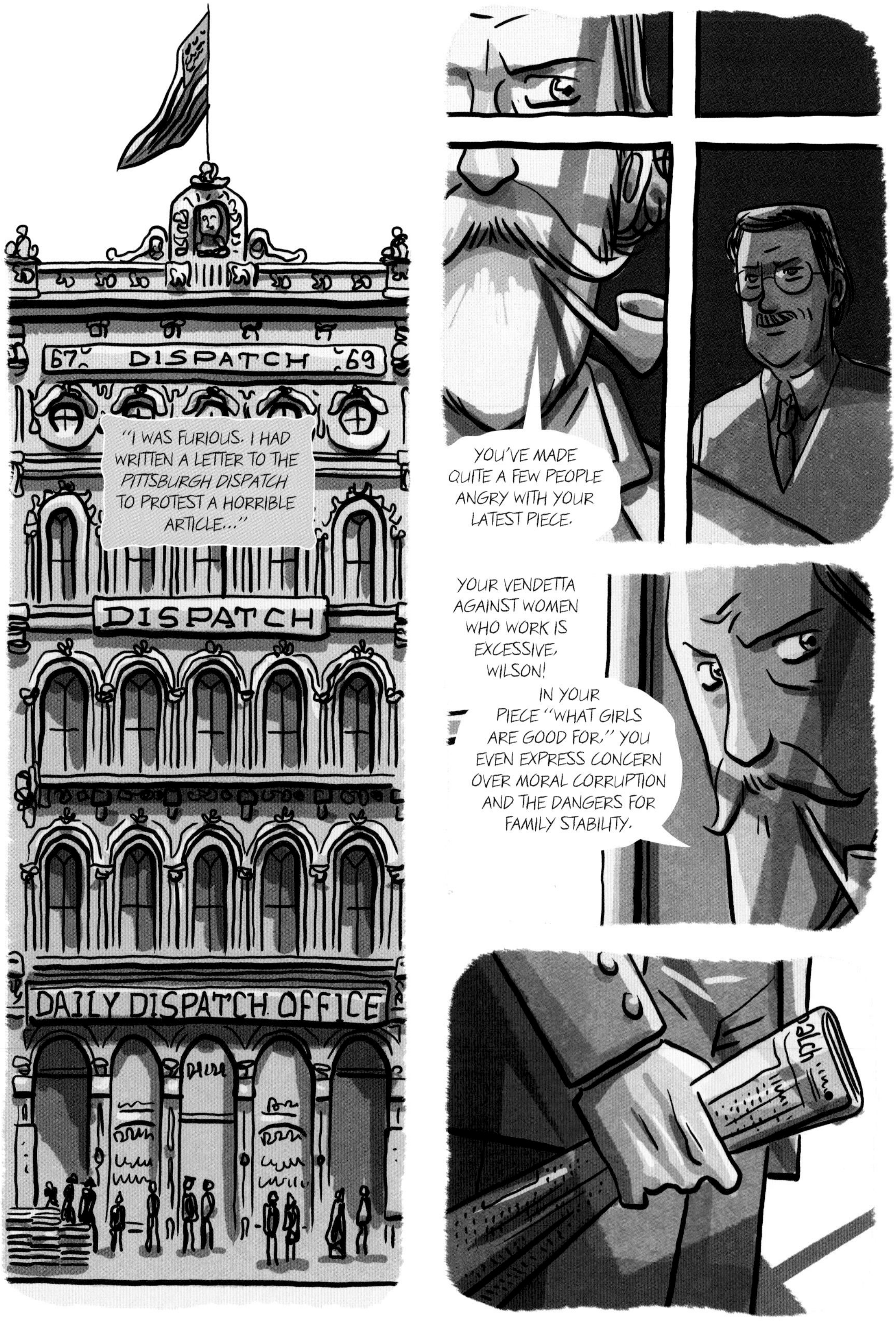
67 DISPATCH 69
"I WAS FURIOUS. I HAD WRITTEN A LETTER TO THE PITTSBURGH DISPATCH TO PROTEST A HORRIBLE ARTICLE..."
DISPATCH
DAILY DISPATCH OFFICE
YOU'VE MADE QUITE A FEW PEOPLE ANGRY WITH YOUR LATEST PIECE.
YOUR VENDETTA AGAINST WOMEN WHO WORK IS EXCESSIVE, WILSON!
IN YOUR PIECE "WHAT GIRLS ARE GOOD FOR," YOU EVEN EXPRESS CONCERN OVER MORAL CORRUPTION AND THE DANGERS FOR FAMILY STABILITY.

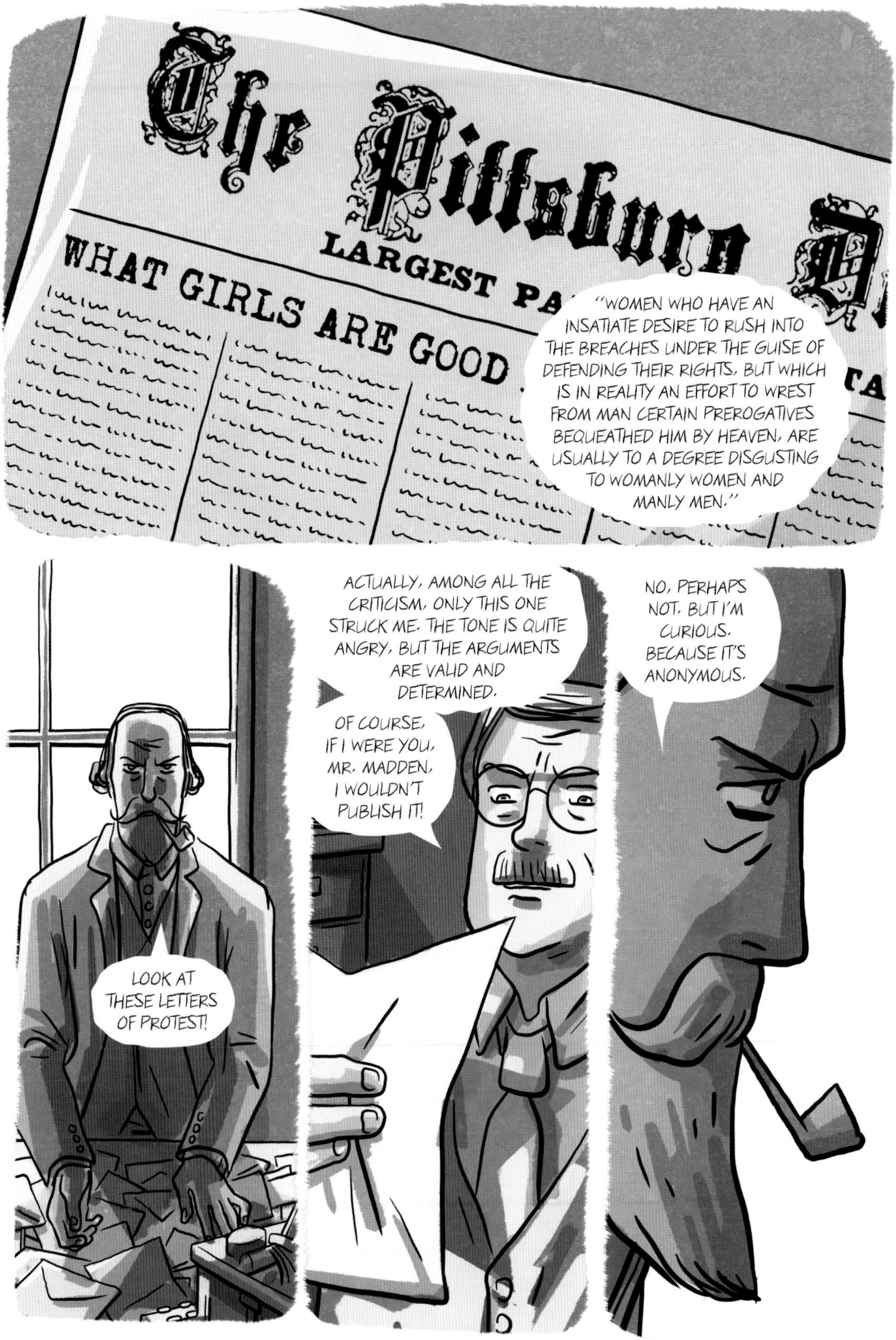
The Pittsburg Dispatch
LARGEST PA
WHAT GIRLS ARE GOOD
"WOMEN WHO HAVE AN INSATIATE DESIRE TO RUSH INTO THE BREACHES UNDER THE GUISE OF DEFENDING THEIR RIGHTS, BUT WHICH IS IN REALITY AN EFFORT TO WREST FROM MAN CERTAIN PREROGATIVES BEQUEATHED HIM BY HEAVEN, ARE USUALLY TO A DEGREE DISGUSTING TO WOMANLY WOMEN AND MANLY MEN."
LOOK AT THESE LETTERS OF PROTEST!
ACTUALLY, AMONG ALL THE CRITICISM, ONLY THIS ONE STRUCK ME. THE TONE IS QUITE ANGRY, BUT THE ARGUMENTS ARE VALID AND DETERMINED.
OF COURSE, IF I WERE YOU, MR. MADDEN, I WOULDN'T PUBLISH IT!
NO, PERHAPS NOT. BUT I'M CURIOUS. BECAUSE IT'S ANONYMOUS.

"WHO'S BEHIND THE SIGNATURE OF **LONELY ORPHAN GIRL?**"

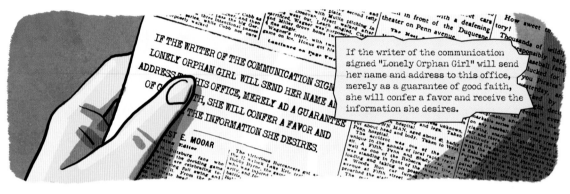

IF THE WRITER OF THE COMMUNICATION SIGN LONELY ORPHAN GIRL WILL SEND HER NAME A ADDRESS HIS OFFICE, MERELY AD A GUARANTEE OF G TH, SHE WILL CONFER A FAVOR AND THE INFORMATION SHE DESIRES.

If the writer of the communication signed "Lonely Orphan Girl" will send her name and address to this office, merely as a guarantee of good faith, she will confer a favor and receive the information she desires.

"DID YOU GO?"

OF COURSE. I MEANT WHAT I WROTE.

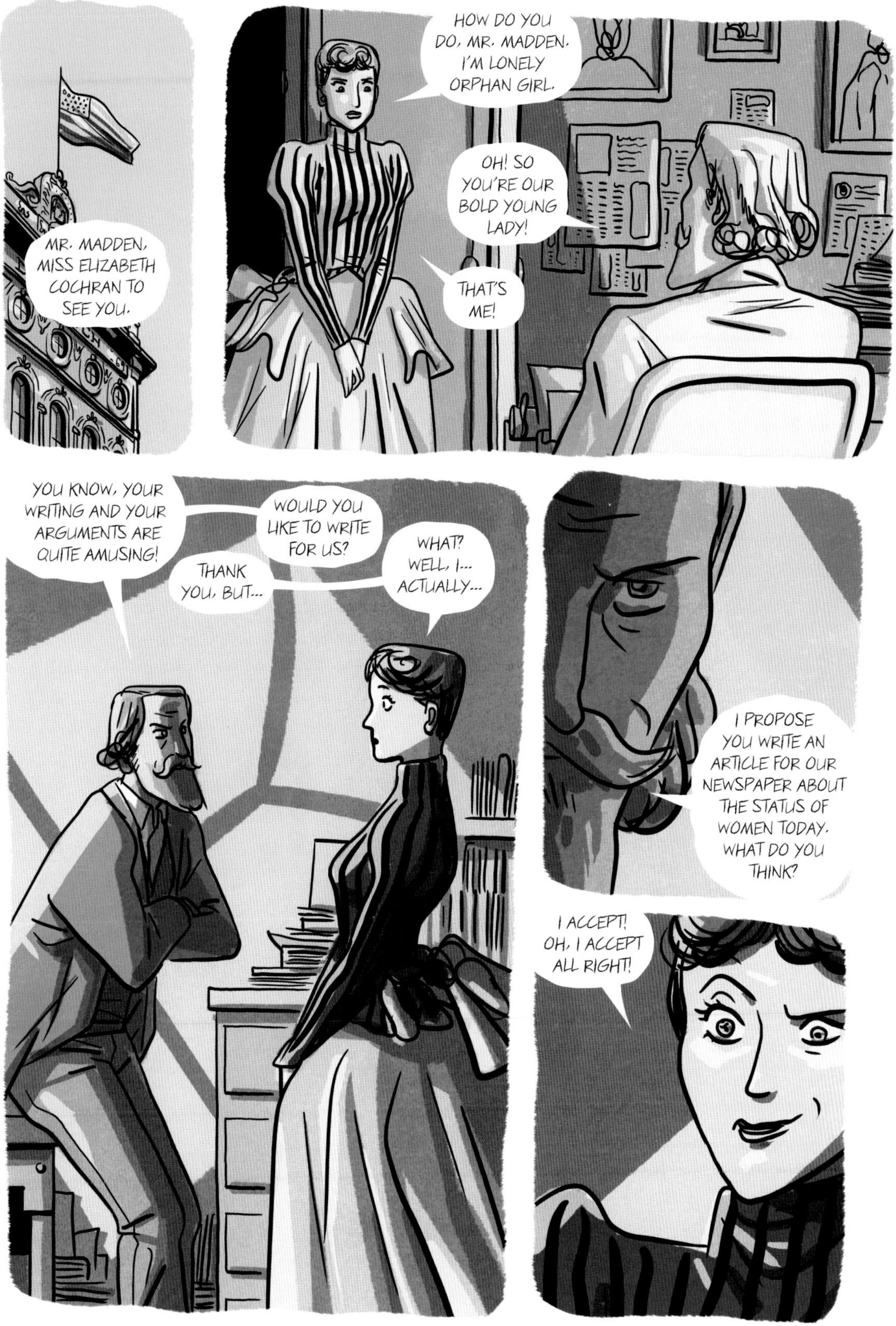
MR. MADDEN, MISS ELIZABETH COCHRAN TO SEE YOU.
HOW DO YOU DO, MR. MADDEN. I'M LONELY ORPHAN GIRL.
OH! SO YOU'RE OUR BOLD YOUNG LADY!
THAT'S ME!
YOU KNOW, YOUR WRITING AND YOUR ARGUMENTS ARE QUITE AMUSING!
THANK YOU, BUT...
WOULD YOU LIKE TO WRITE FOR US?
WHAT? WELL, I... ACTUALLY...
I PROPOSE YOU WRITE AN ARTICLE FOR OUR NEWSPAPER ABOUT THE STATUS OF WOMEN TODAY. WHAT DO YOU THINK?
I ACCEPT! OH, I ACCEPT ALL RIGHT!

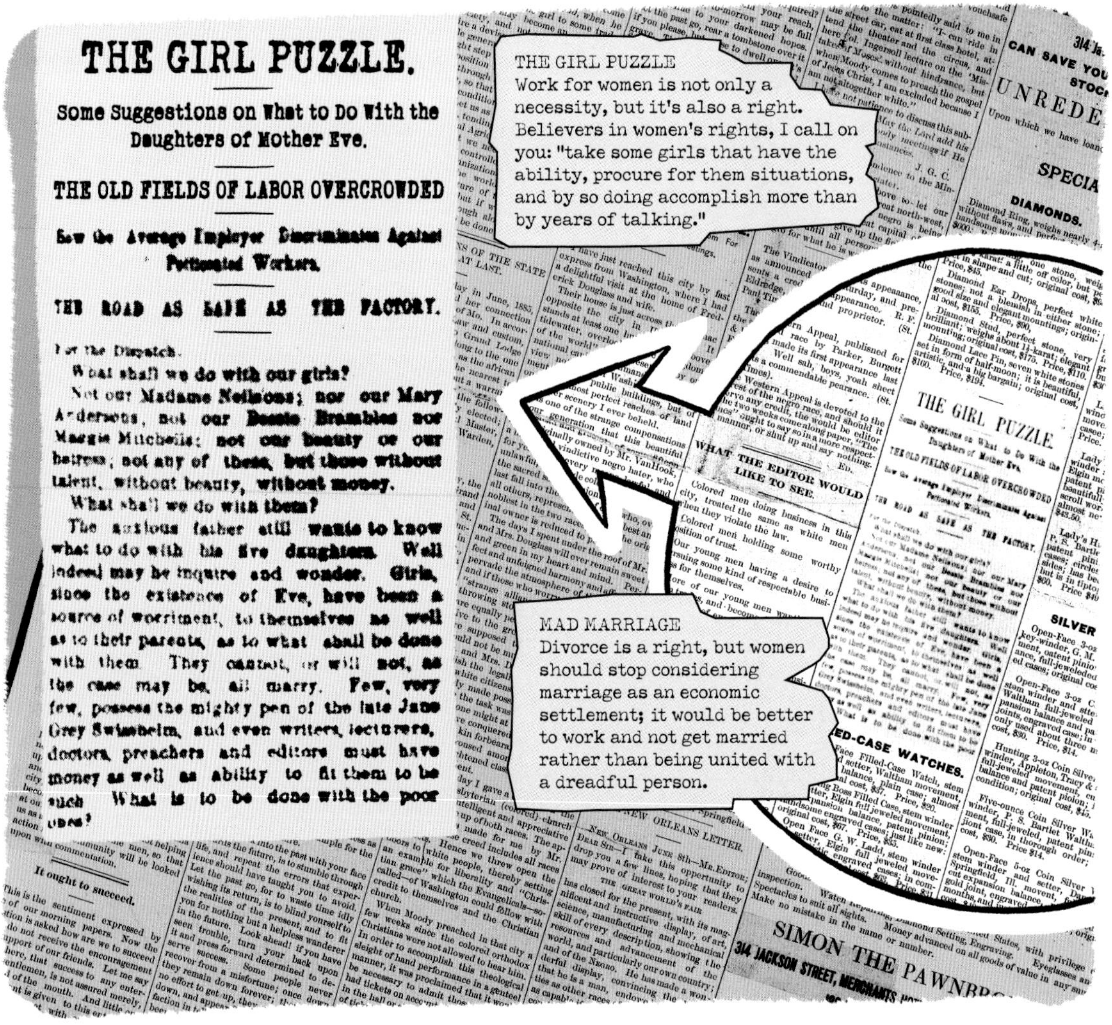

THE GIRL PUZZLE.

Some Suggestions on What to Do With the Daughters of Mother Eve.

THE OLD FIELDS OF LABOR OVERCROWDED

How the Average Employer Discriminates Against Petticoated Workers.

THE ROAD AS SAFE AS THE FACTORY.

For the Dispatch.

What shall we do with our girls?

Not our Madame Neilsons; nor our Mary Andersons, not our Bessie Brambles nor Maggie Mitchells; not our beauty or our heiress; not any of these, but those without talent, without beauty, without money.

What shall we do with them?

The anxious father still wants to know what to do with his five daughters. Well indeed may he inquire and wonder. Girls, since the existence of Eve, have been a source of worriment, to themselves as well as to their parents, as to what shall be done with them. They cannot, or will not, as the case may be, all marry. Few, very few, possess the mighty pen of the late Jane Grey Swisshelm, and even writers, lecturers, doctors, preachers and editors must have money as well as ability to fit them to be such. What is to be done with the poor ones?

THE GIRL PUZZLE
Work for women is not only a necessity, but it's also a right. Believers in women's rights, I call on you: "take some girls that have the ability, procure for them situations, and by so doing accomplish more than by years of talking."
MAD MARRIAGE
Divorce is a right, but women should stop considering marriage as an economic settlement; it would be better to work and not get married rather than being united with a dreadful person.

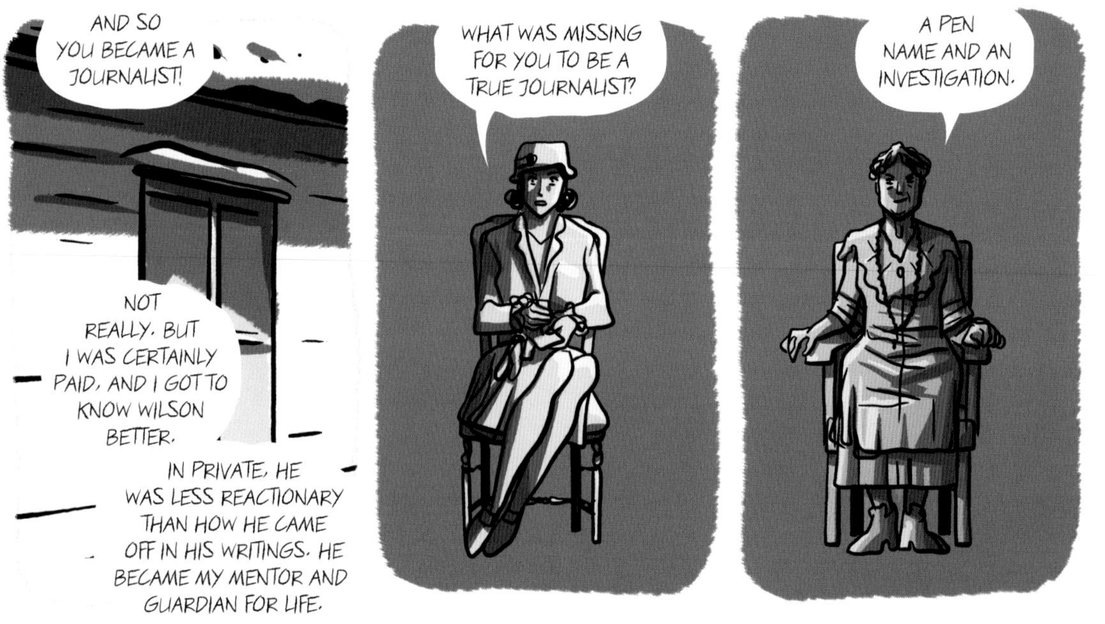
AND SO YOU BECAME A JOURNALIST!
NOT REALLY. BUT I WAS CERTAINLY PAID, AND I GOT TO KNOW WILSON BETTER.
IN PRIVATE, HE WAS LESS REACTIONARY THAN HOW HE CAME OFF IN HIS WRITINGS. HE BECAME MY MENTOR AND GUARDIAN FOR LIFE.
WHAT WAS MISSING FOR YOU TO BE A TRUE JOURNALIST?
A PEN NAME AND AN INVESTIGATION.

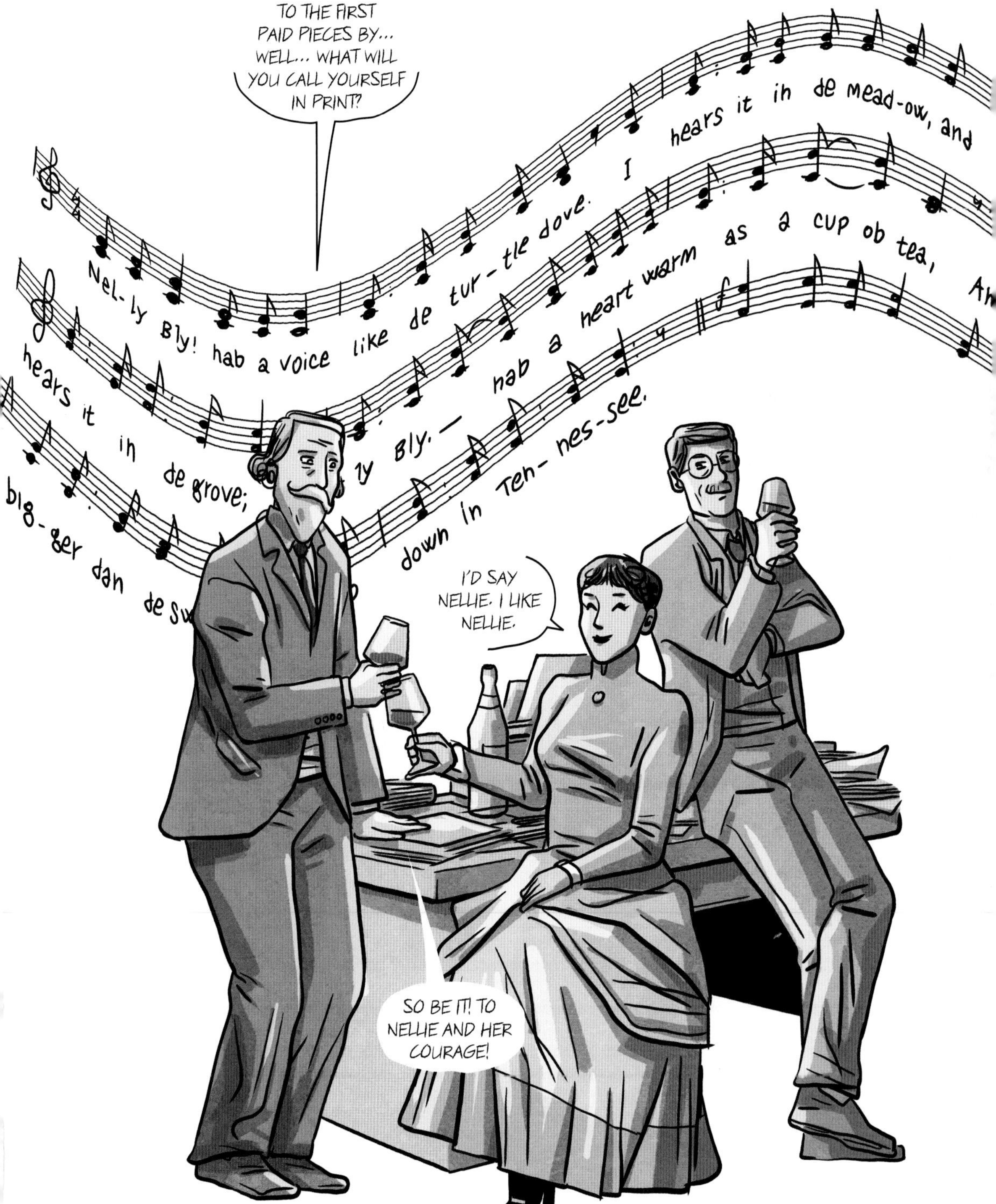
TO THE FIRST PAID PIECES BY... WELL... WHAT WILL YOU CALL YOURSELF IN PRINT?
Nel-ly Bly! hab a voice like de tur-tle dove. I hears it in de mead-ow, and
hears it in de grove;
ly Bly. — hab a heart warm as a cup ob tea,
down in Ten- nes-see.
big-ger dan de su
I'D SAY NELLIE. I LIKE NELLIE.
SO BE IT! TO NELLIE AND HER COURAGE!

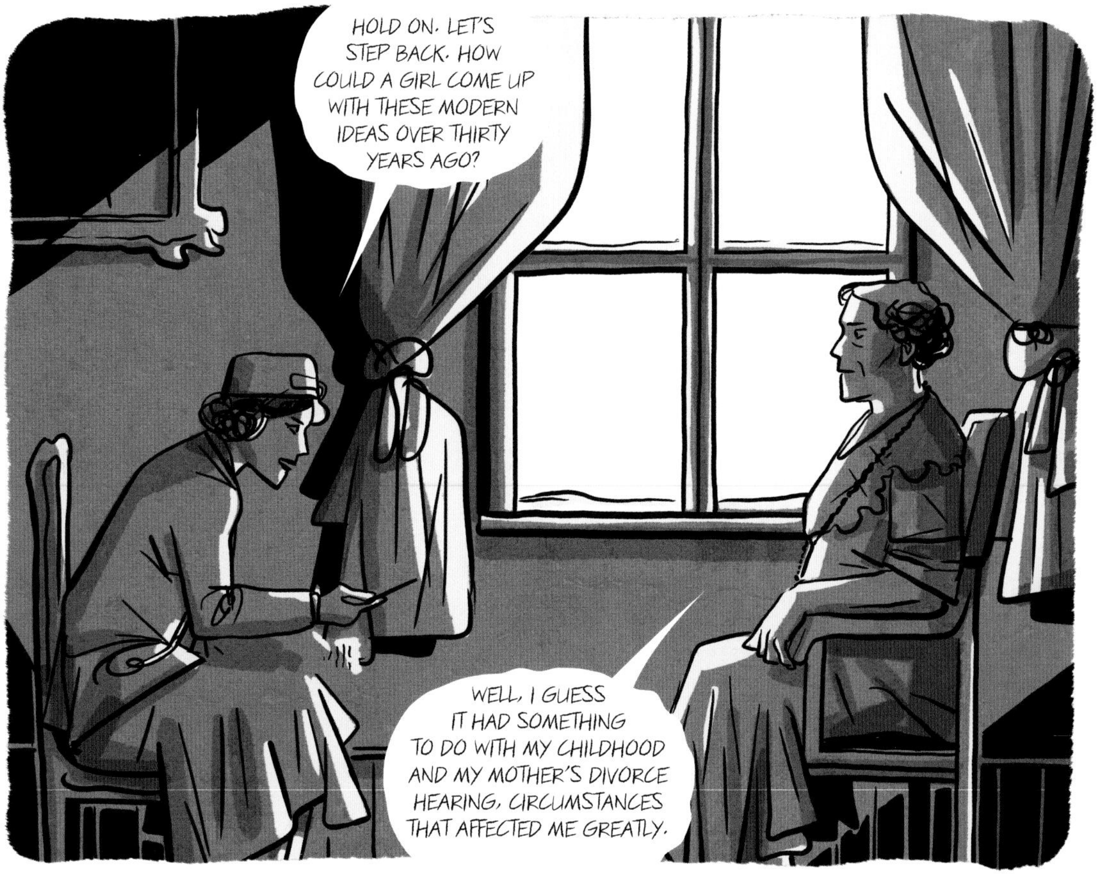
HOLD ON. LET'S STEP BACK. HOW COULD A GIRL COME UP WITH THESE MODERN IDEAS OVER THIRTY YEARS AGO?
WELL, I GUESS IT HAD SOMETHING TO DO WITH MY CHILDHOOD AND MY MOTHER'S DIVORCE HEARING, CIRCUMSTANCES THAT AFFECTED ME GREATLY.

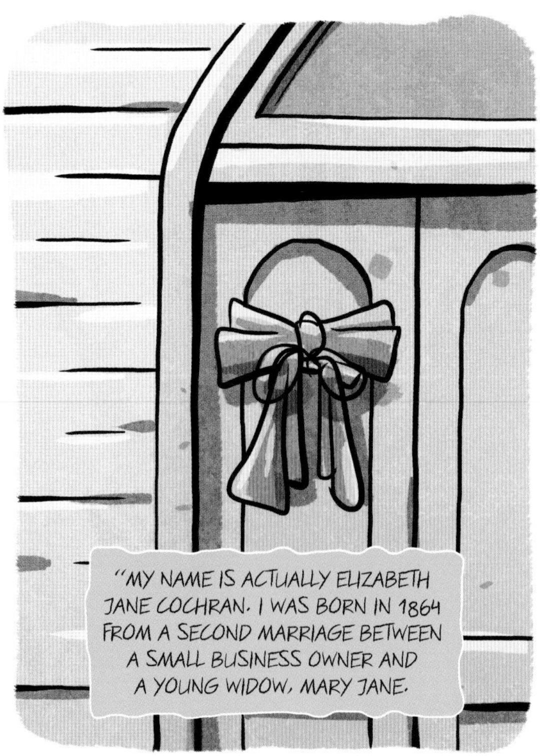
"MY NAME IS ACTUALLY ELIZABETH JANE COCHRAN. I WAS BORN IN 1864 FROM A SECOND MARRIAGE BETWEEN A SMALL BUSINESS OWNER AND A YOUNG WIDOW, MARY JANE.

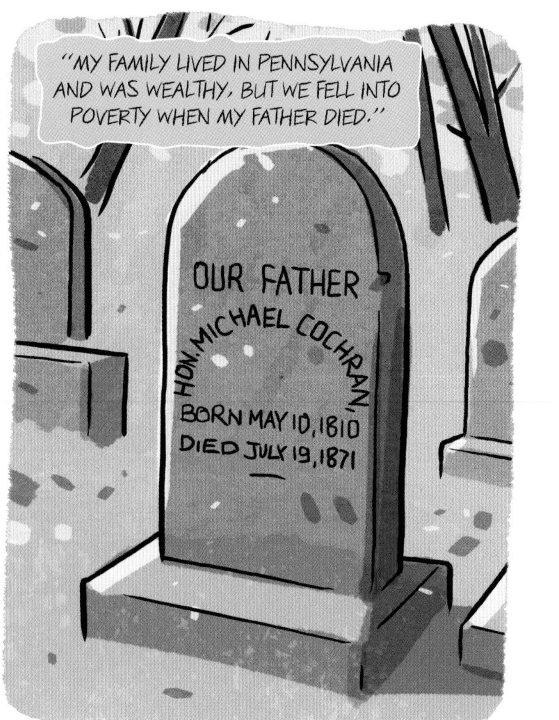
"MY FAMILY LIVED IN PENNSYLVANIA AND WAS WEALTHY, BUT WE FELL INTO POVERTY WHEN MY FATHER DIED."
OUR FATHER
HON. MICHAEL COCHRAN.
BORN MAY 10, 1810
DIED JULY 19, 1871

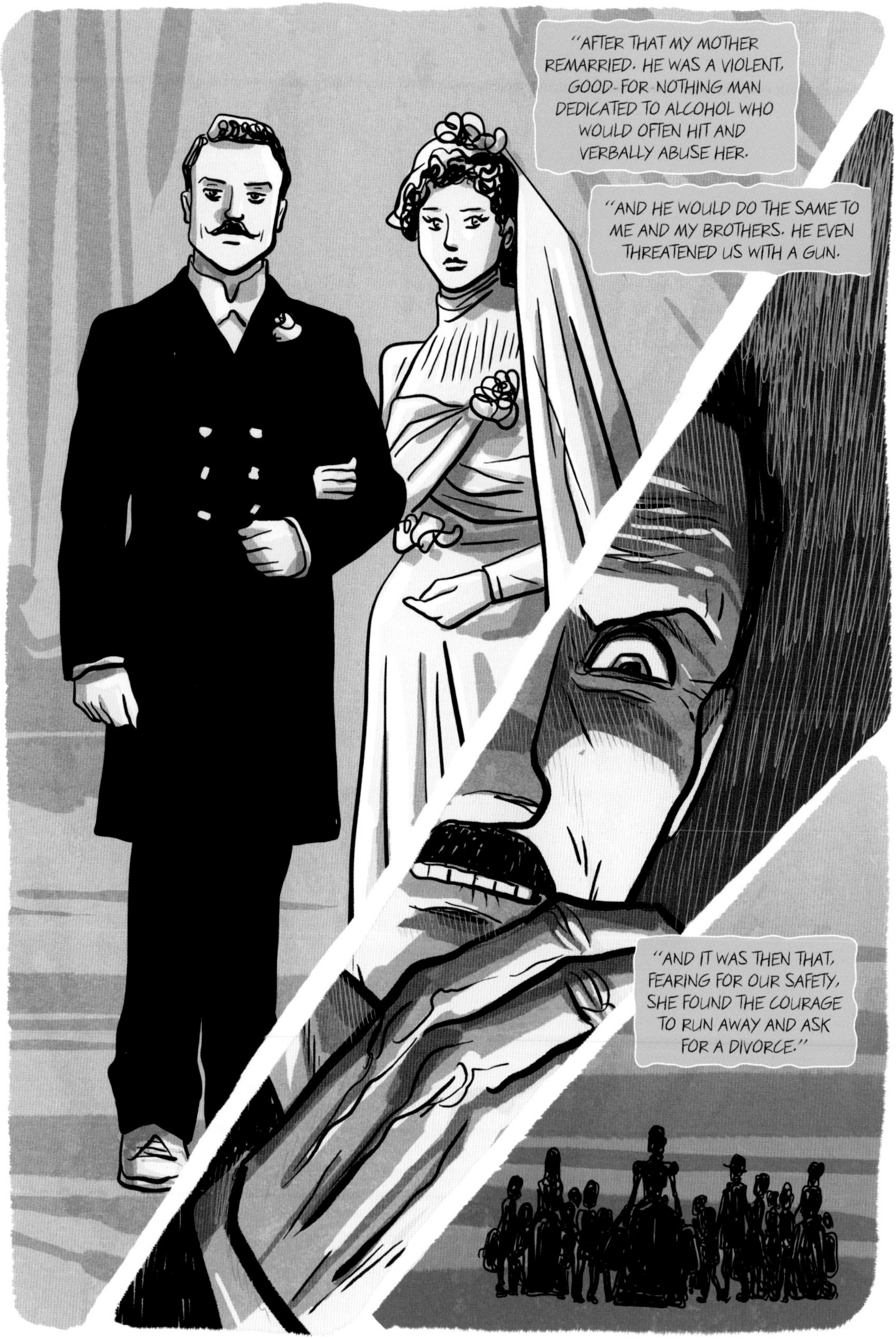
"AFTER THAT MY MOTHER REMARRIED. HE WAS A VIOLENT, GOOD-FOR-NOTHING MAN DEDICATED TO ALCOHOL WHO WOULD OFTEN HIT AND VERBALLY ABUSE HER.
"AND HE WOULD DO THE SAME TO ME AND MY BROTHERS. HE EVEN THREATENED US WITH A GUN.
"AND IT WAS THEN THAT, FEARING FOR OUR SAFETY, SHE FOUND THE COURAGE TO RUN AWAY AND ASK FOR A DIVORCE."

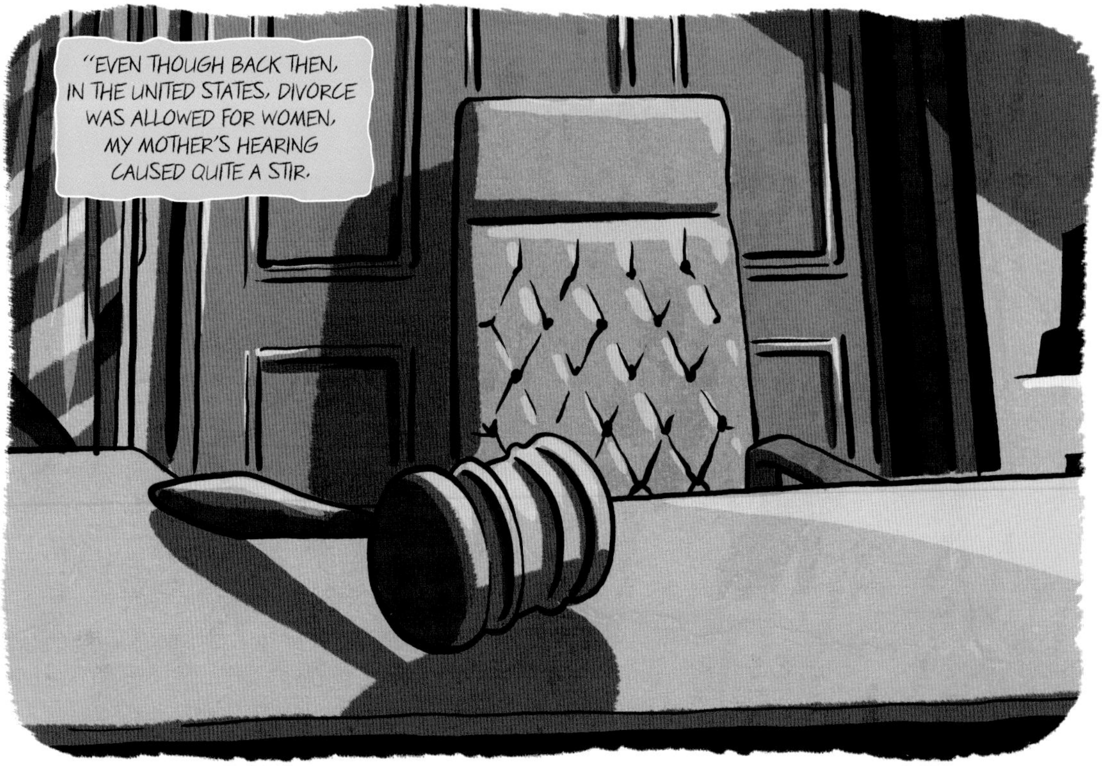
"EVEN THOUGH BACK THEN, IN THE UNITED STATES, DIVORCE WAS ALLOWED FOR WOMEN, MY MOTHER'S HEARING CAUSED QUITE A STIR.

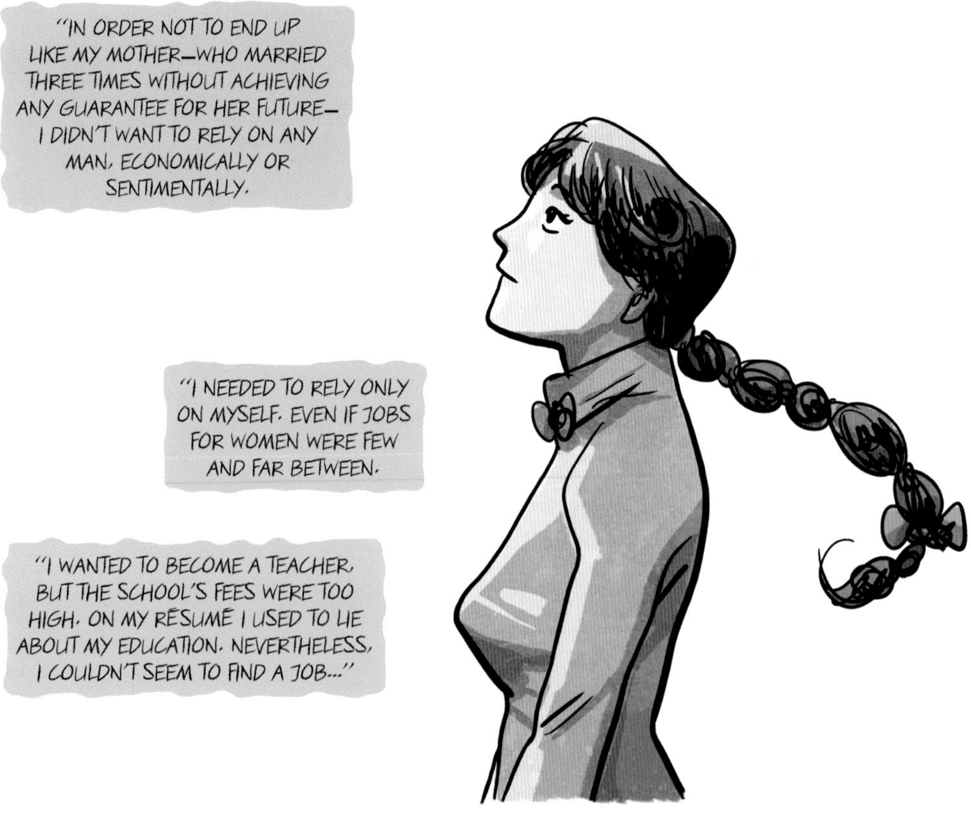
"IN ORDER NOT TO END UP LIKE MY MOTHER—WHO MARRIED THREE TIMES WITHOUT ACHIEVING ANY GUARANTEE FOR HER FUTURE—I DIDN'T WANT TO RELY ON ANY MAN, ECONOMICALLY OR SENTIMENTALLY.
"I NEEDED TO RELY ONLY ON MYSELF. EVEN IF JOBS FOR WOMEN WERE FEW AND FAR BETWEEN.
"I WANTED TO BECOME A TEACHER, BUT THE SCHOOL'S FEES WERE TOO HIGH. ON MY RÉSUMÉ I USED TO LIE ABOUT MY EDUCATION. NEVERTHELESS, I COULDN'T SEEM TO FIND A JOB..."

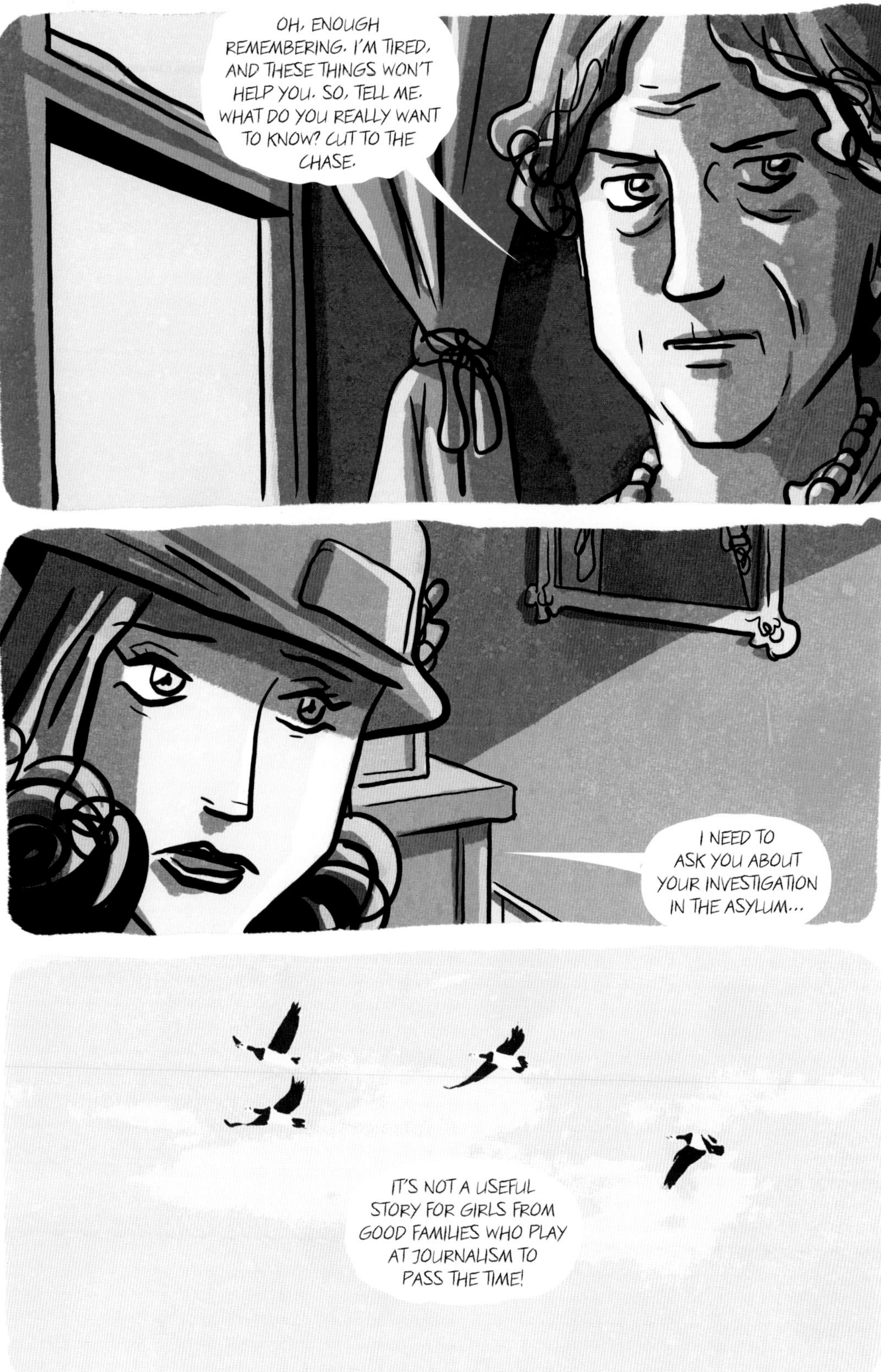
OH, ENOUGH REMEMBERING. I'M TIRED, AND THESE THINGS WON'T HELP YOU. SO, TELL ME. WHAT DO YOU REALLY WANT TO KNOW? CUT TO THE CHASE.
I NEED TO ASK YOU ABOUT YOUR INVESTIGATION IN THE ASYLUM...
IT'S NOT A USEFUL STORY FOR GIRLS FROM GOOD FAMILIES WHO PLAY AT JOURNALISM TO PASS THE TIME!

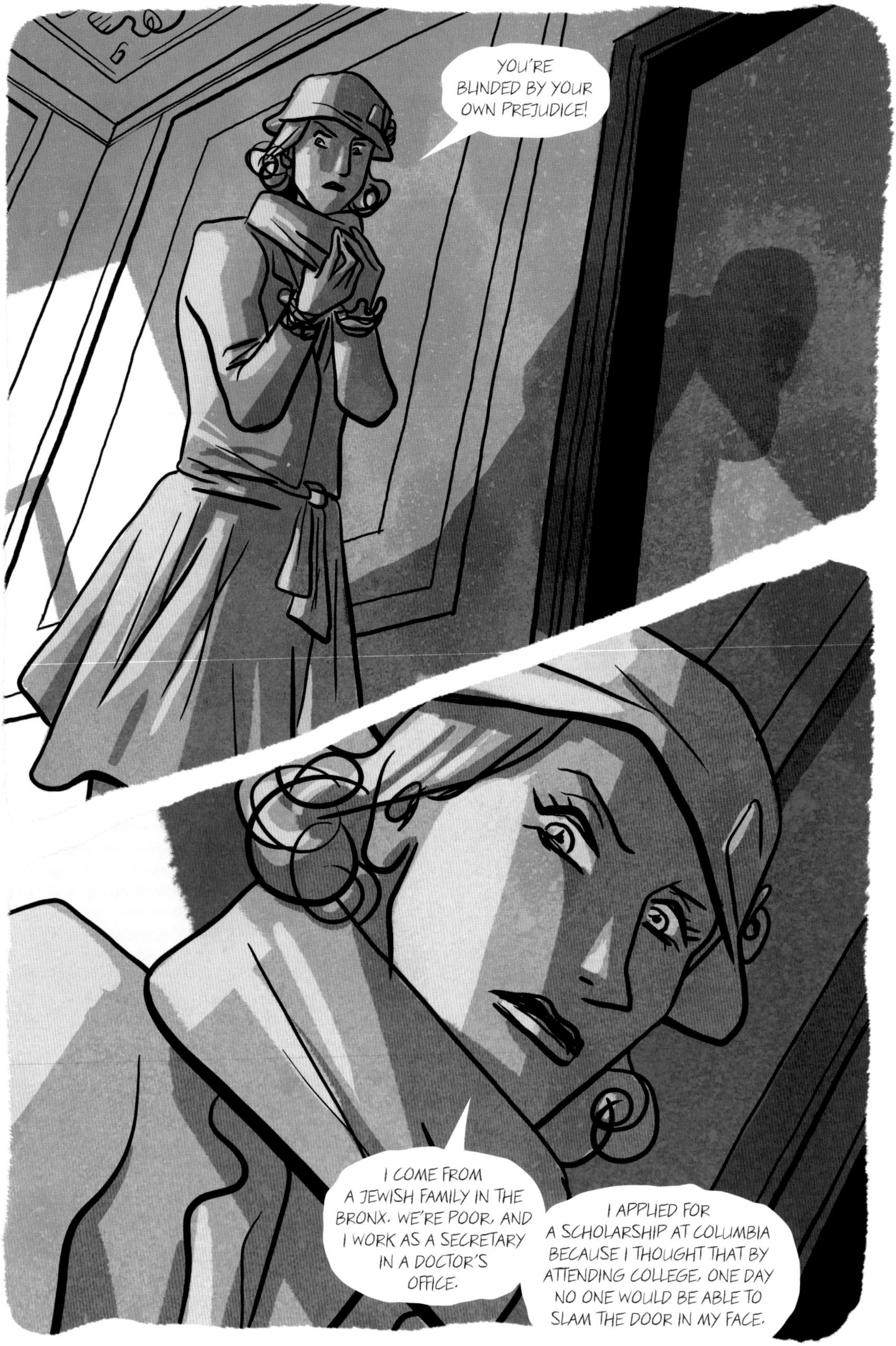

YOU'RE BLINDED BY YOUR OWN PREJUDICE!
I COME FROM A JEWISH FAMILY IN THE BRONX. WE'RE POOR, AND I WORK AS A SECRETARY IN A DOCTOR'S OFFICE.
I APPLIED FOR A SCHOLARSHIP AT COLUMBIA BECAUSE I THOUGHT THAT BY ATTENDING COLLEGE, ONE DAY NO ONE WOULD BE ABLE TO SLAM THE DOOR IN MY FACE.

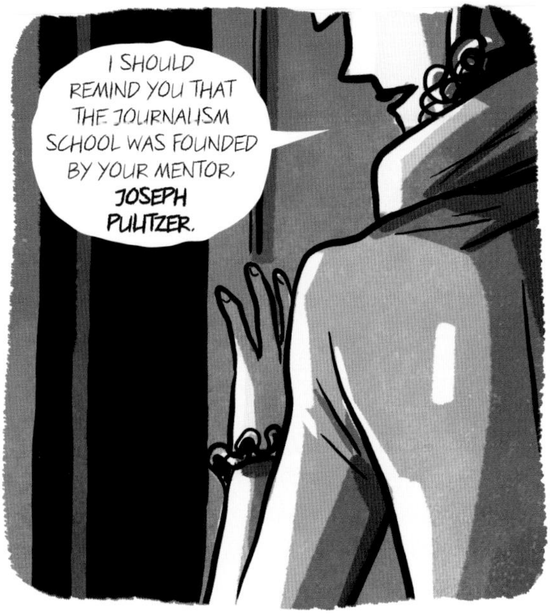
I SHOULD REMIND YOU THAT THE JOURNALISM SCHOOL WAS FOUNDED BY YOUR MENTOR, **JOSEPH PULITZER.**

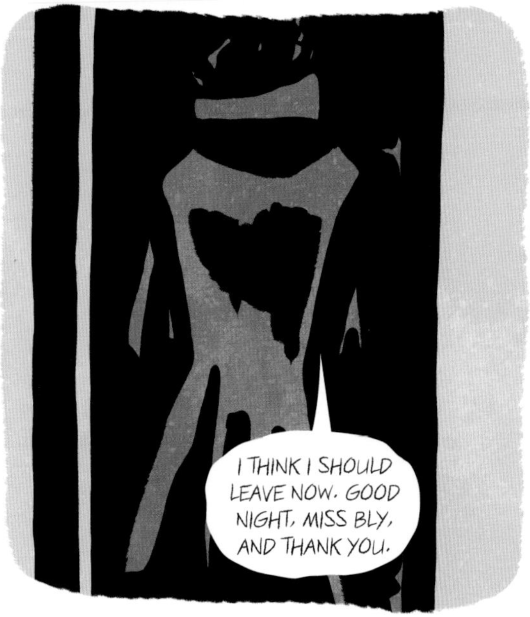
I THINK I SHOULD LEAVE NOW. GOOD NIGHT, MISS BLY, AND THANK YOU.

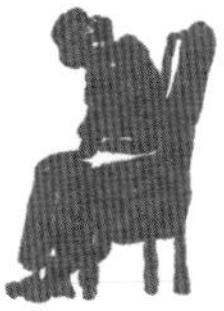

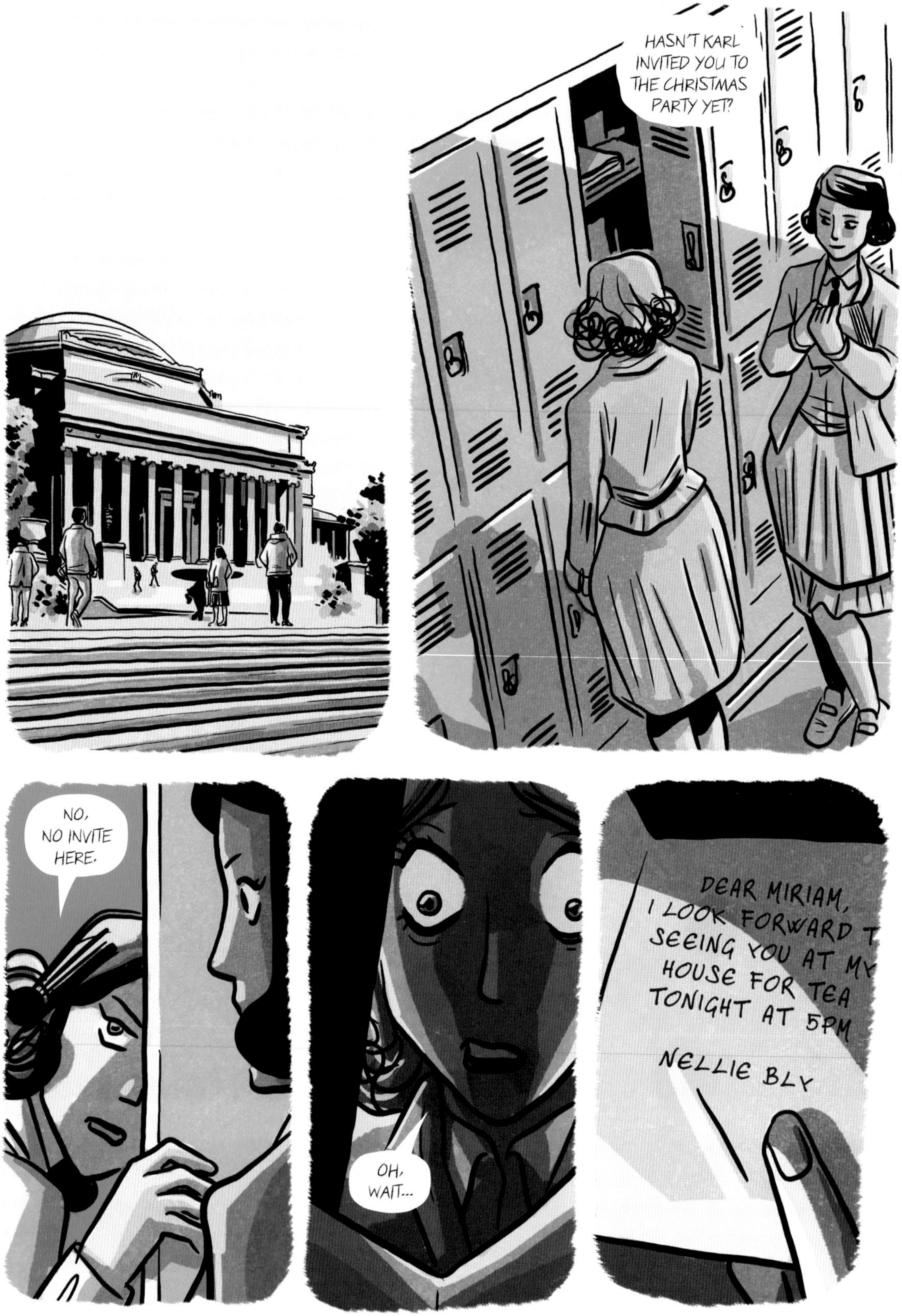
HASN'T KARL INVITED YOU TO THE CHRISTMAS PARTY YET?
NO, NO INVITE HERE.
OH, WAIT...
DEAR MIRIAM,
I LOOK FORWARD T
SEEING YOU AT MY
HOUSE FOR TEA
TONIGHT AT 5PM
NELLIE BLY

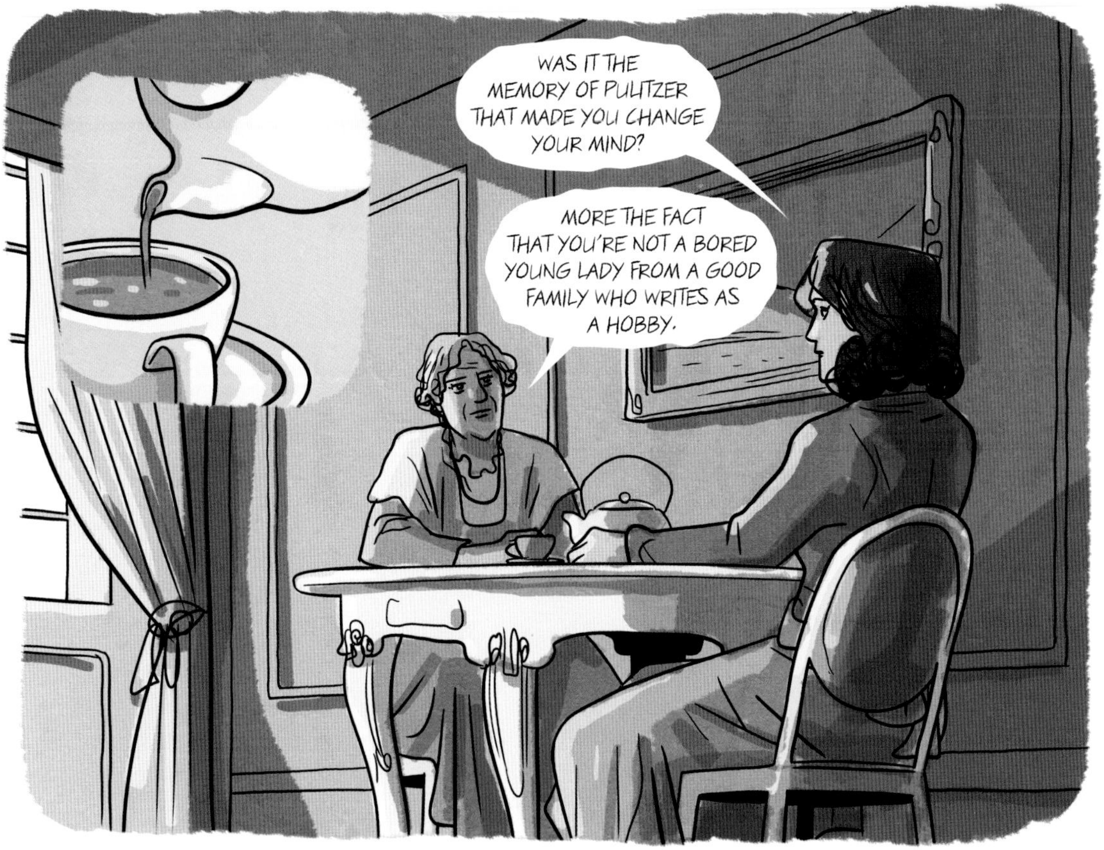
WAS IT THE MEMORY OF PULITZER THAT MADE YOU CHANGE YOUR MIND?
MORE THE FACT THAT YOU'RE NOT A BORED YOUNG LADY FROM A GOOD FAMILY WHO WRITES AS A HOBBY.

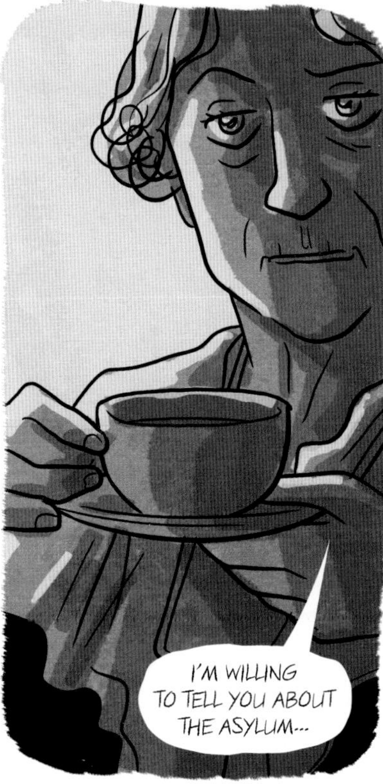
I'M WILLING TO TELL YOU ABOUT THE ASYLUM...

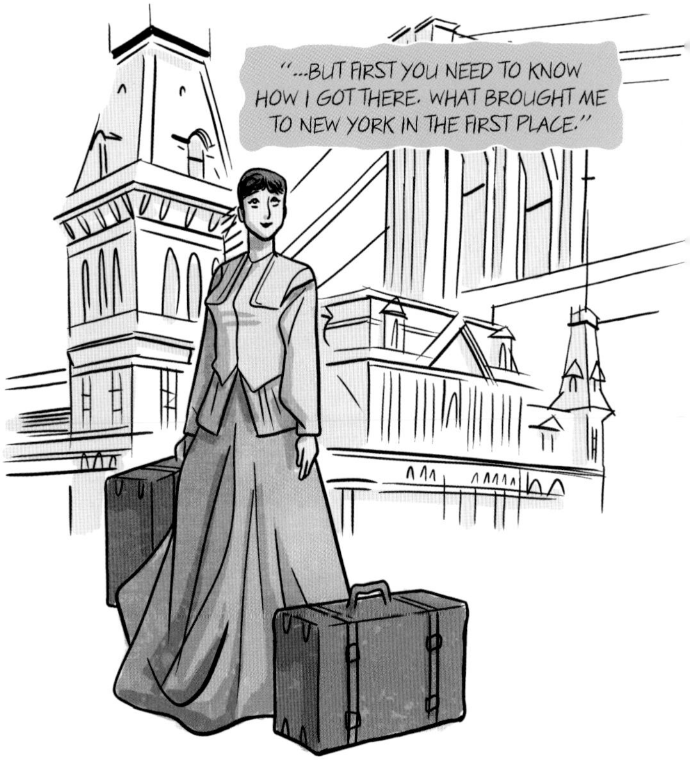
"...BUT FIRST YOU NEED TO KNOW HOW I GOT THERE. WHAT BROUGHT ME TO NEW YORK IN THE FIRST PLACE."

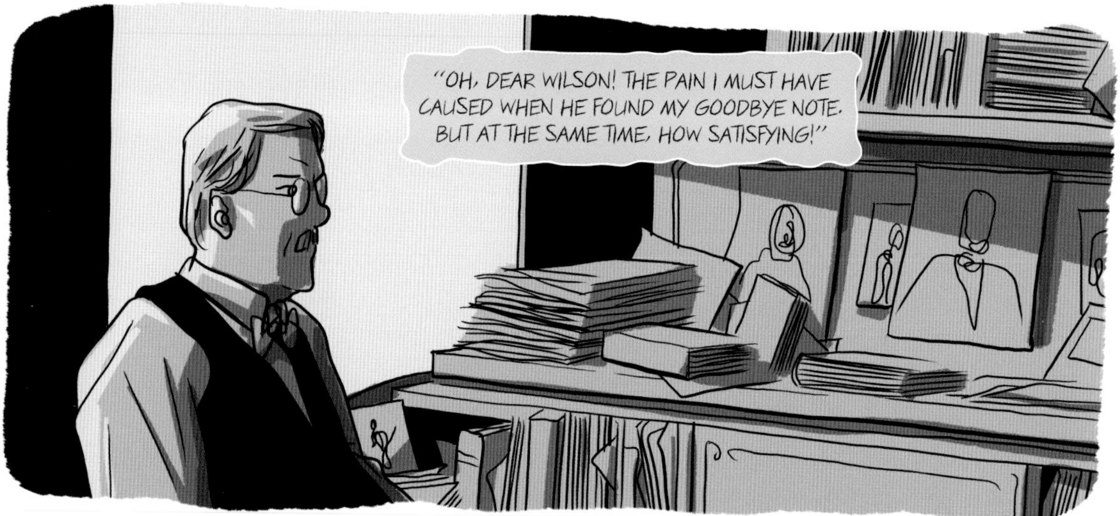
"OH, DEAR WILSON! THE PAIN I MUST HAVE CAUSED WHEN HE FOUND MY GOODBYE NOTE. BUT AT THE SAME TIME, HOW SATISFYING!"

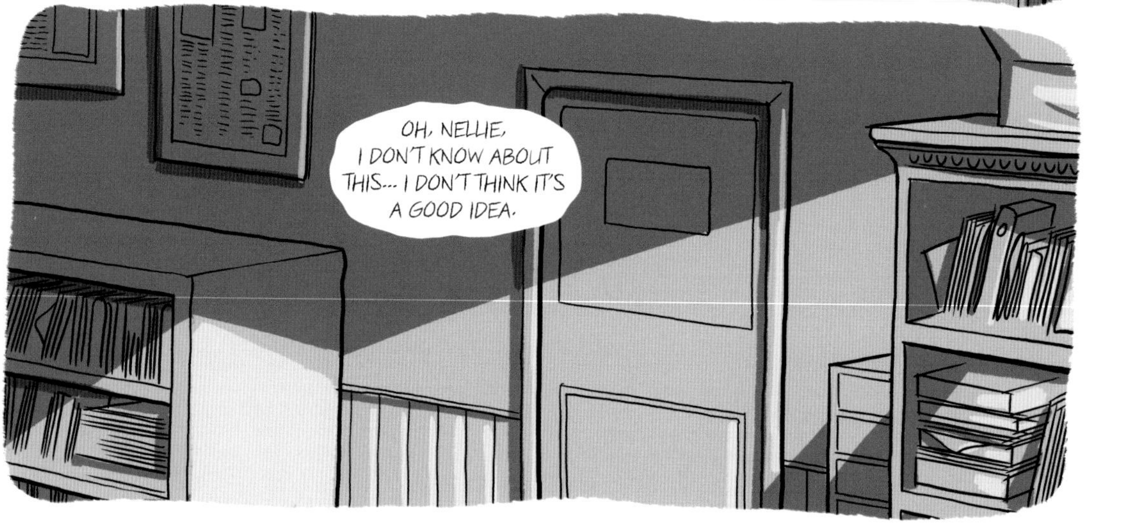
OH, NELLIE, I DON'T KNOW ABOUT THIS... I DON'T THINK IT'S A GOOD IDEA.

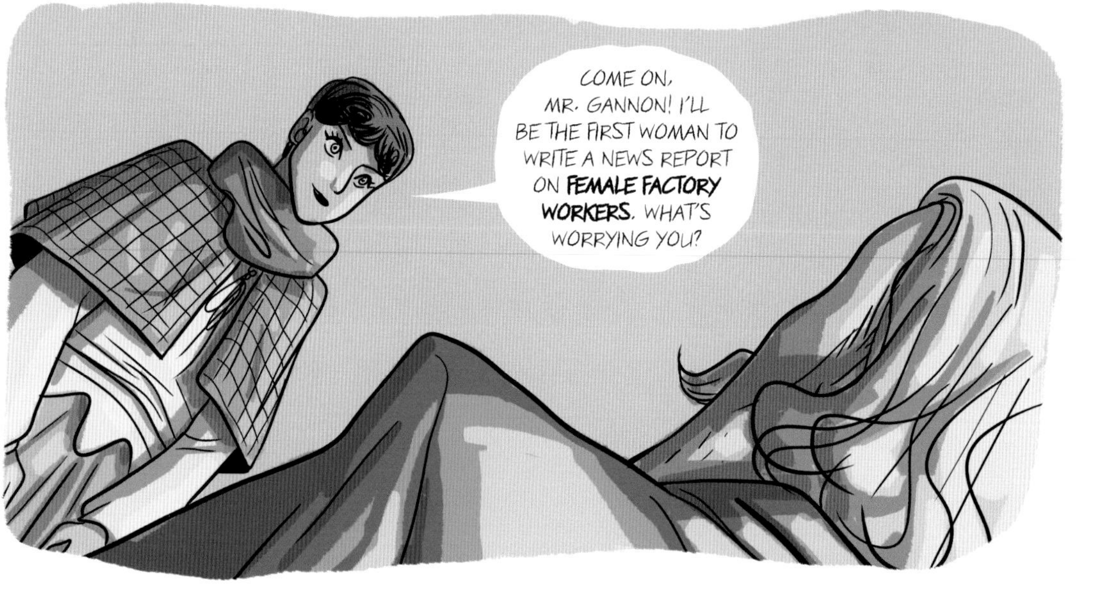
COME ON, MR. GANNON! I'LL BE THE FIRST WOMAN TO WRITE A NEWS REPORT ON **FEMALE FACTORY WORKERS**. WHAT'S WORRYING YOU?

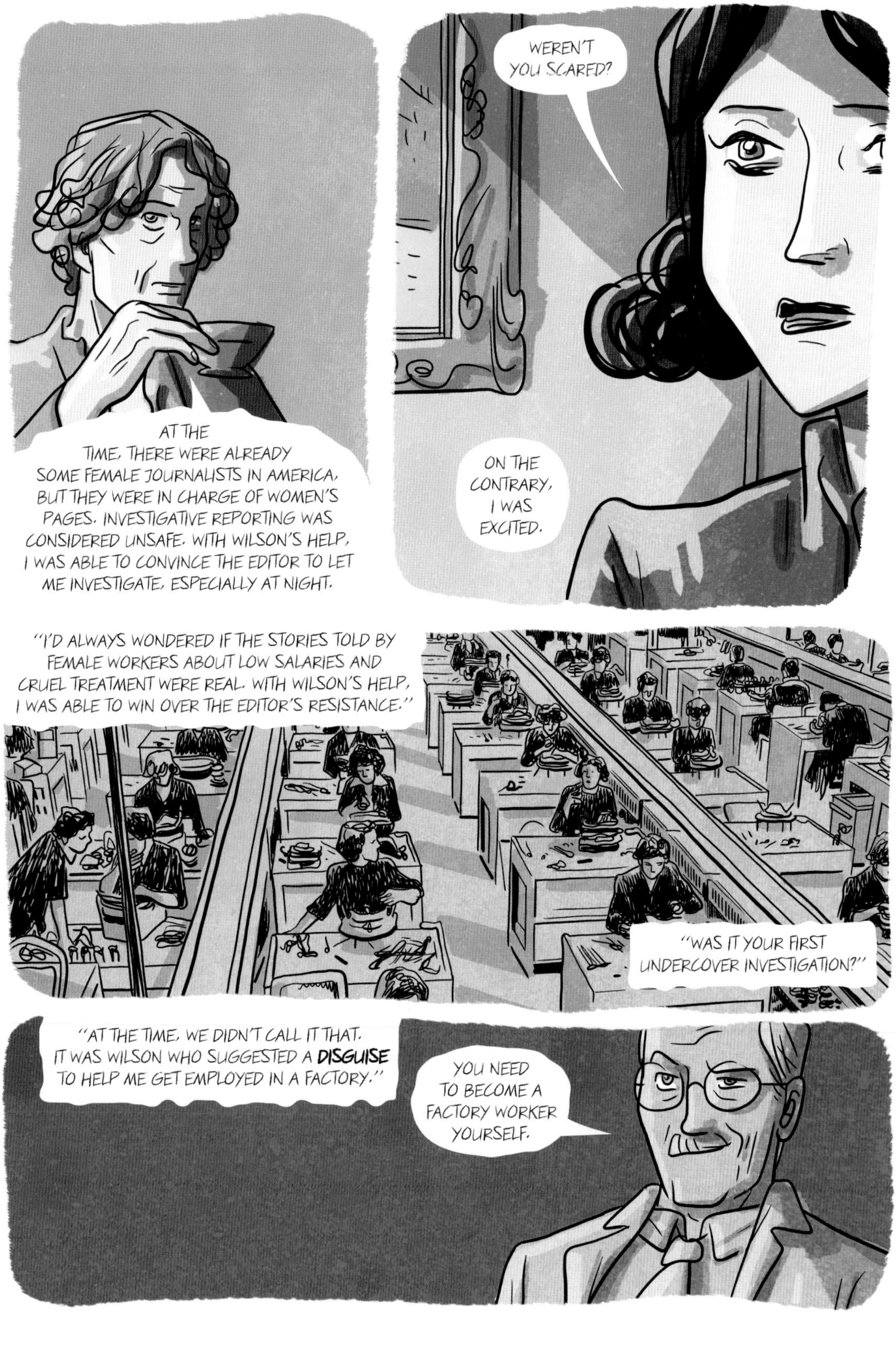
AT THE TIME, THERE WERE ALREADY SOME FEMALE JOURNALISTS IN AMERICA, BUT THEY WERE IN CHARGE OF WOMEN'S PAGES. INVESTIGATIVE REPORTING WAS CONSIDERED UNSAFE. WITH WILSON'S HELP, I WAS ABLE TO CONVINCE THE EDITOR TO LET ME INVESTIGATE, ESPECIALLY AT NIGHT.
WEREN'T YOU SCARED?
ON THE CONTRARY, I WAS EXCITED.
"I'D ALWAYS WONDERED IF THE STORIES TOLD BY FEMALE WORKERS ABOUT LOW SALARIES AND CRUEL TREATMENT WERE REAL. WITH WILSON'S HELP, I WAS ABLE TO WIN OVER THE EDITOR'S RESISTANCE."
"WAS IT YOUR FIRST UNDERCOVER INVESTIGATION?"
"AT THE TIME, WE DIDN'T CALL IT THAT. IT WAS WILSON WHO SUGGESTED A **DISGUISE** TO HELP ME GET EMPLOYED IN A FACTORY."
YOU NEED TO BECOME A FACTORY WORKER YOURSELF.

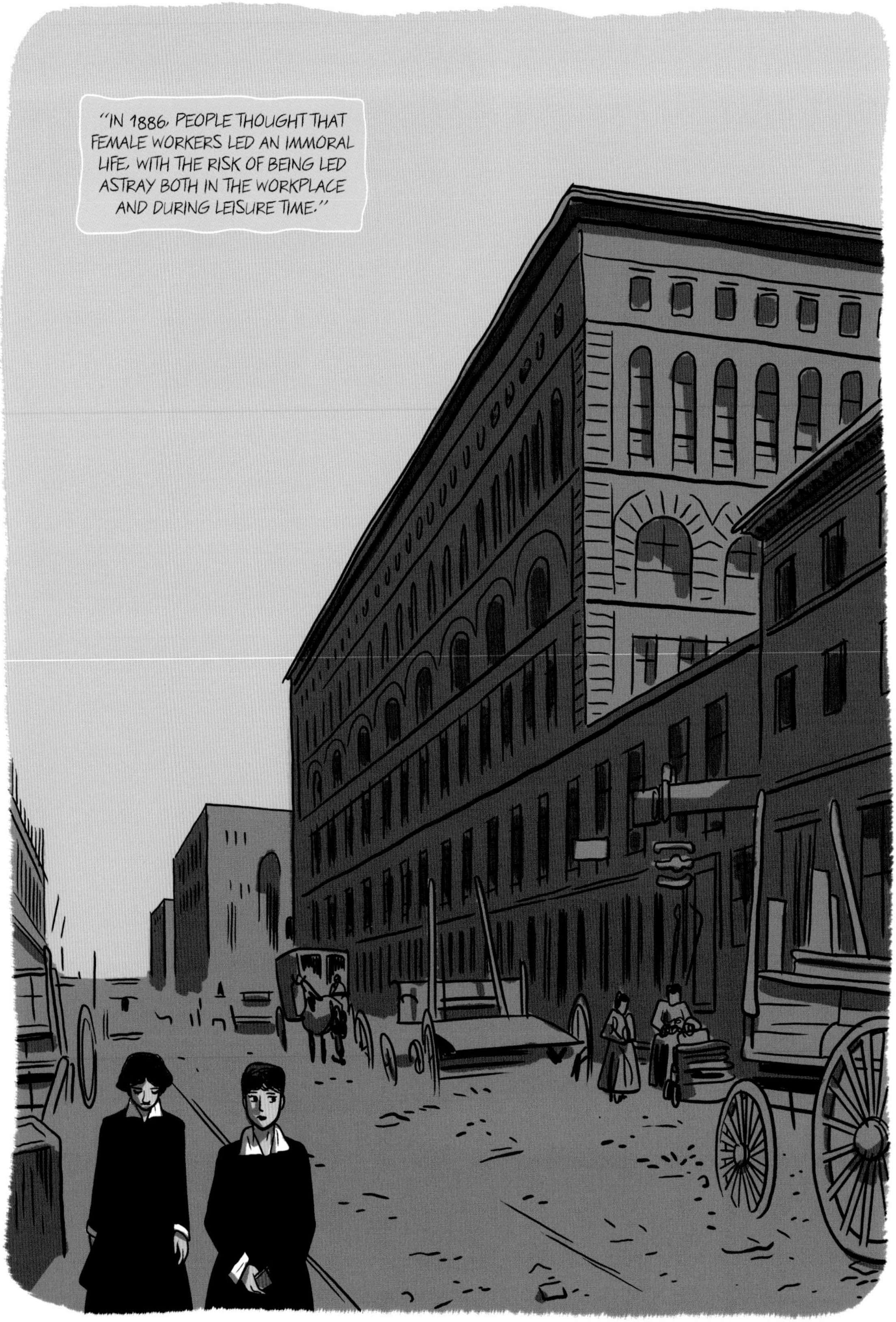
"IN 1886, PEOPLE THOUGHT THAT FEMALE WORKERS LED AN IMMORAL LIFE, WITH THE RISK OF BEING LED ASTRAY BOTH IN THE WORKPLACE AND DURING LEISURE TIME."

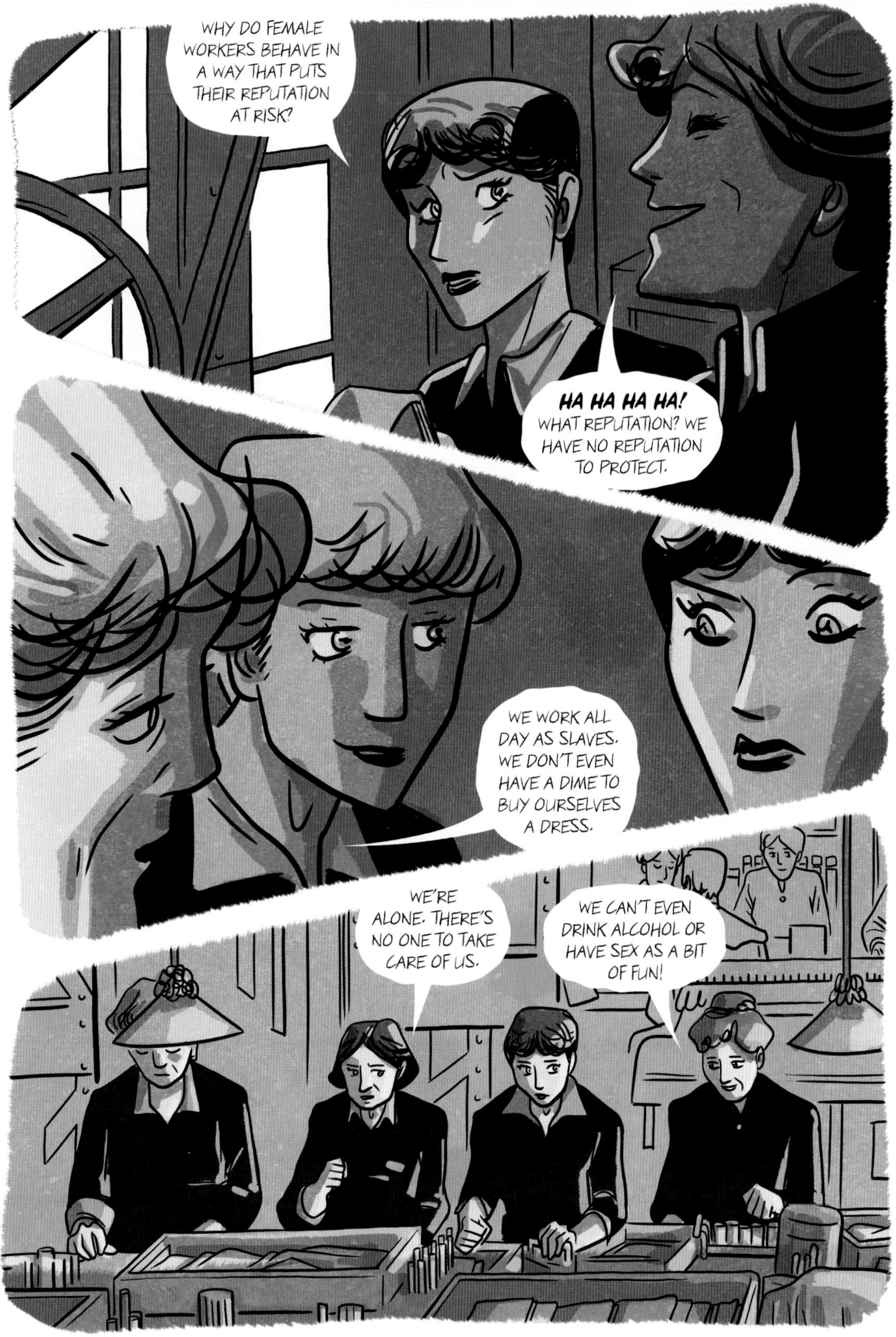
WHY DO FEMALE WORKERS BEHAVE IN A WAY THAT PUTS THEIR REPUTATION AT RISK?
HA HA HA HA! WHAT REPUTATION? WE HAVE NO REPUTATION TO PROTECT.
WE WORK ALL DAY AS SLAVES. WE DON'T EVEN HAVE A DIME TO BUY OURSELVES A DRESS.
WE'RE ALONE. THERE'S NO ONE TO TAKE CARE OF US.
WE CAN'T EVEN DRINK ALCOHOL OR HAVE SEX AS A BIT OF FUN!

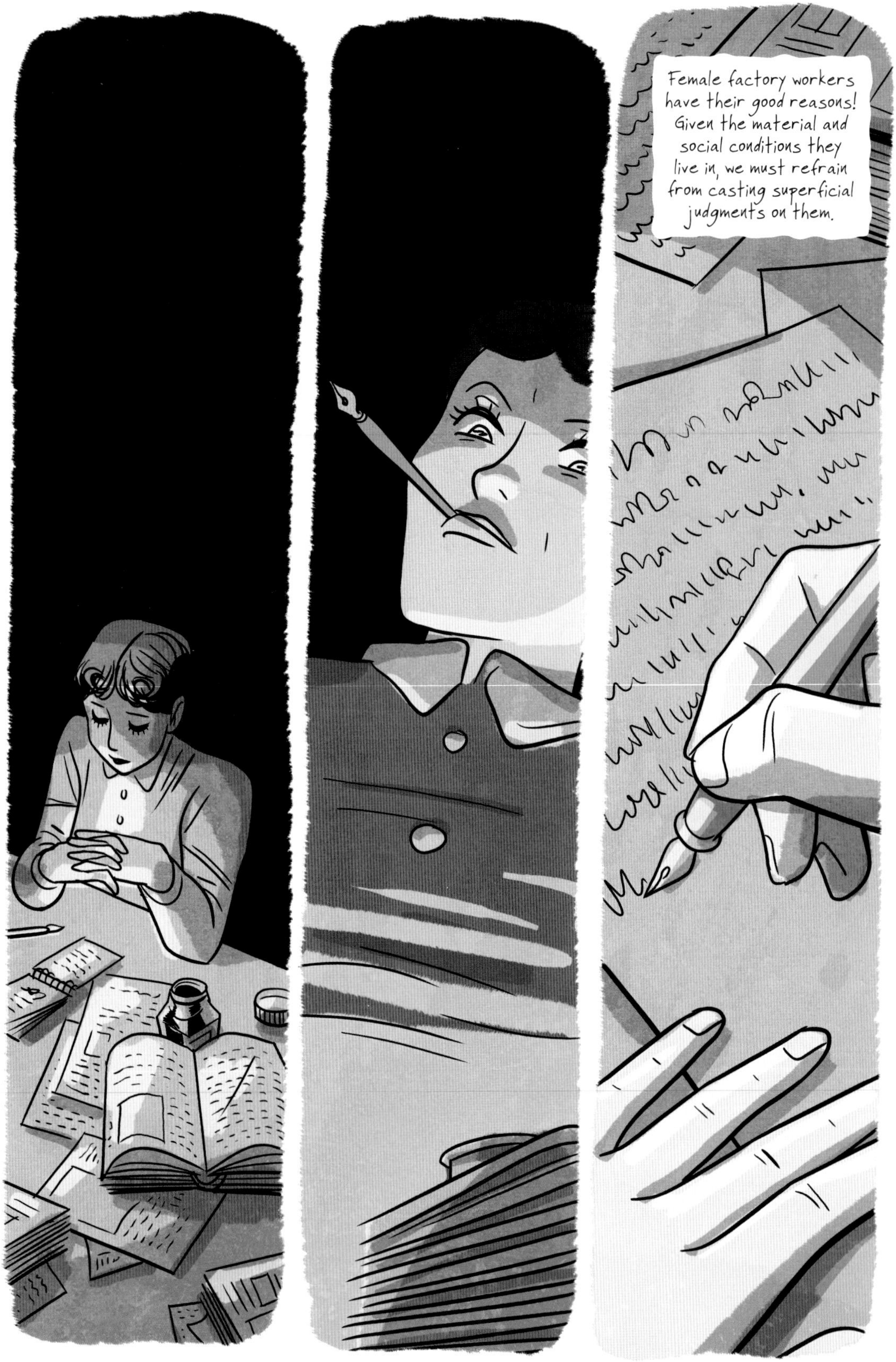
Female factory workers have their good reasons! Given the material and social conditions they live in, we must refrain from casting superficial judgments on them.

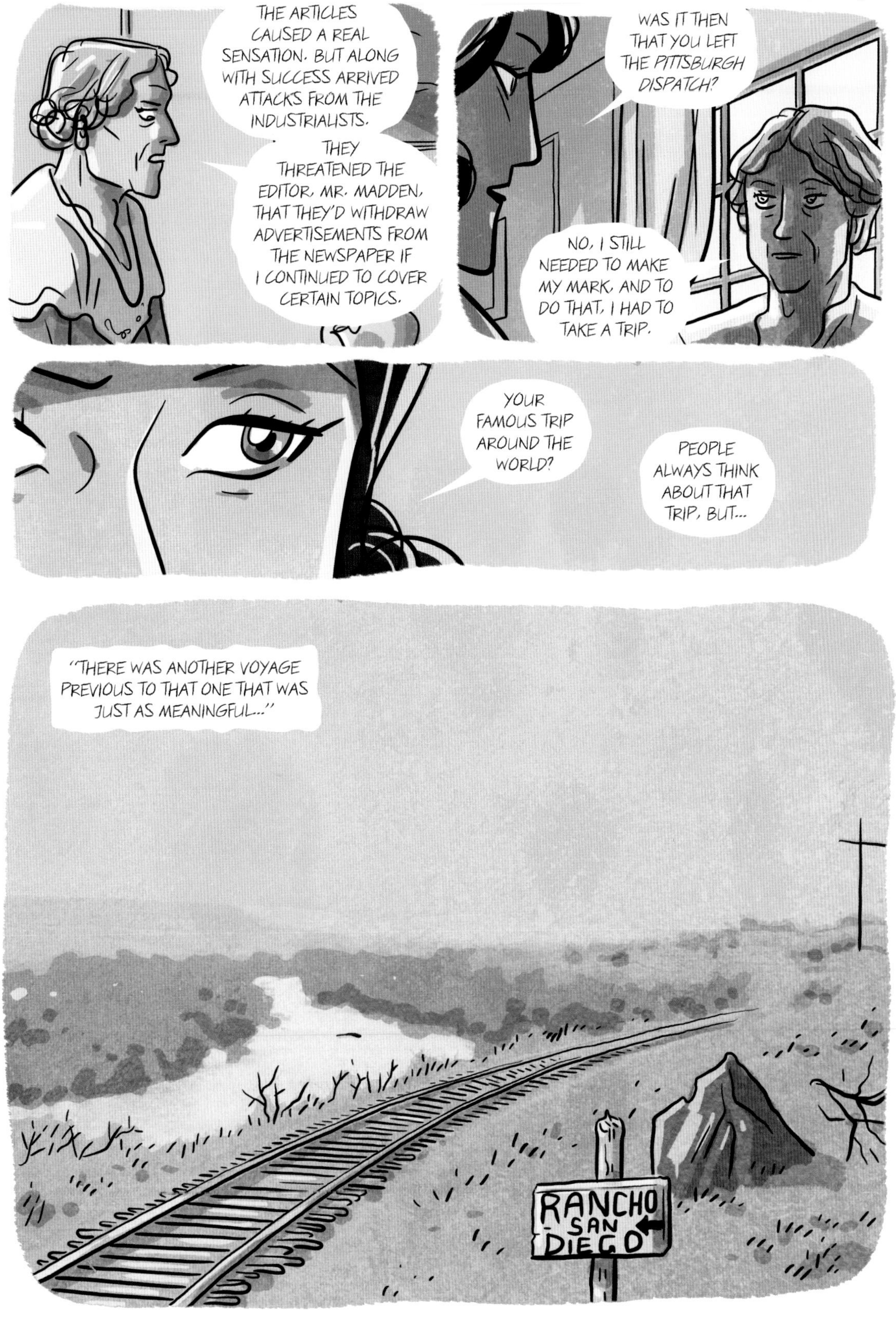
THE ARTICLES CAUSED A REAL SENSATION. BUT ALONG WITH SUCCESS ARRIVED ATTACKS FROM THE INDUSTRIALISTS.
THEY THREATENED THE EDITOR, MR. MADDEN, THAT THEY'D WITHDRAW ADVERTISEMENTS FROM THE NEWSPAPER IF I CONTINUED TO COVER CERTAIN TOPICS.
WAS IT THEN THAT YOU LEFT THE *PITTSBURGH DISPATCH*?
NO, I STILL NEEDED TO MAKE MY MARK, AND TO DO THAT, I HAD TO TAKE A TRIP.
YOUR FAMOUS TRIP AROUND THE WORLD?
PEOPLE ALWAYS THINK ABOUT THAT TRIP, BUT...
"THERE WAS ANOTHER VOYAGE PREVIOUS TO THAT ONE THAT WAS JUST AS MEANINGFUL..."
RANCHO SAN DIEGO

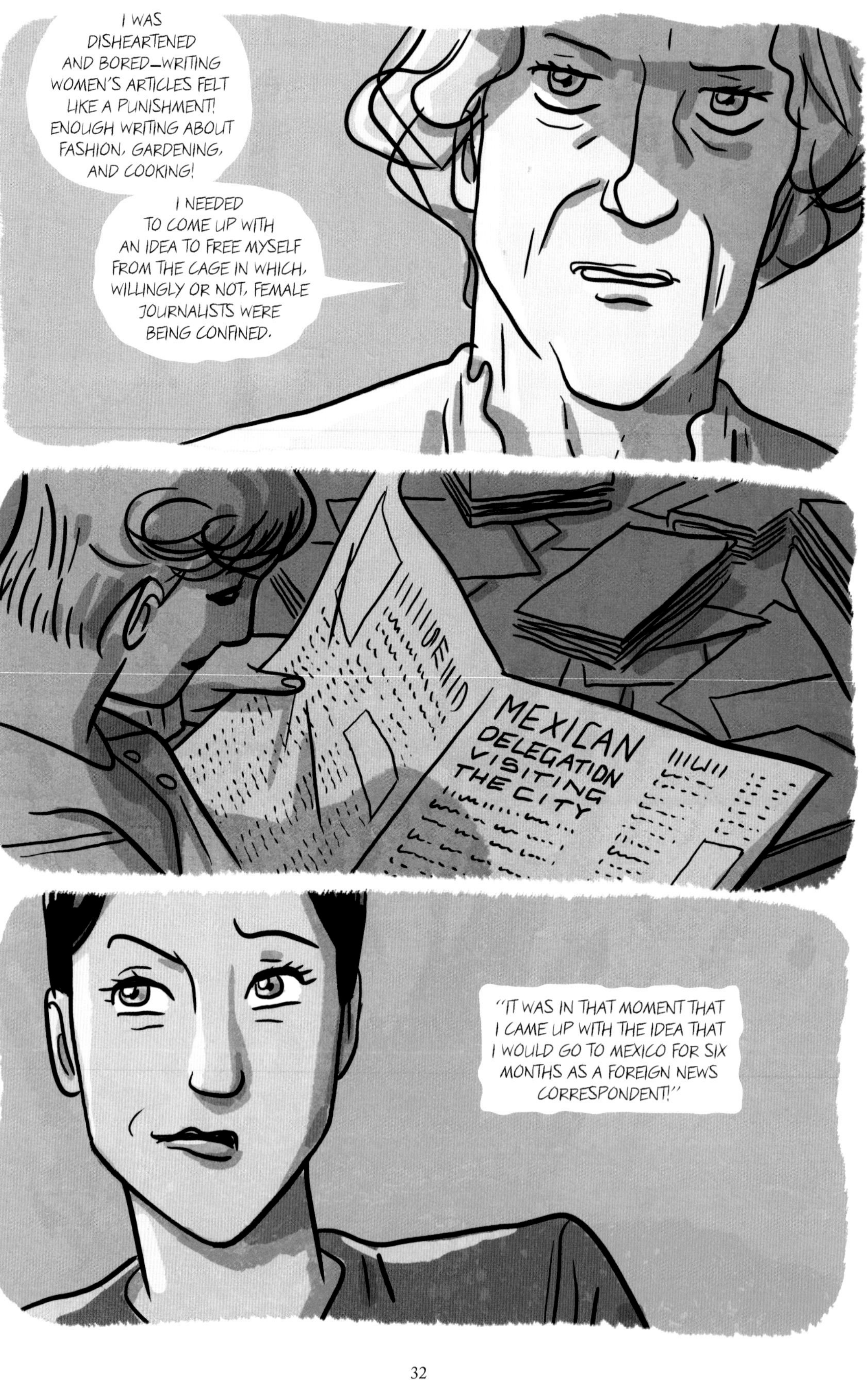
I WAS DISHEARTENED AND BORED—WRITING WOMEN'S ARTICLES FELT LIKE A PUNISHMENT! ENOUGH WRITING ABOUT FASHION, GARDENING, AND COOKING!
I NEEDED TO COME UP WITH AN IDEA TO FREE MYSELF FROM THE CAGE IN WHICH, WILLINGLY OR NOT, FEMALE JOURNALISTS WERE BEING CONFINED.
MEXICAN DELEGATION VISITING THE CITY
"IT WAS IN THAT MOMENT THAT I CAME UP WITH THE IDEA THAT I WOULD GO TO MEXICO FOR SIX MONTHS AS A FOREIGN NEWS CORRESPONDENT!"

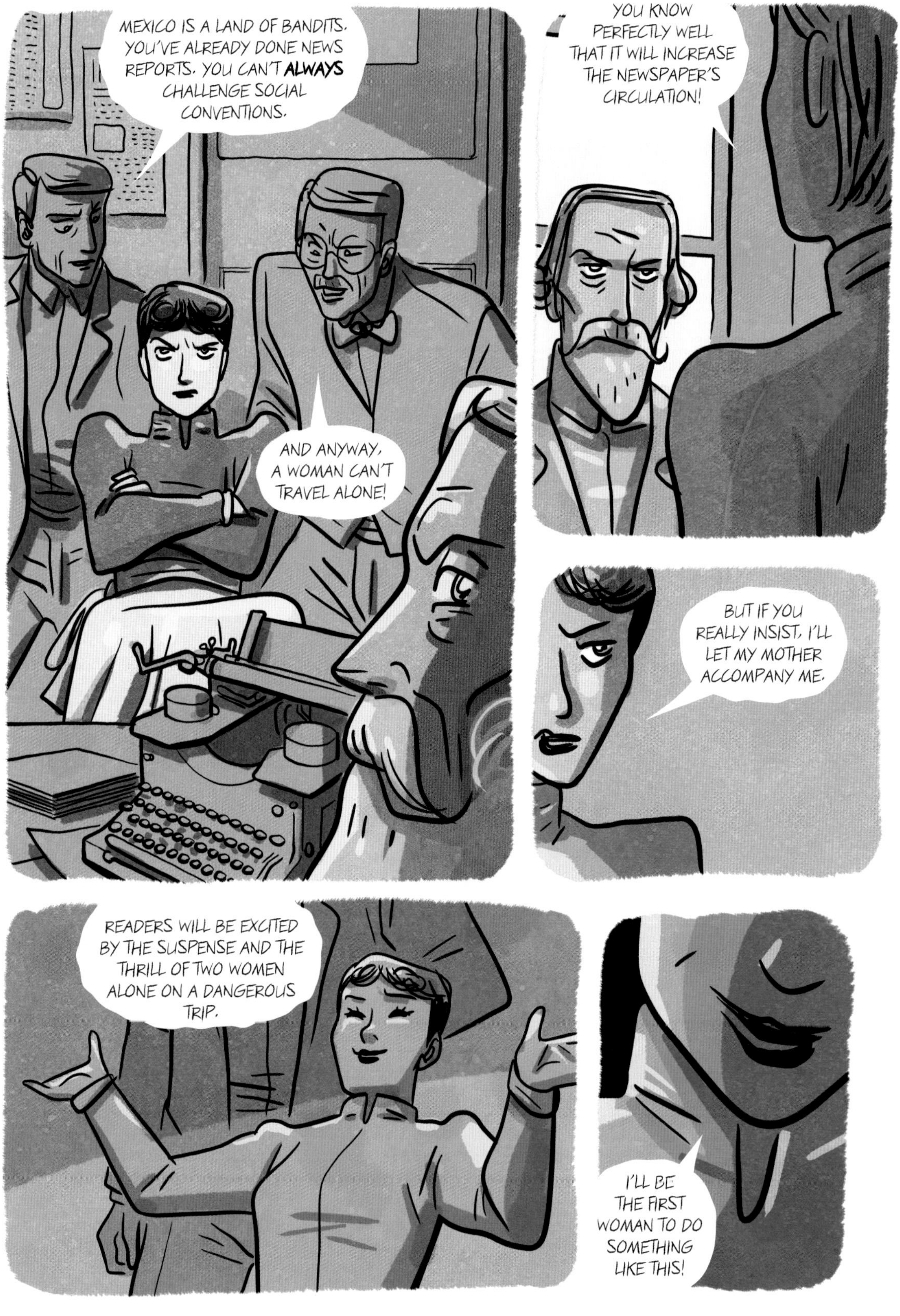
MEXICO IS A LAND OF BANDITS. YOU'VE ALREADY DONE NEWS REPORTS. YOU CAN'T **ALWAYS** CHALLENGE SOCIAL CONVENTIONS.
AND ANYWAY, A WOMAN CAN'T TRAVEL ALONE!
YOU KNOW PERFECTLY WELL THAT IT WILL INCREASE THE NEWSPAPER'S CIRCULATION!
BUT IF YOU REALLY INSIST, I'LL LET MY MOTHER ACCOMPANY ME.
READERS WILL BE EXCITED BY THE SUSPENSE AND THE THRILL OF TWO WOMEN ALONE ON A DANGEROUS TRIP.
I'LL BE THE FIRST WOMAN TO DO SOMETHING LIKE THIS!

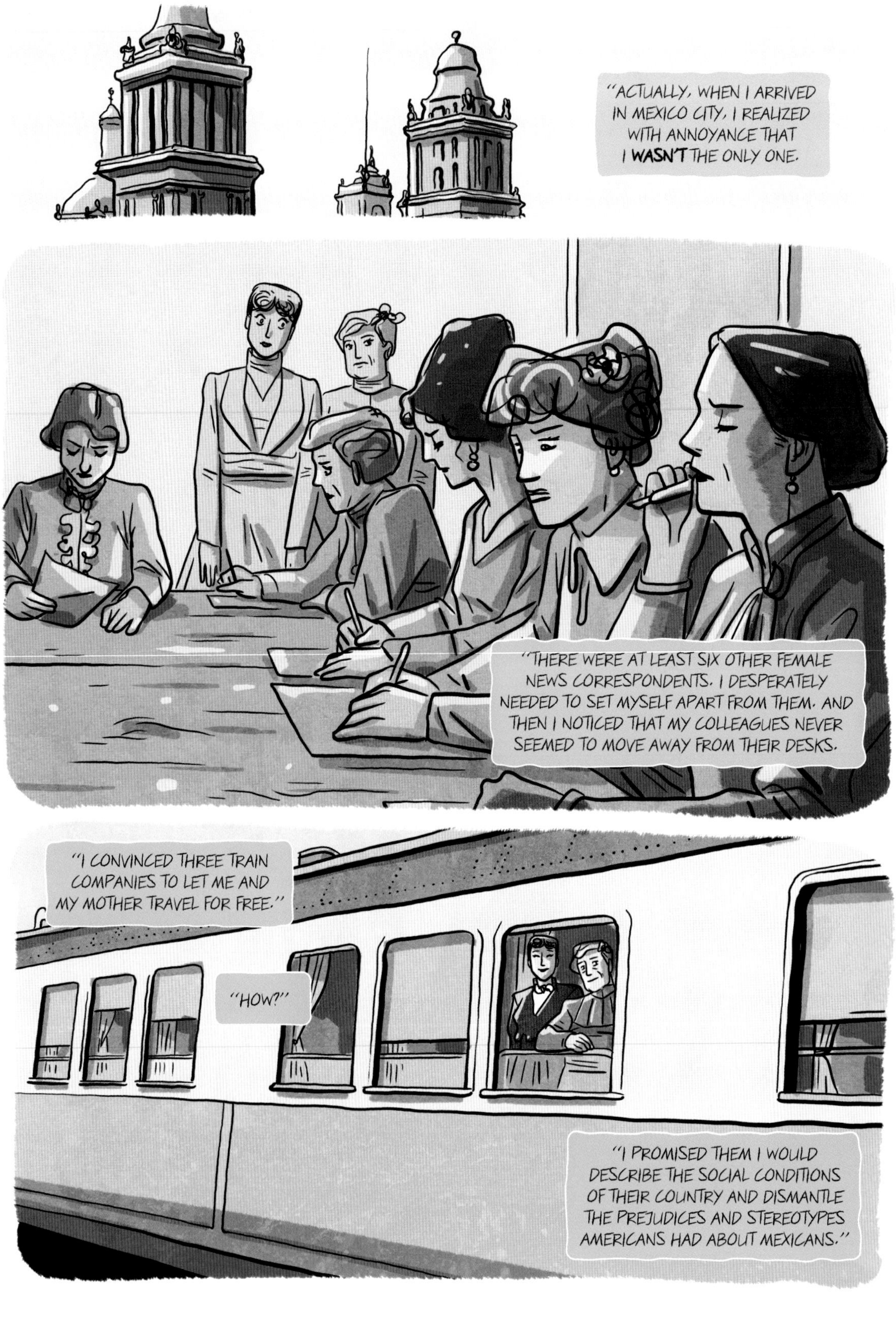
"ACTUALLY, WHEN I ARRIVED IN MEXICO CITY, I REALIZED WITH ANNOYANCE THAT I **WASN'T** THE ONLY ONE.
"THERE WERE AT LEAST SIX OTHER FEMALE NEWS CORRESPONDENTS. I DESPERATELY NEEDED TO SET MYSELF APART FROM THEM. AND THEN I NOTICED THAT MY COLLEAGUES NEVER SEEMED TO MOVE AWAY FROM THEIR DESKS.
"I CONVINCED THREE TRAIN COMPANIES TO LET ME AND MY MOTHER TRAVEL FOR FREE."
"HOW?"
"I PROMISED THEM I WOULD DESCRIBE THE SOCIAL CONDITIONS OF THEIR COUNTRY AND DISMANTLE THE PREJUDICES AND STEREOTYPES AMERICANS HAD ABOUT MEXICANS."

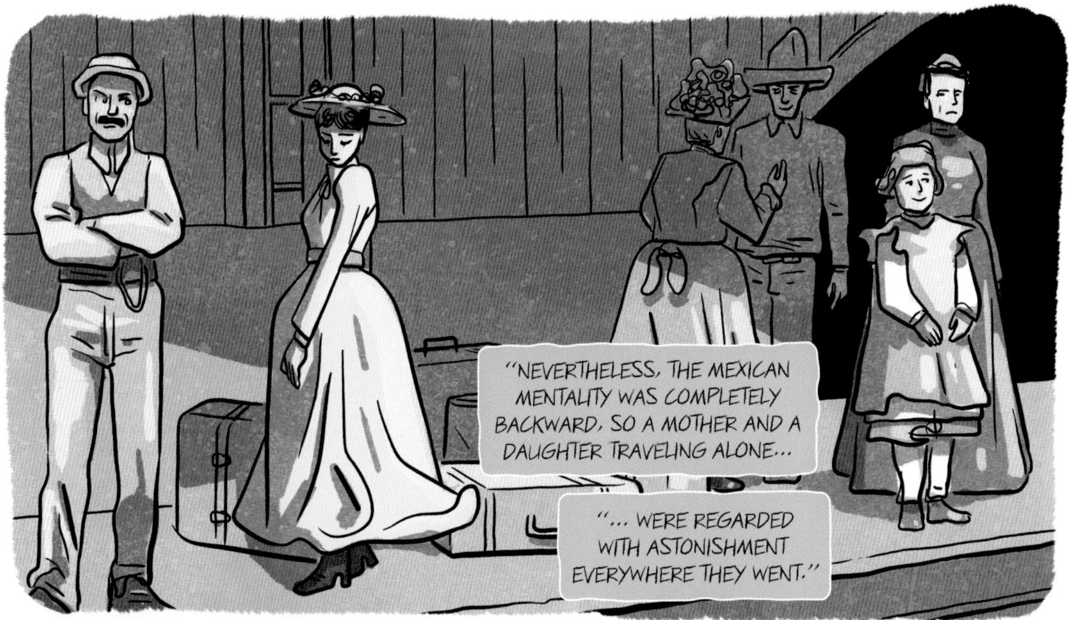
"NEVERTHELESS, THE MEXICAN MENTALITY WAS COMPLETELY BACKWARD, SO A MOTHER AND A DAUGHTER TRAVELING ALONE...
"... WERE REGARDED WITH ASTONISHMENT EVERYWHERE THEY WENT."

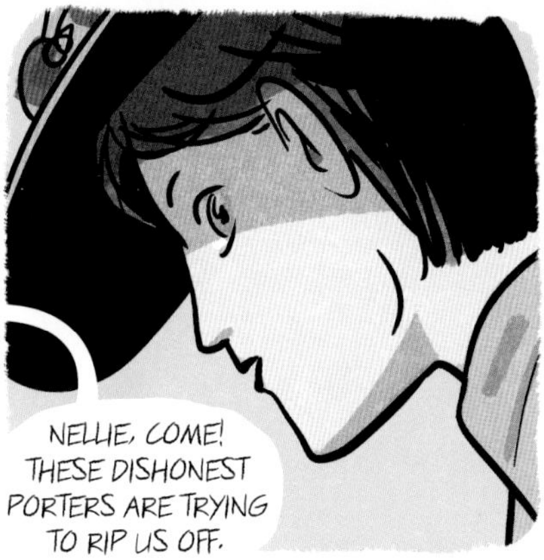
NELLIE, COME! THESE DISHONEST PORTERS ARE TRYING TO RIP US OFF.

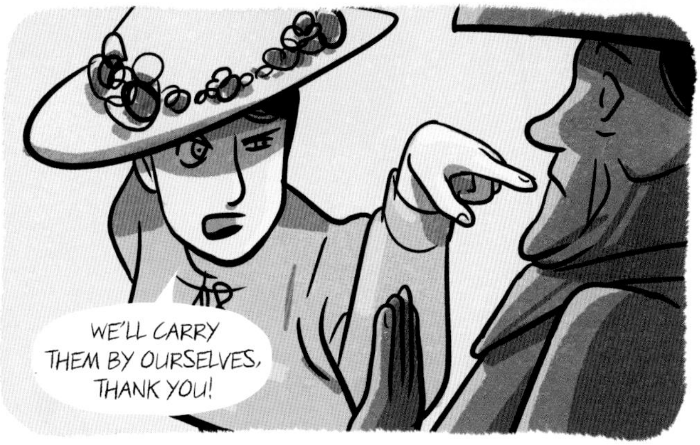
WE'LL CARRY THEM BY OURSELVES, THANK YOU!

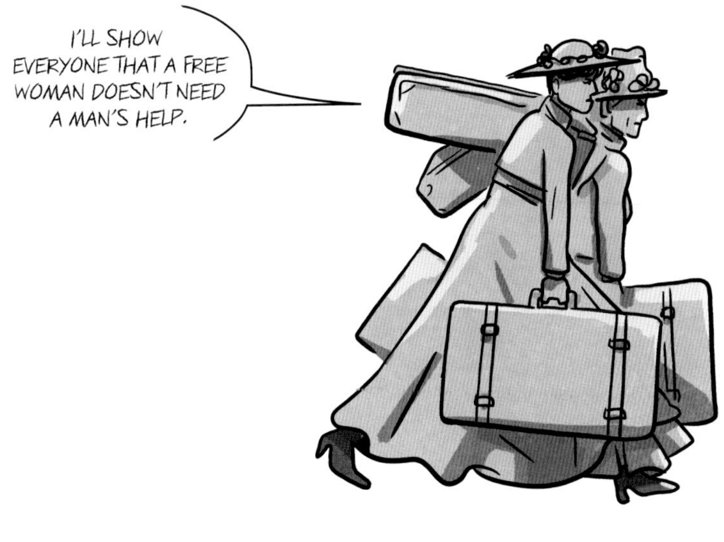
I'LL SHOW EVERYONE THAT A FREE WOMAN DOESN'T NEED A MAN'S HELP.

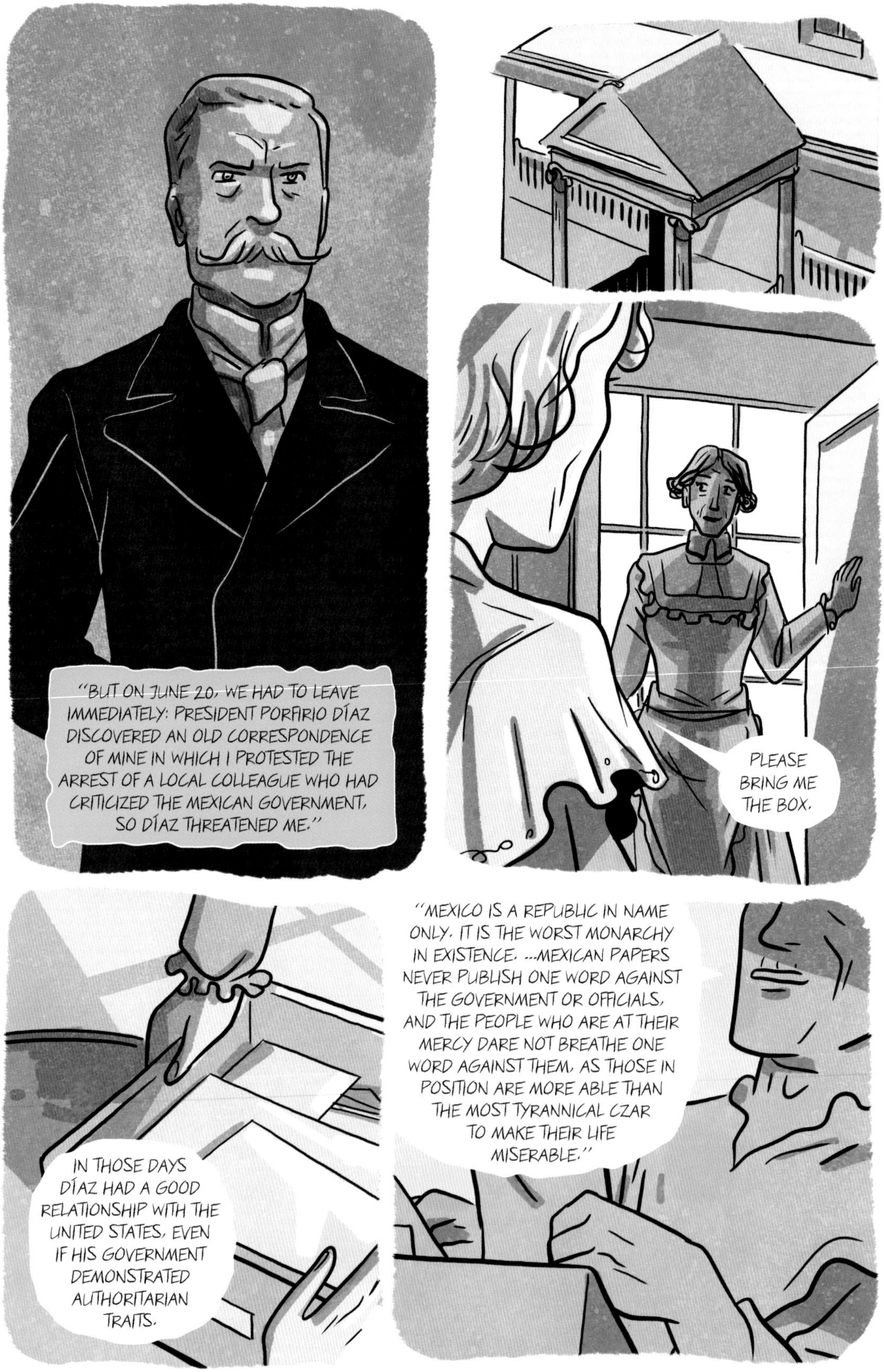
"BUT ON JUNE 20, WE HAD TO LEAVE IMMEDIATELY: PRESIDENT PORFIRIO DÍAZ DISCOVERED AN OLD CORRESPONDENCE OF MINE IN WHICH I PROTESTED THE ARREST OF A LOCAL COLLEAGUE WHO HAD CRITICIZED THE MEXICAN GOVERNMENT, SO DÍAZ THREATENED ME."
PLEASE BRING ME THE BOX.
IN THOSE DAYS DÍAZ HAD A GOOD RELATIONSHIP WITH THE UNITED STATES, EVEN IF HIS GOVERNMENT DEMONSTRATED AUTHORITARIAN TRAITS.
"MEXICO IS A REPUBLIC IN NAME ONLY. IT IS THE WORST MONARCHY IN EXISTENCE. ...MEXICAN PAPERS NEVER PUBLISH ONE WORD AGAINST THE GOVERNMENT OR OFFICIALS, AND THE PEOPLE WHO ARE AT THEIR MERCY DARE NOT BREATHE ONE WORD AGAINST THEM, AS THOSE IN POSITION ARE MORE ABLE THAN THE MOST TYRANNICAL CZAR TO MAKE THEIR LIFE MISERABLE."

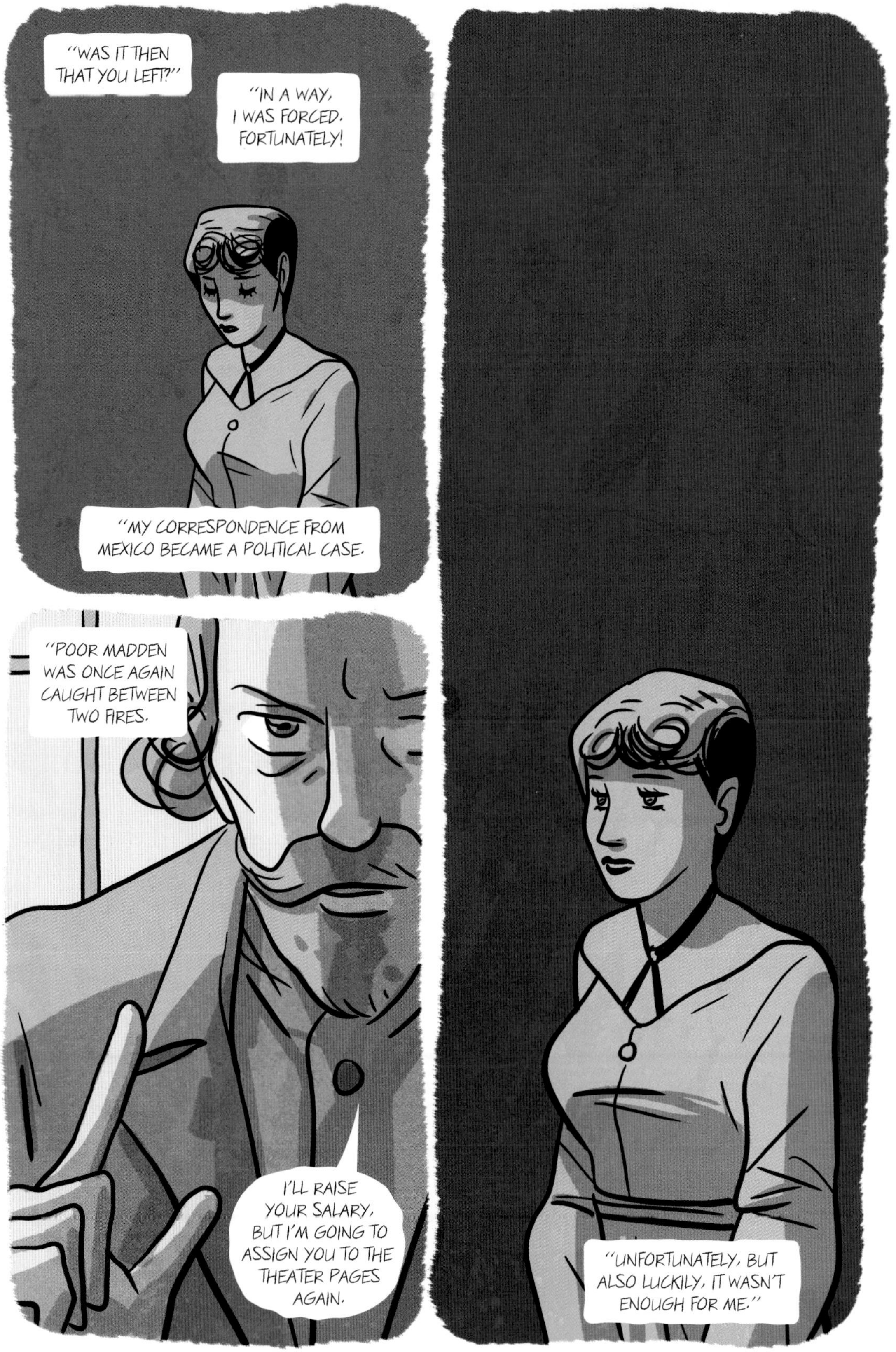
"WAS IT THEN THAT YOU LEFT?"
"IN A WAY, I WAS FORCED. FORTUNATELY!
"MY CORRESPONDENCE FROM MEXICO BECAME A POLITICAL CASE.
"POOR MADDEN WAS ONCE AGAIN CAUGHT BETWEEN TWO FIRES.
I'LL RAISE YOUR SALARY, BUT I'M GOING TO ASSIGN YOU TO THE THEATER PAGES AGAIN.
"UNFORTUNATELY, BUT ALSO LUCKILY, IT WASN'T ENOUGH FOR ME."

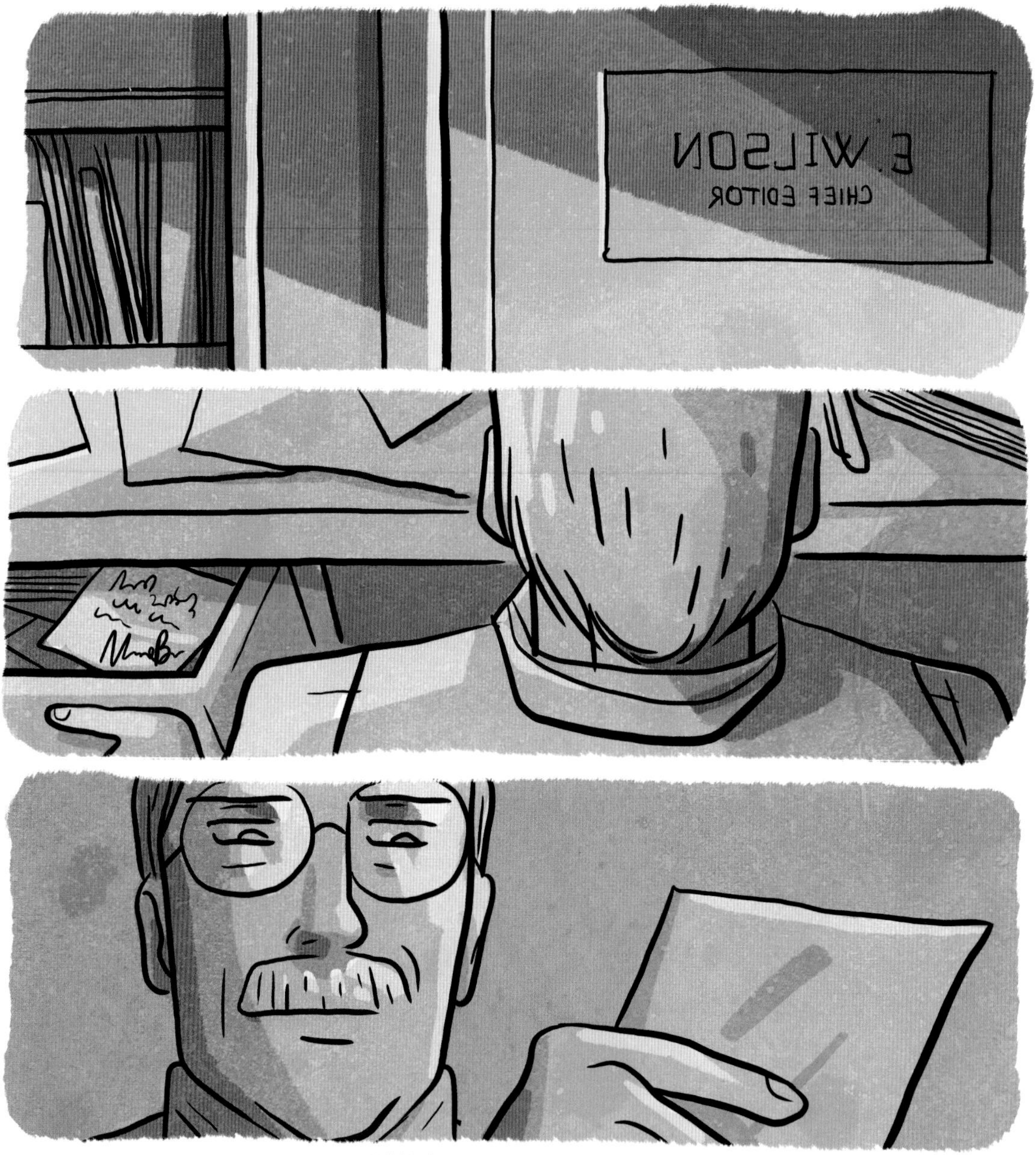
E. WILSON
CHIEF EDITOR
Dear Erasmus,
I'm going to New York.
You'll hear about me.

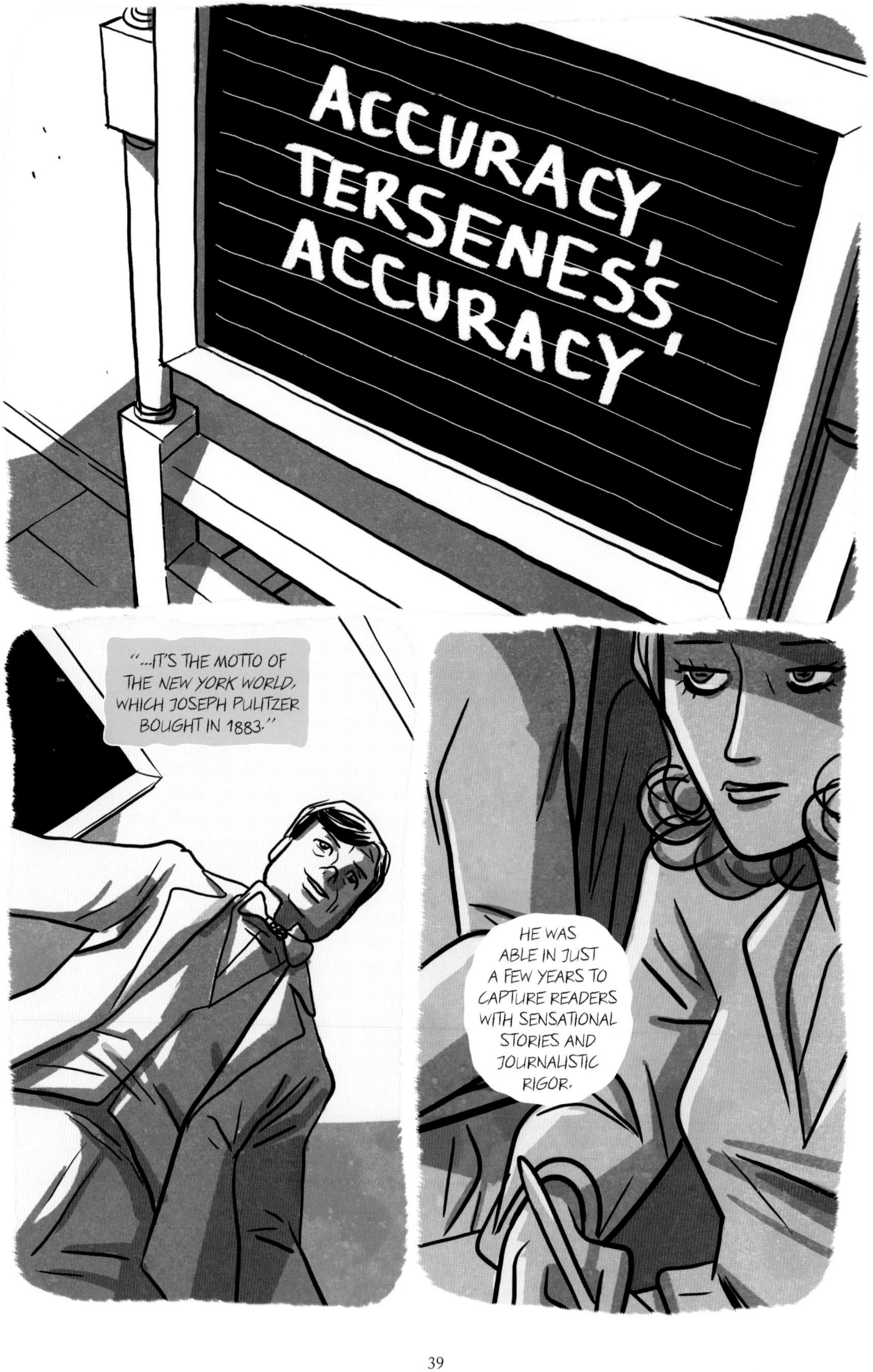
ACCURACY, TERSENESS, ACCURACY'
"...IT'S THE MOTTO OF THE NEW YORK WORLD, WHICH JOSEPH PULITZER BOUGHT IN 1883."
HE WAS ABLE IN JUST A FEW YEARS TO CAPTURE READERS WITH SENSATIONAL STORIES AND JOURNALISTIC RIGOR.

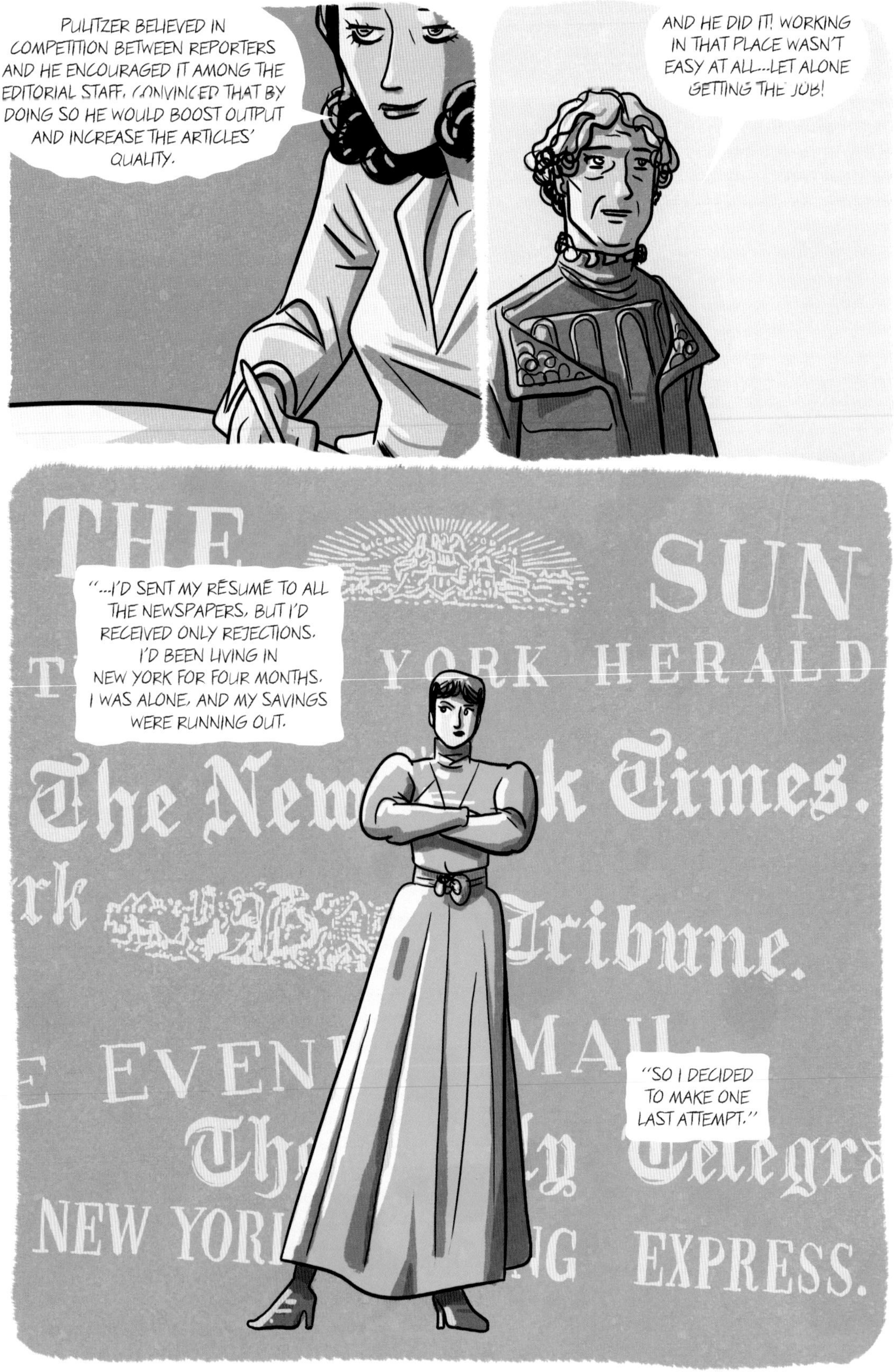
PULITZER BELIEVED IN COMPETITION BETWEEN REPORTERS AND HE ENCOURAGED IT AMONG THE EDITORIAL STAFF, CONVINCED THAT BY DOING SO HE WOULD BOOST OUTPUT AND INCREASE THE ARTICLES' QUALITY.
AND HE DID IT! WORKING IN THAT PLACE WASN'T EASY AT ALL...LET ALONE GETTING THE JOB!
THE SUN
YORK HERALD
"...I'D SENT MY RÉSUMÉ TO ALL THE NEWSPAPERS, BUT I'D RECEIVED ONLY REJECTIONS. I'D BEEN LIVING IN NEW YORK FOR FOUR MONTHS. I WAS ALONE, AND MY SAVINGS WERE RUNNING OUT.
Tribune.
"SO I DECIDED TO MAKE ONE LAST ATTEMPT."
EXPRESS.

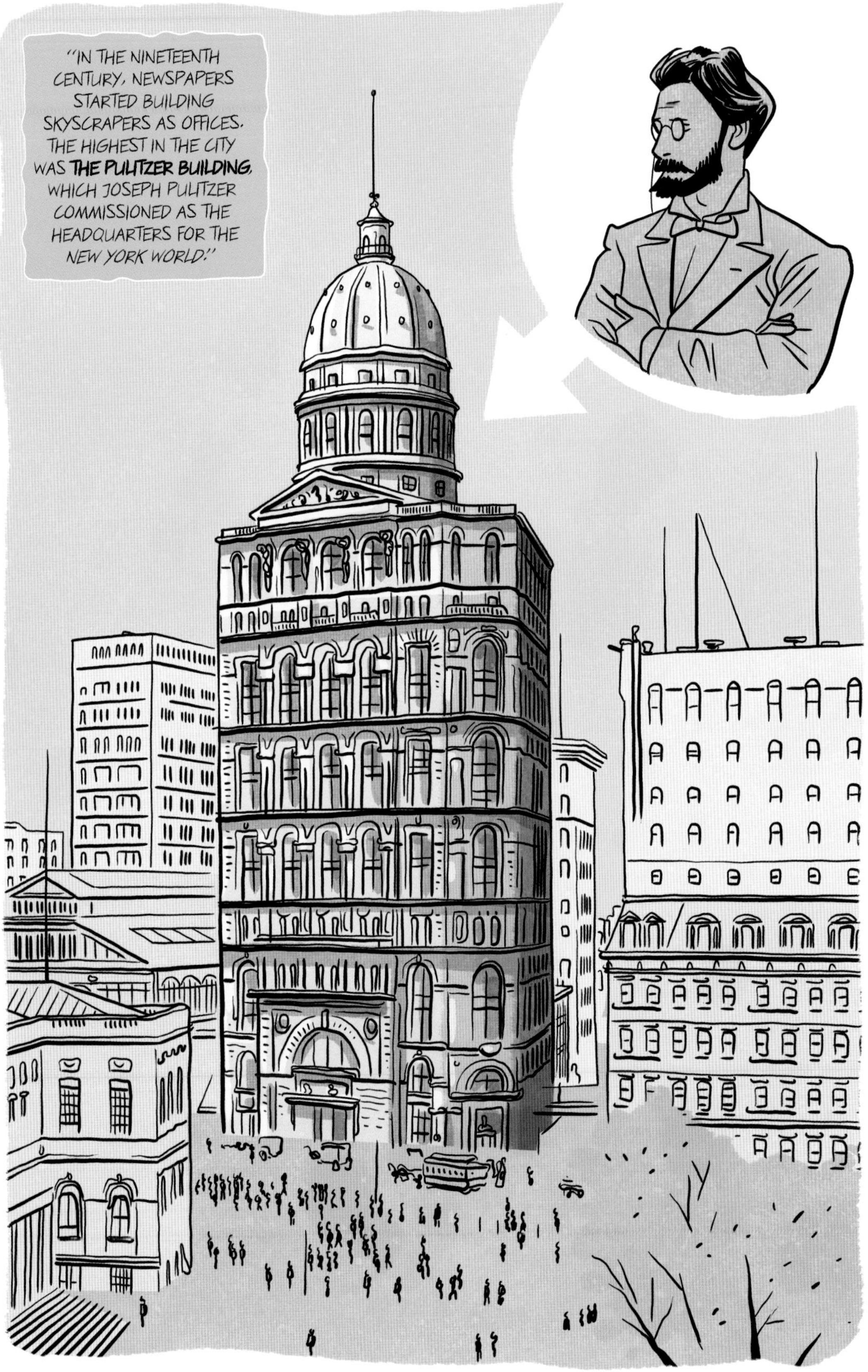
"IN THE NINETEENTH CENTURY, NEWSPAPERS STARTED BUILDING SKYSCRAPERS AS OFFICES. THE HIGHEST IN THE CITY WAS **THE PULITZER BUILDING**, WHICH JOSEPH PULITZER COMMISSIONED AS THE HEADQUARTERS FOR THE *NEW YORK WORLD*."

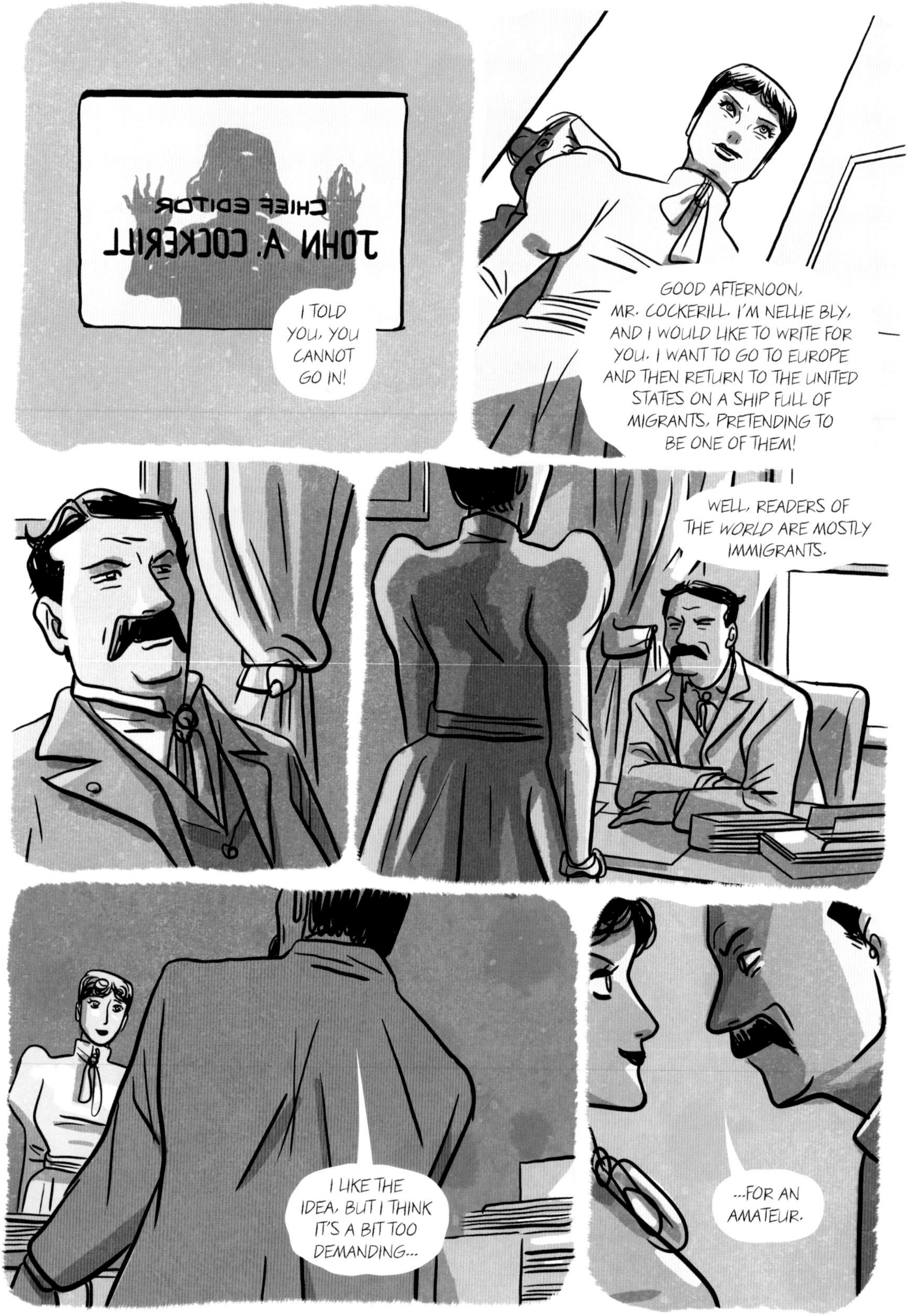
CHIEF EDITOR
JOHN A. COCKERILL
I TOLD YOU, YOU CANNOT GO IN!
GOOD AFTERNOON, MR. COCKERILL. I'M NELLIE BLY, AND I WOULD LIKE TO WRITE FOR YOU. I WANT TO GO TO EUROPE AND THEN RETURN TO THE UNITED STATES ON A SHIP FULL OF MIGRANTS, PRETENDING TO BE ONE OF THEM!
WELL, READERS OF THE *WORLD* ARE MOSTLY IMMIGRANTS.
I LIKE THE IDEA, BUT I THINK IT'S A BIT TOO DEMANDING...
...FOR AN AMATEUR.

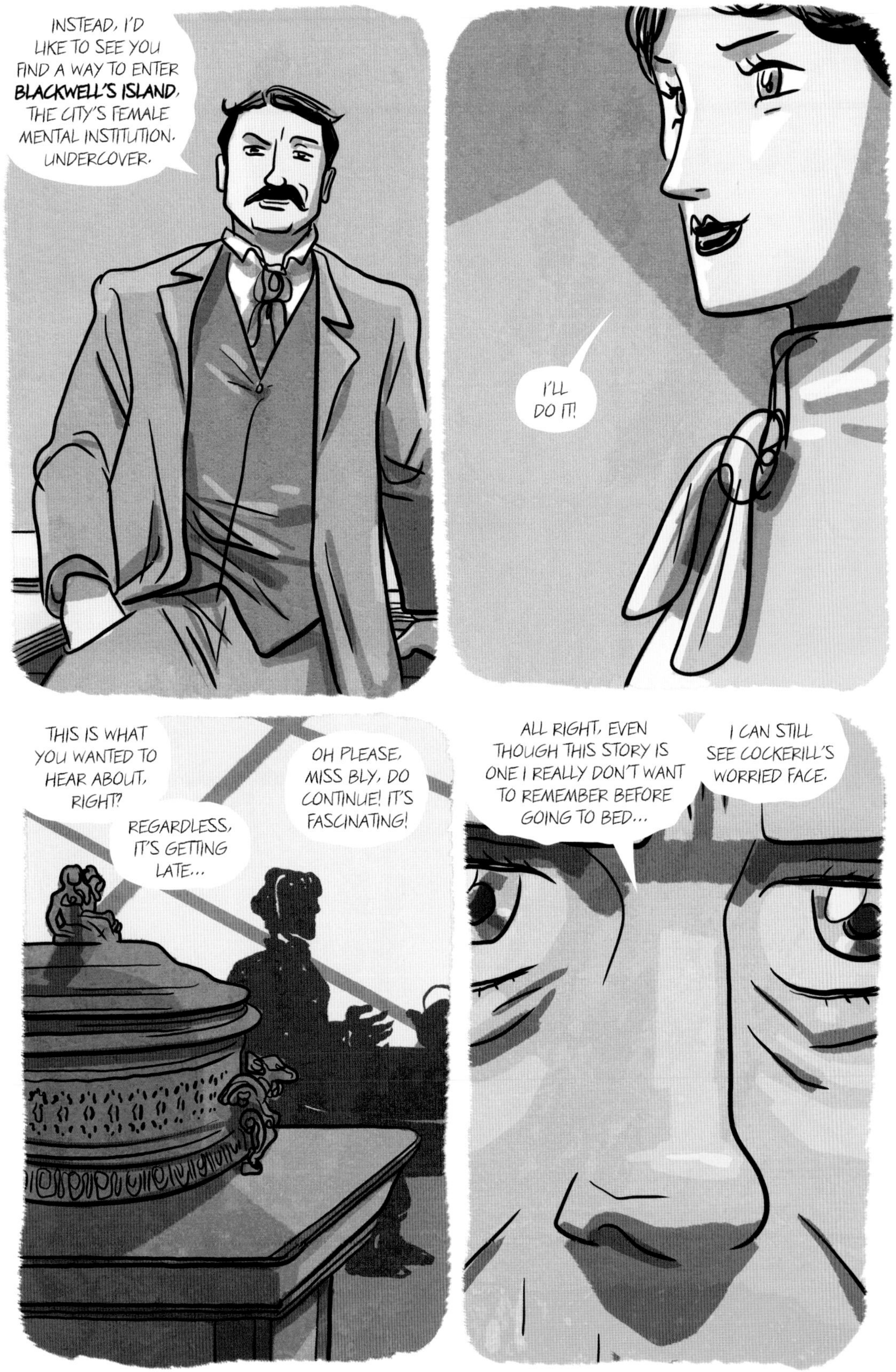
INSTEAD, I'D LIKE TO SEE YOU FIND A WAY TO ENTER **BLACKWELL'S ISLAND**, THE CITY'S FEMALE MENTAL INSTITUTION. UNDERCOVER.
I'LL DO IT!
THIS IS WHAT YOU WANTED TO HEAR ABOUT, RIGHT?
REGARDLESS, IT'S GETTING LATE...
OH PLEASE, MISS BLY, DO CONTINUE! IT'S FASCINATING!
ALL RIGHT, EVEN THOUGH THIS STORY IS ONE I REALLY DON'T WANT TO REMEMBER BEFORE GOING TO BED...
I CAN STILL SEE COCKERILL'S WORRIED FACE.

THE NEWSPAPER HAS COVERED THE INSTITUTION IN THE PAST. WE SUSPECT THAT PATIENTS ARE BEING MISTREATED, BUT TO HAVE PROOF, WE NEED TO GET INSIDE. ARE YOU UP TO IT, NELLIE?

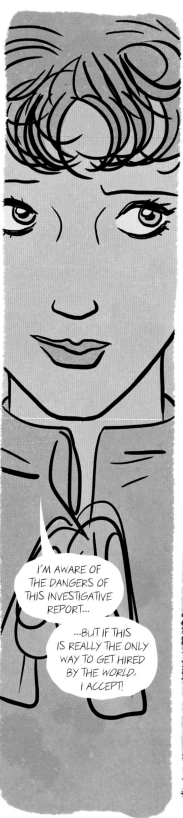

I'M AWARE OF THE DANGERS OF THIS INVESTIGATIVE REPORT...

...BUT IF THIS IS REALLY THE ONLY WAY TO GET HIRED BY THE WORLD, I ACCEPT!

YOU'VE GOT GUTS, GIRL. I'M SERIOUS!

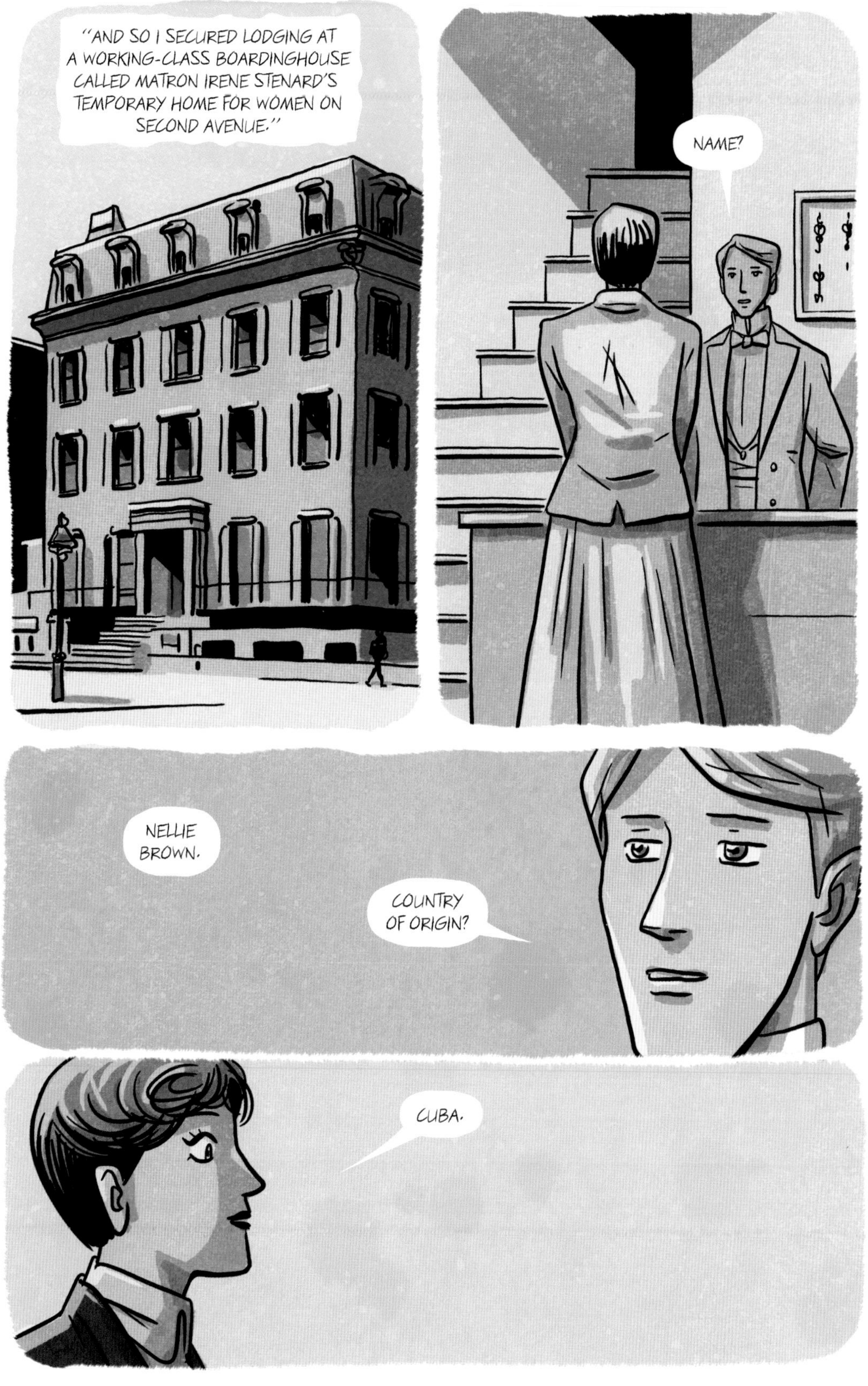
"AND SO I SECURED LODGING AT A WORKING-CLASS BOARDINGHOUSE CALLED MATRON IRENE STENARD'S TEMPORARY HOME FOR WOMEN ON SECOND AVENUE."
NAME?
NELLIE BROWN.
COUNTRY OF ORIGIN?
CUBA.

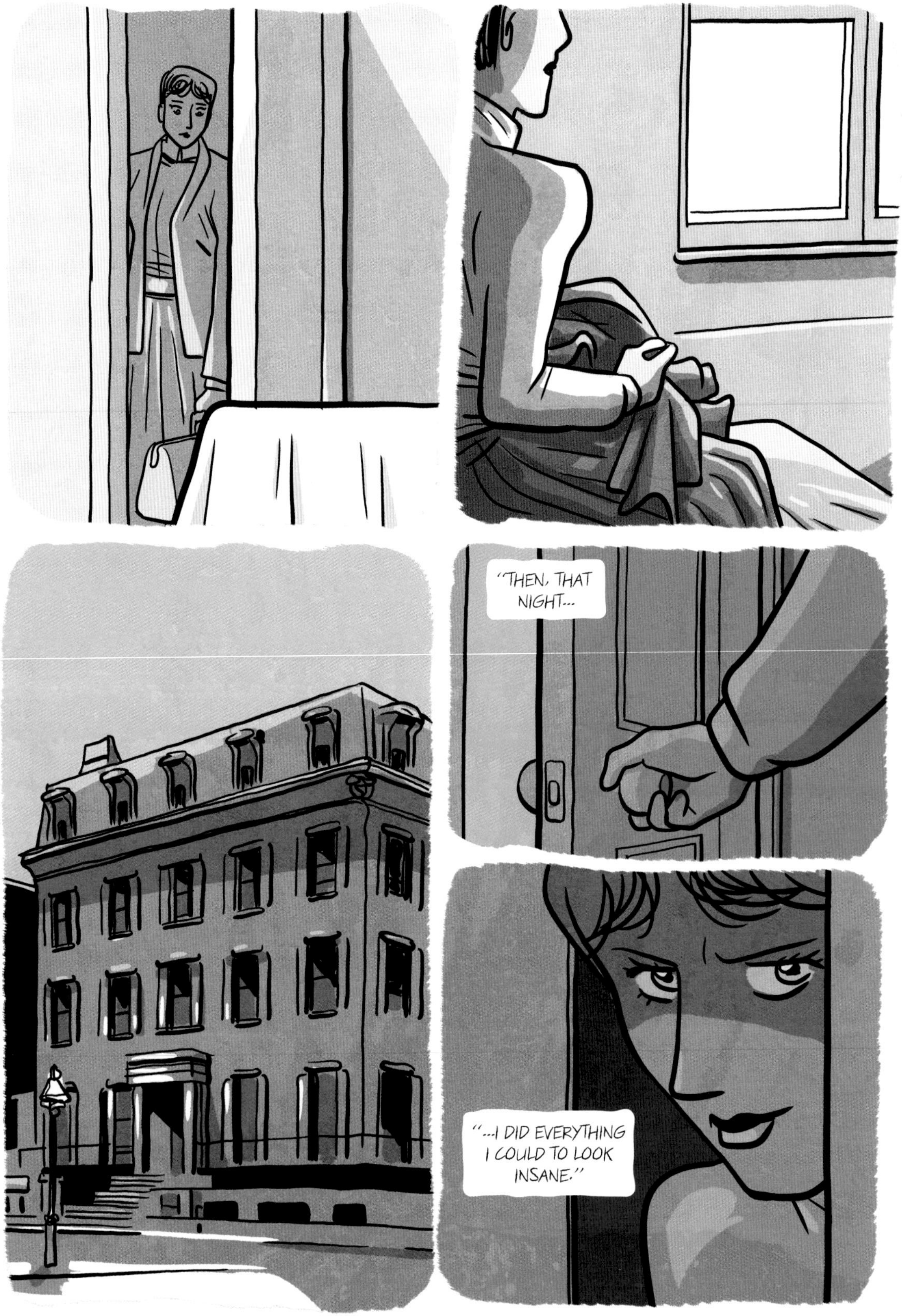
"THEN, THAT NIGHT...
"...I DID EVERYTHING I COULD TO LOOK INSANE."

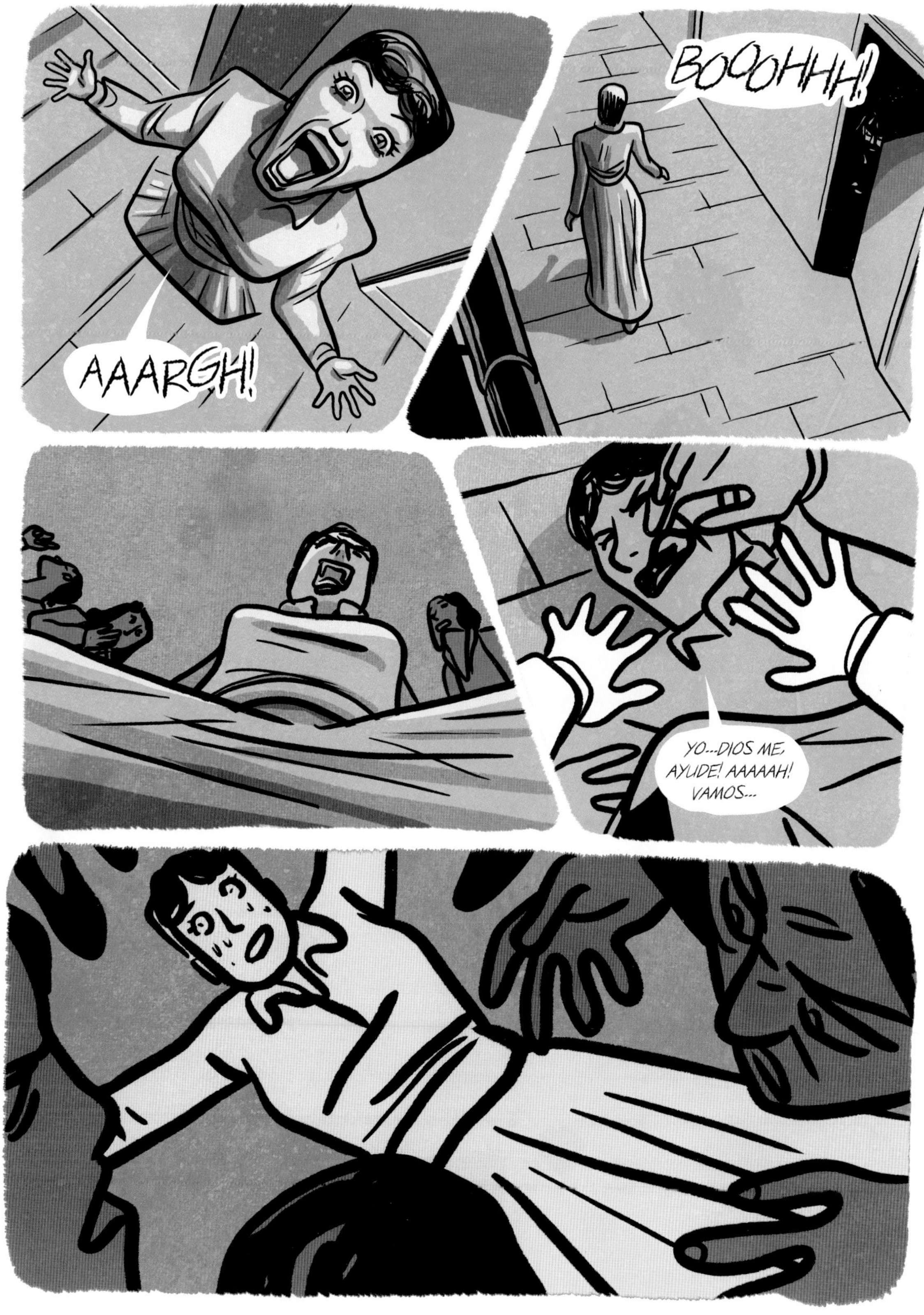
AAARGH!
BOOOHHH!
YO...DIOS ME, AYUDE! AAAAAH! VAMOS...

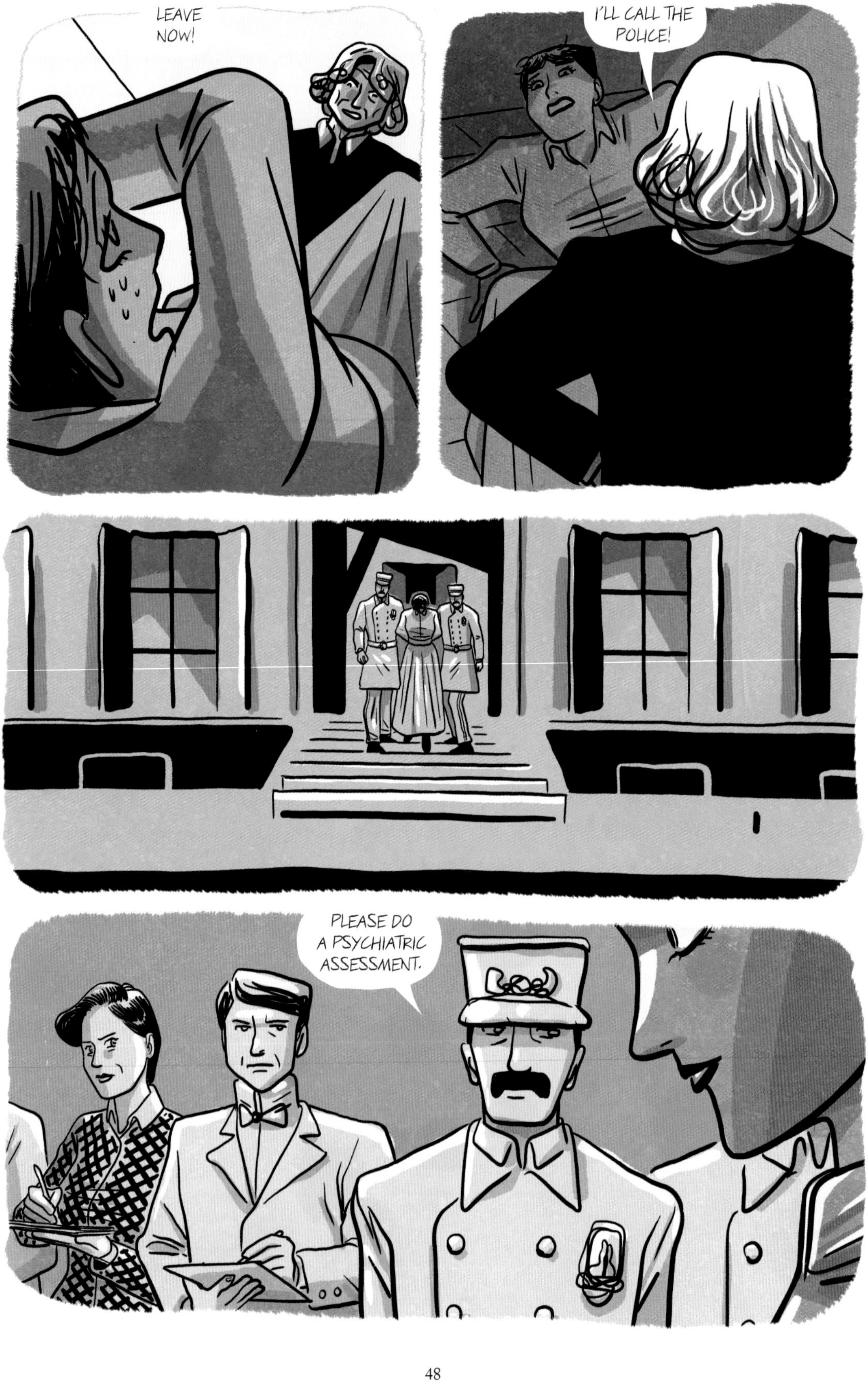
LEAVE NOW!
I'LL CALL THE POLICE!
PLEASE DO A PSYCHIATRIC ASSESSMENT.

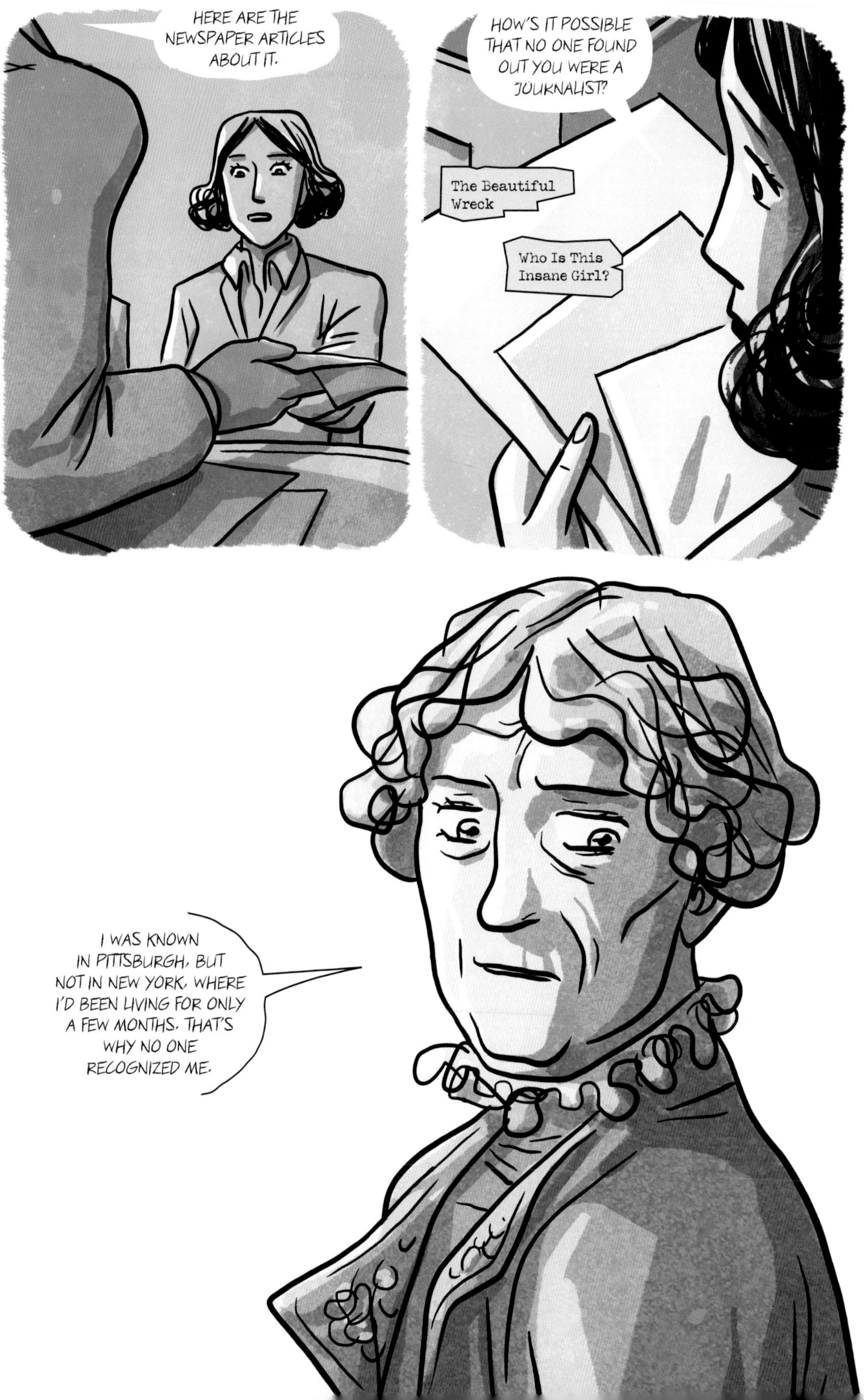
HERE ARE THE NEWSPAPER ARTICLES ABOUT IT.
HOW'S IT POSSIBLE THAT NO ONE FOUND OUT YOU WERE A JOURNALIST?
The Beautiful Wreck
Who Is This Insane Girl?
I WAS KNOWN IN PITTSBURGH, BUT NOT IN NEW YORK, WHERE I'D BEEN LIVING FOR ONLY A FEW MONTHS. THAT'S WHY NO ONE RECOGNIZED ME.

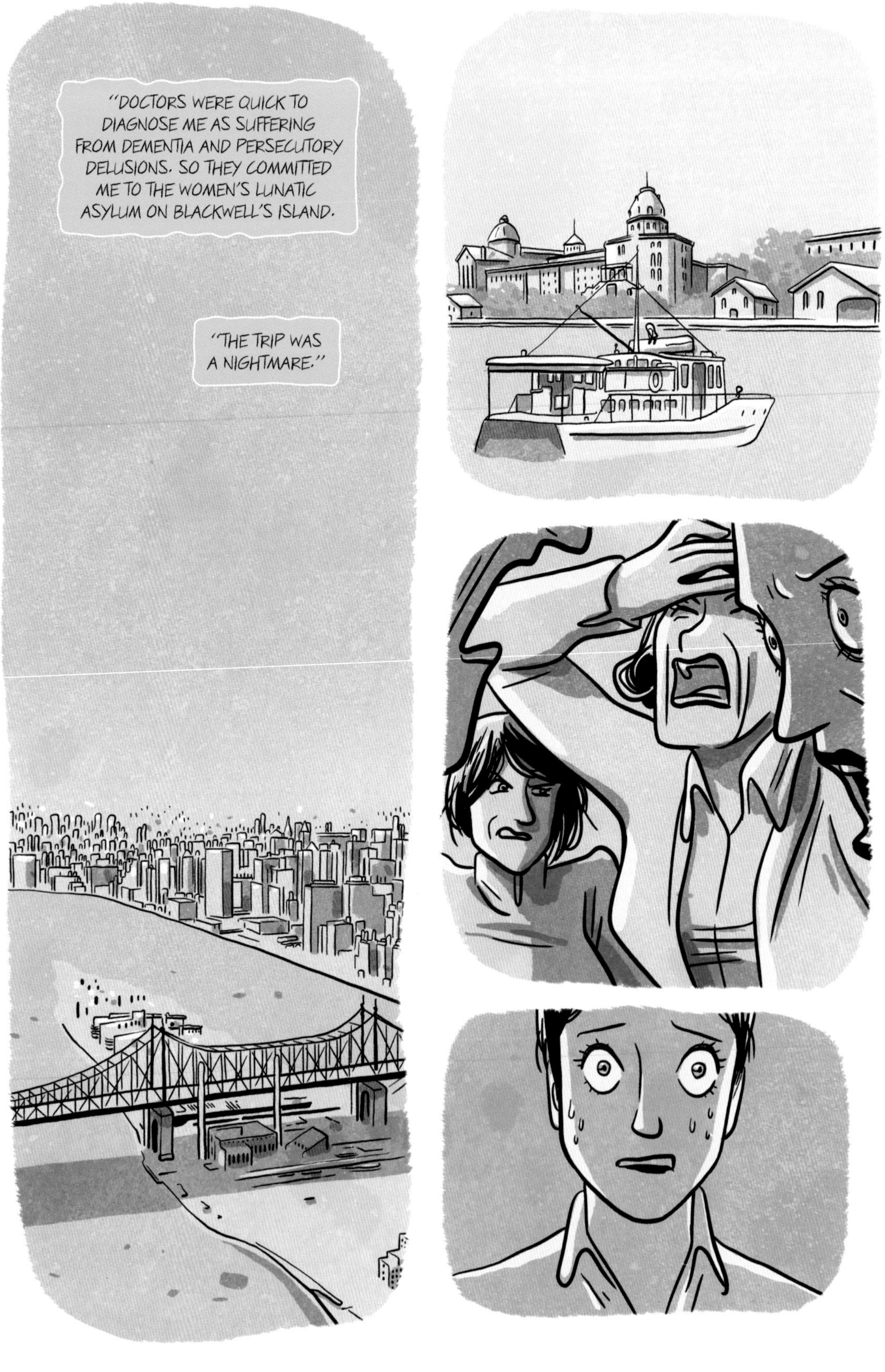
"DOCTORS WERE QUICK TO DIAGNOSE ME AS SUFFERING FROM DEMENTIA AND PERSECUTORY DELUSIONS. SO THEY COMMITTED ME TO THE WOMEN'S LUNATIC ASYLUM ON BLACKWELL'S ISLAND.
"THE TRIP WAS A NIGHTMARE."

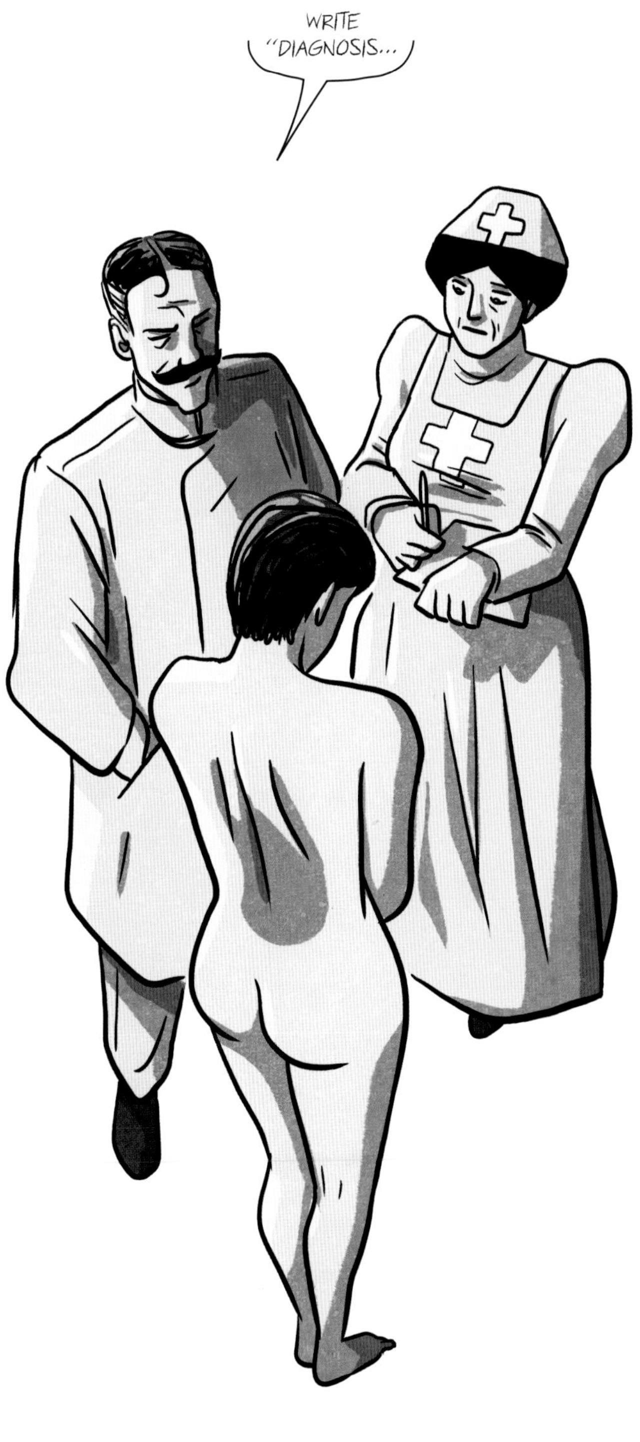
WRITE "DIAGNOSIS...

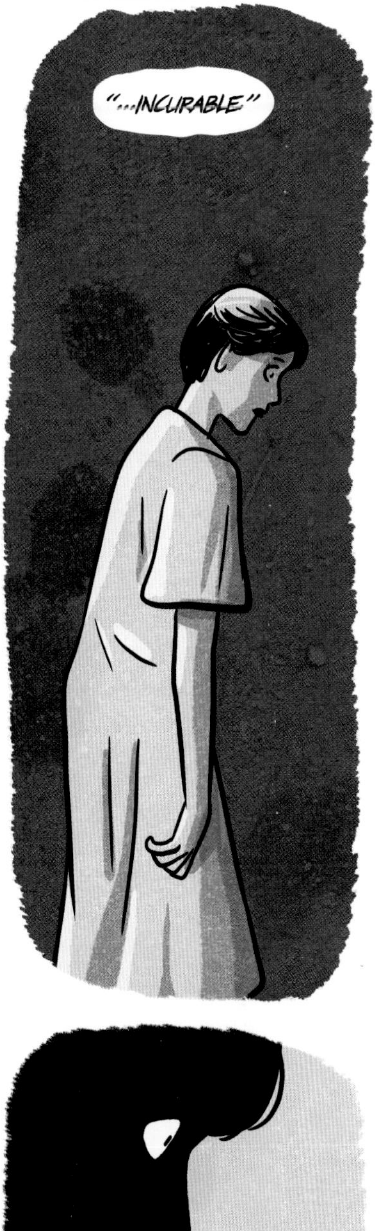
"...INCURABLE"

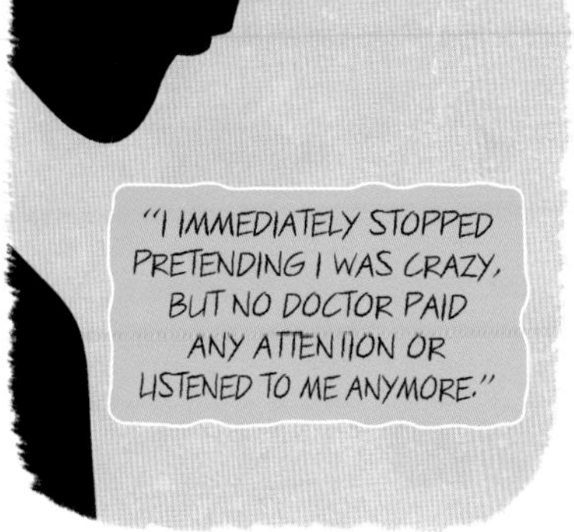
"I IMMEDIATELY STOPPED PRETENDING I WAS CRAZY, BUT NO DOCTOR PAID ANY ATTENTION OR LISTENED TO ME ANYMORE."

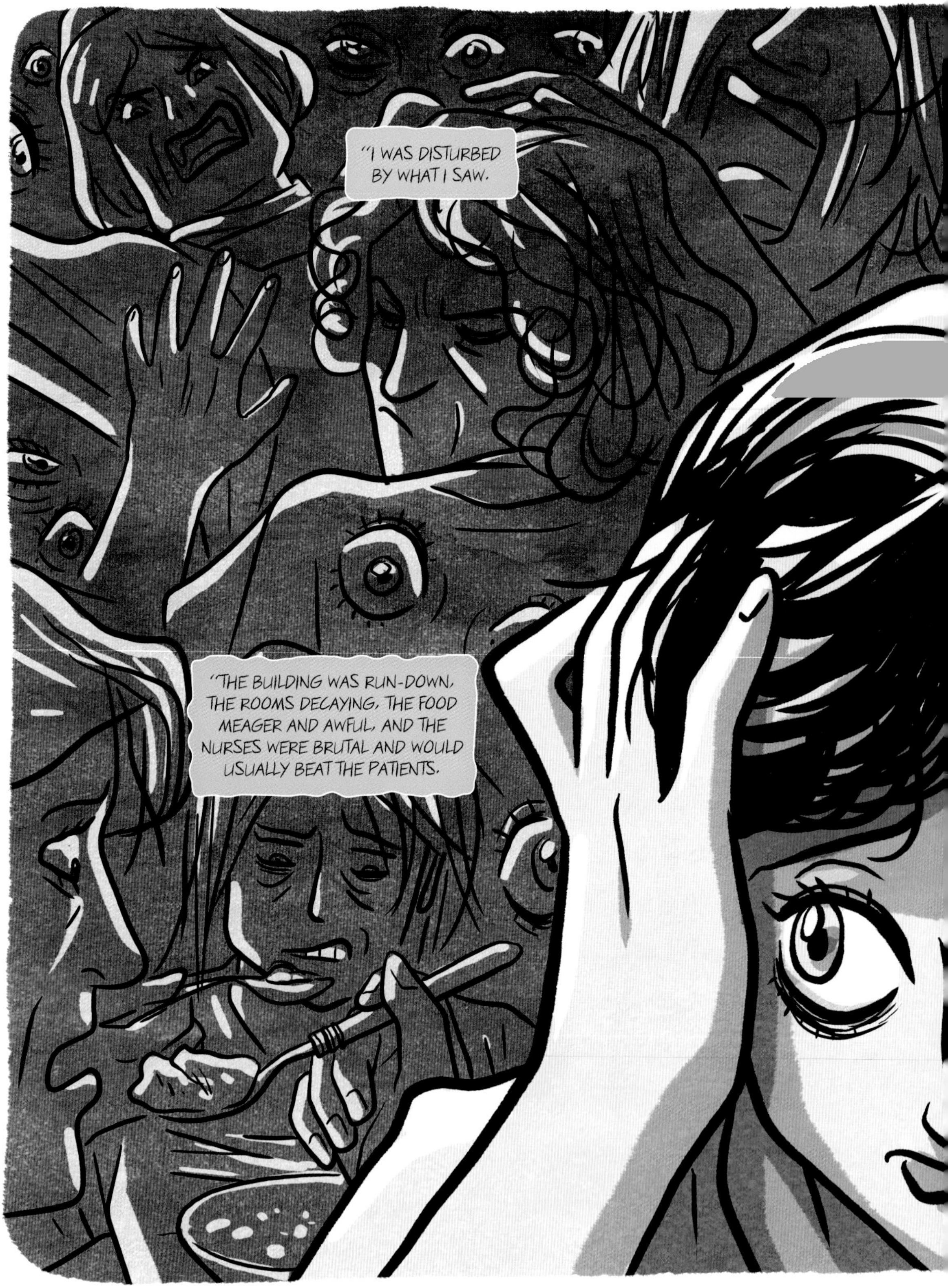
"I WAS DISTURBED BY WHAT I SAW.
"THE BUILDING WAS RUN-DOWN, THE ROOMS DECAYING, THE FOOD MEAGER AND AWFUL, AND THE NURSES WERE BRUTAL AND WOULD USUALLY BEAT THE PATIENTS.

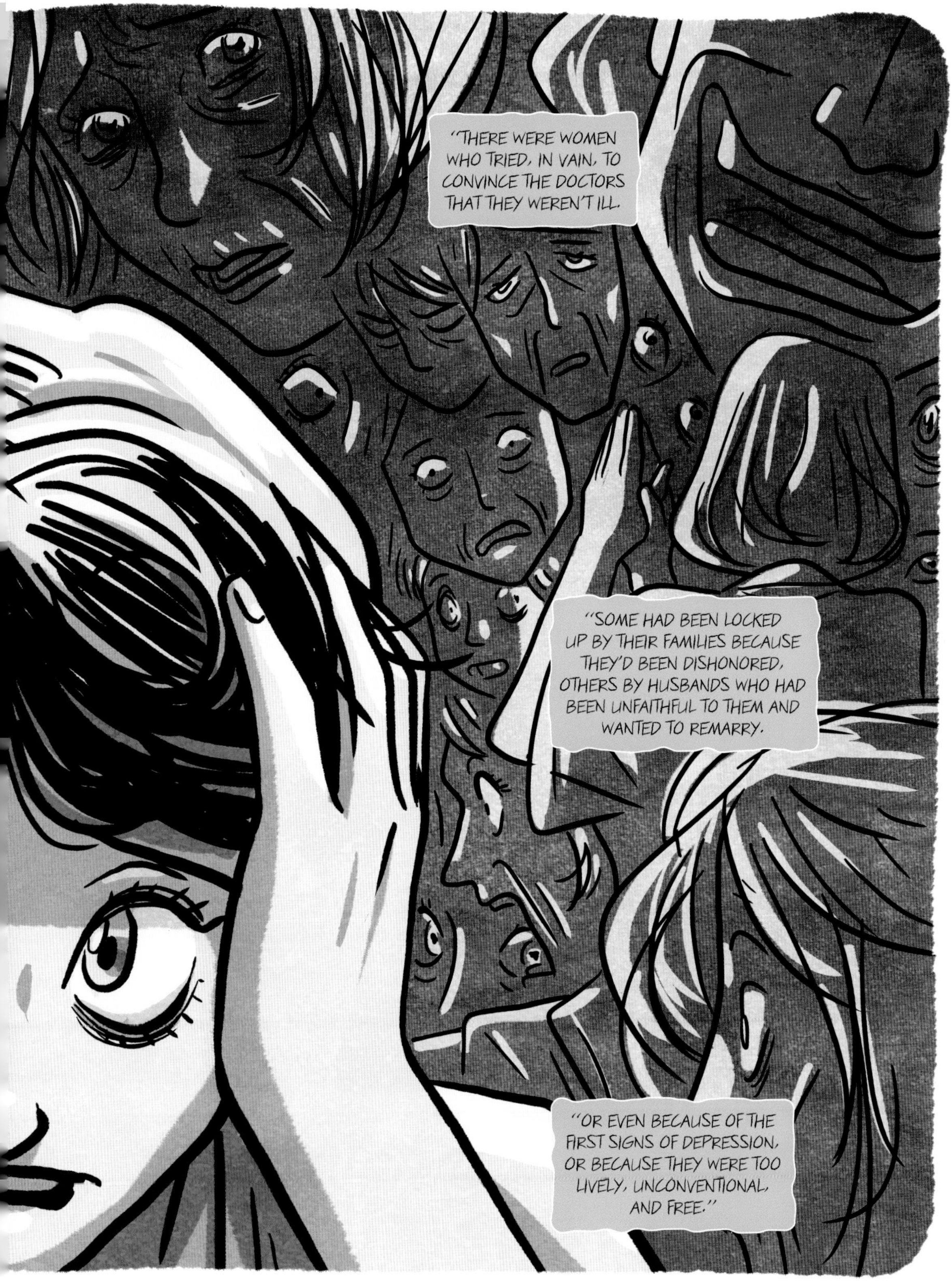
"THERE WERE WOMEN WHO TRIED, IN VAIN, TO CONVINCE THE DOCTORS THAT THEY WEREN'T ILL.
"SOME HAD BEEN LOCKED UP BY THEIR FAMILIES BECAUSE THEY'D BEEN DISHONORED, OTHERS BY HUSBANDS WHO HAD BEEN UNFAITHFUL TO THEM AND WANTED TO REMARRY.
"OR EVEN BECAUSE OF THE FIRST SIGNS OF DEPRESSION, OR BECAUSE THEY WERE TOO LIVELY, UNCONVENTIONAL, AND FREE."

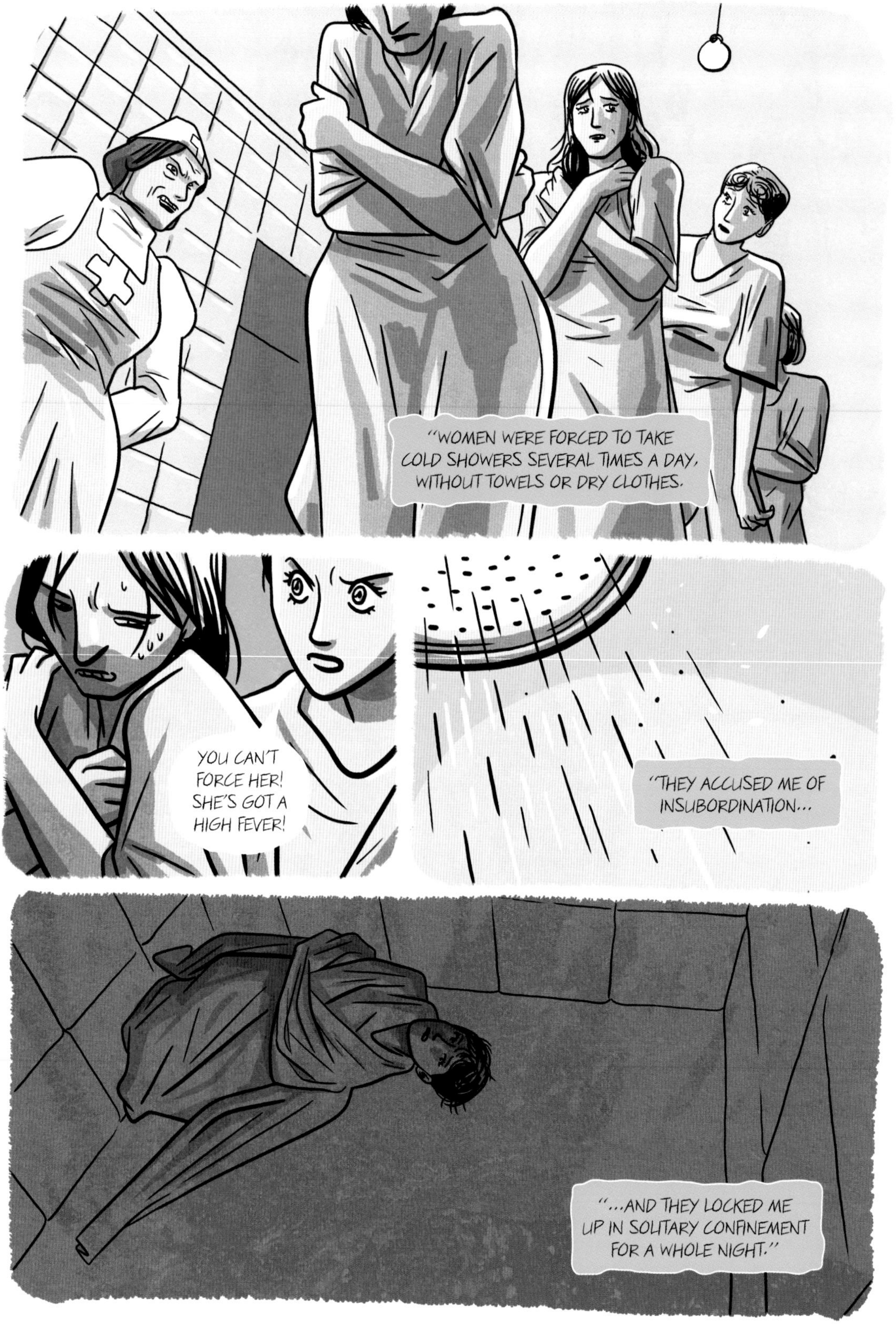
"WOMEN WERE FORCED TO TAKE COLD SHOWERS SEVERAL TIMES A DAY, WITHOUT TOWELS OR DRY CLOTHES.
YOU CAN'T FORCE HER! SHE'S GOT A HIGH FEVER!
"THEY ACCUSED ME OF INSUBORDINATION...
"...AND THEY LOCKED ME UP IN SOLITARY CONFINEMENT FOR A WHOLE NIGHT."

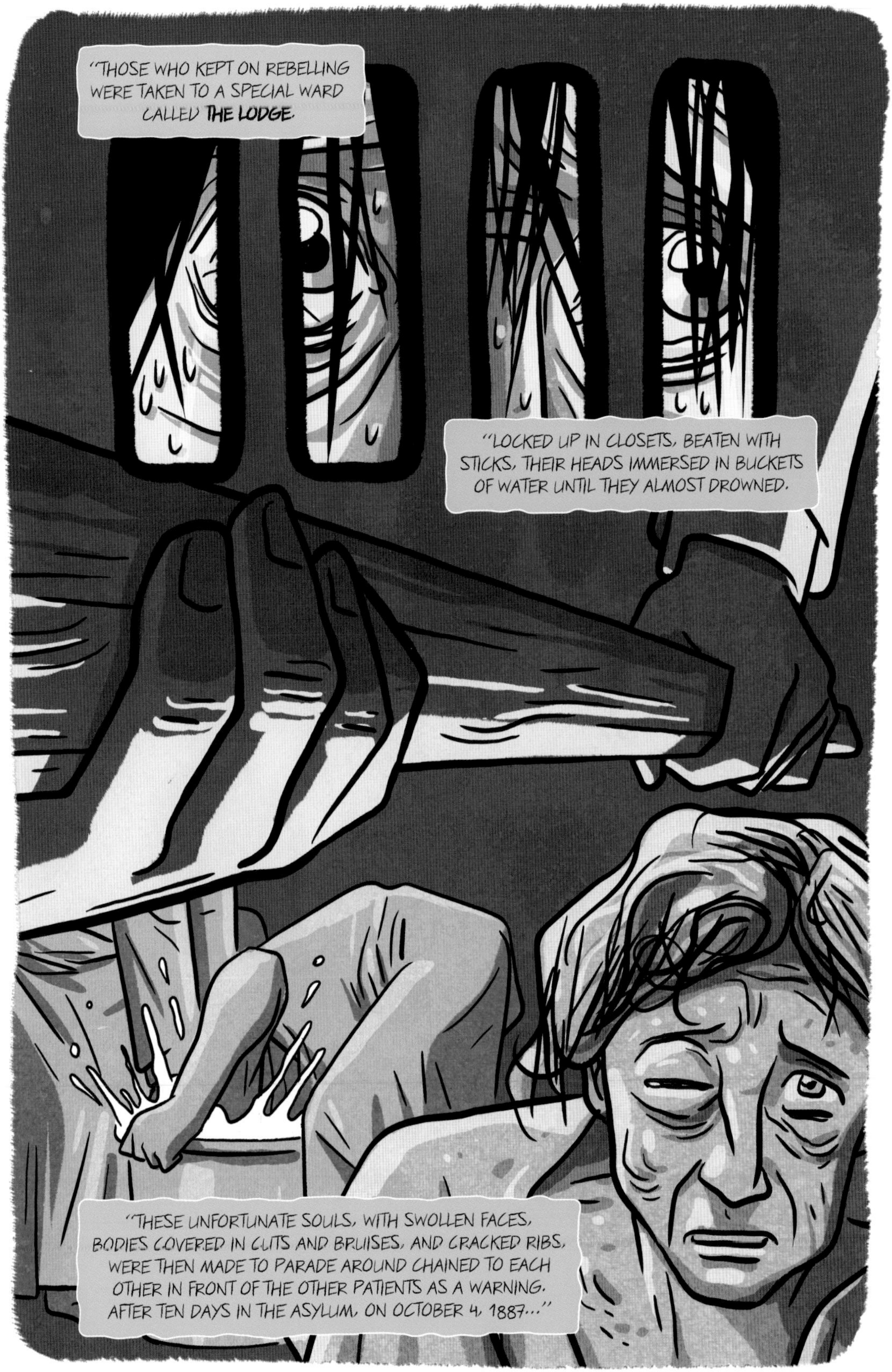
"THOSE WHO KEPT ON REBELLING WERE TAKEN TO A SPECIAL WARD CALLED **THE LODGE**.
"LOCKED UP IN CLOSETS, BEATEN WITH STICKS, THEIR HEADS IMMERSED IN BUCKETS OF WATER UNTIL THEY ALMOST DROWNED.
"THESE UNFORTUNATE SOULS, WITH SWOLLEN FACES, BODIES COVERED IN CUTS AND BRUISES, AND CRACKED RIBS, WERE THEN MADE TO PARADE AROUND CHAINED TO EACH OTHER IN FRONT OF THE OTHER PATIENTS AS A WARNING. AFTER TEN DAYS IN THE ASYLUM, ON OCTOBER 4, 1887..."

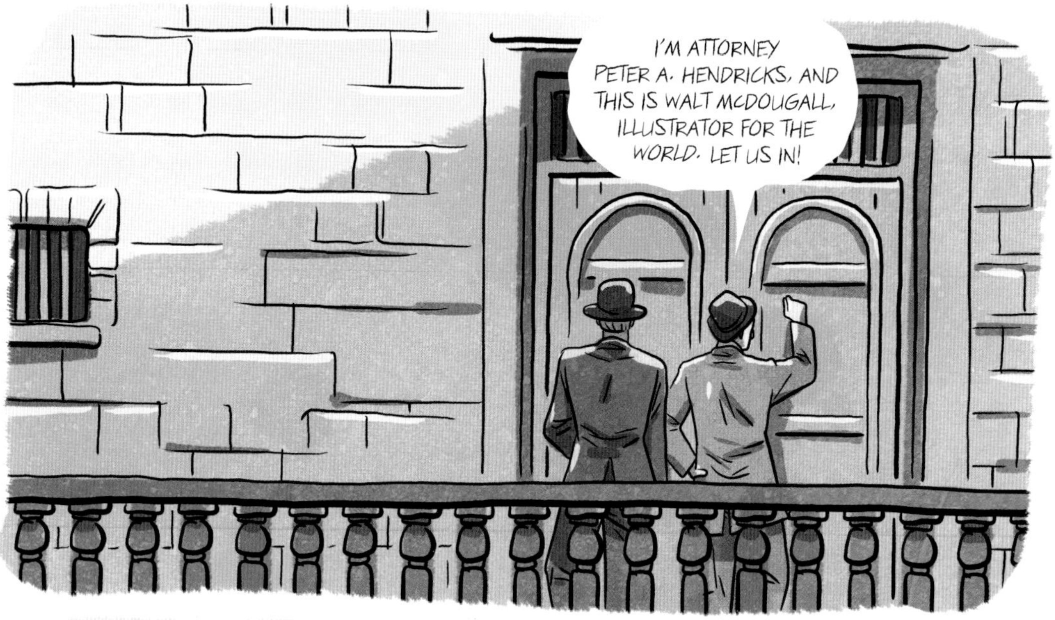
I'M ATTORNEY PETER A. HENDRICKS, AND THIS IS WALT McDOUGALL, ILLUSTRATOR FOR THE WORLD. LET US IN!

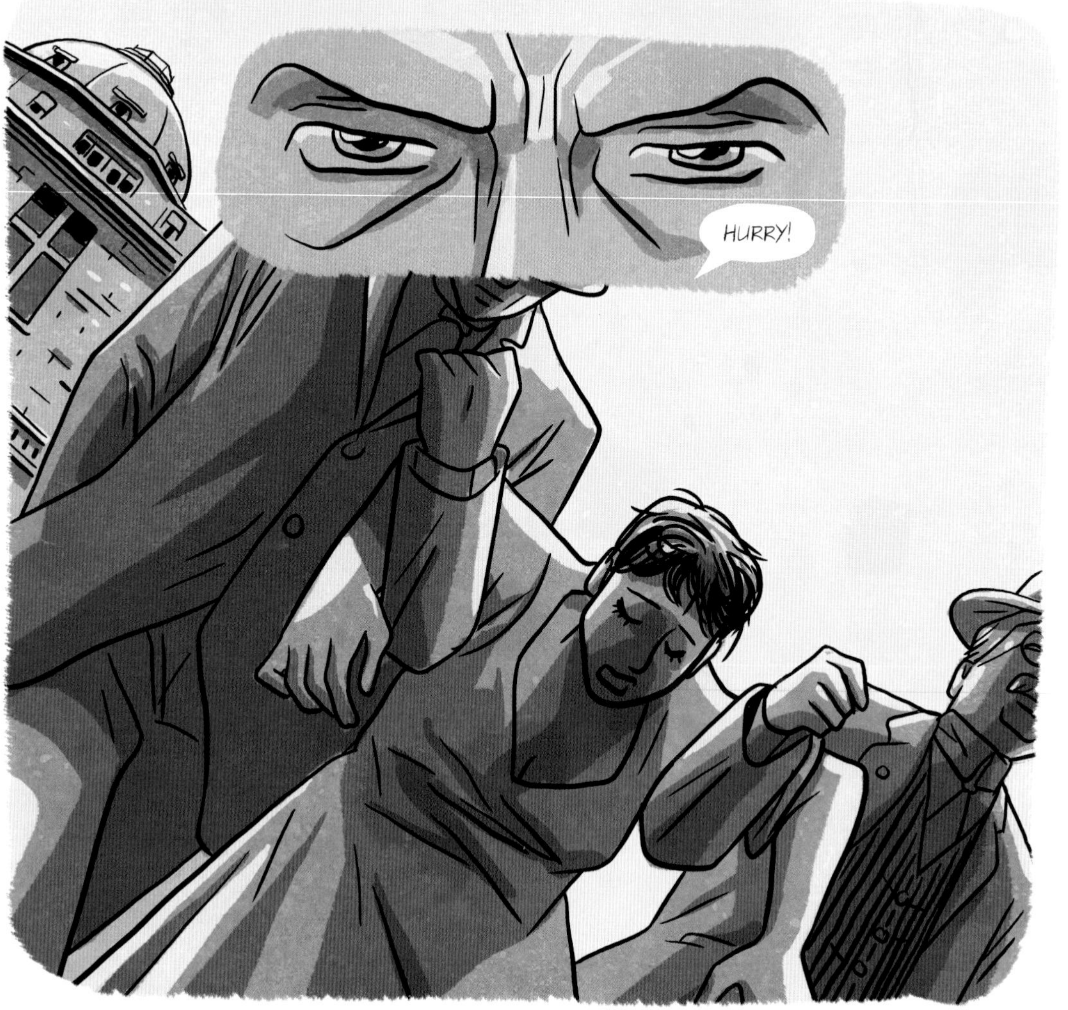
HURRY!

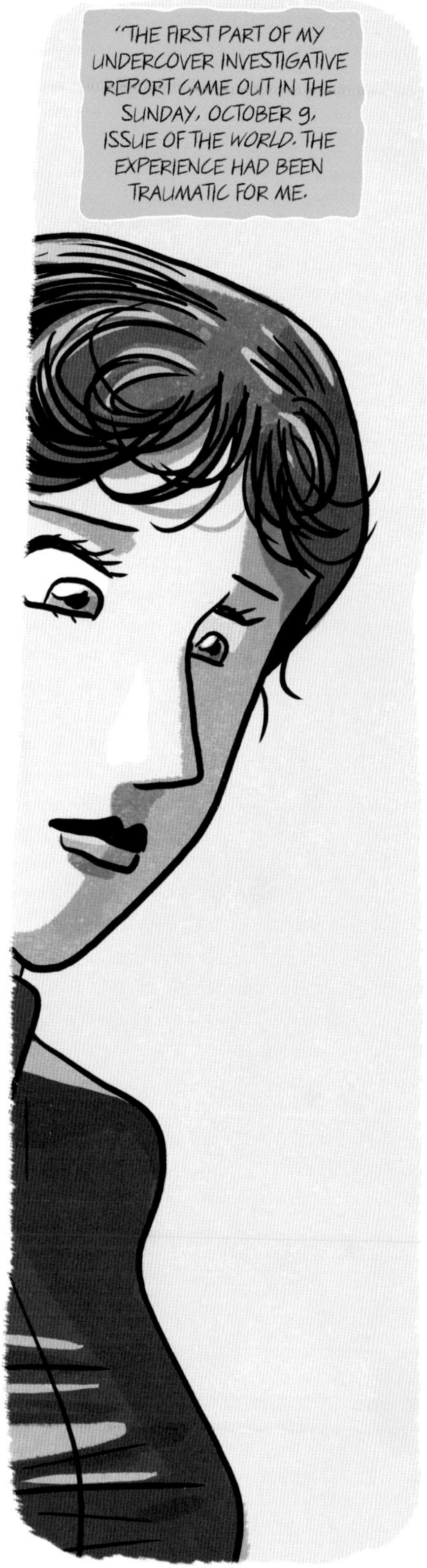
"THE FIRST PART OF MY UNDERCOVER INVESTIGATIVE REPORT CAME OUT IN THE SUNDAY, OCTOBER 9, ISSUE OF THE *WORLD*. THE EXPERIENCE HAD BEEN TRAUMATIC FOR ME.

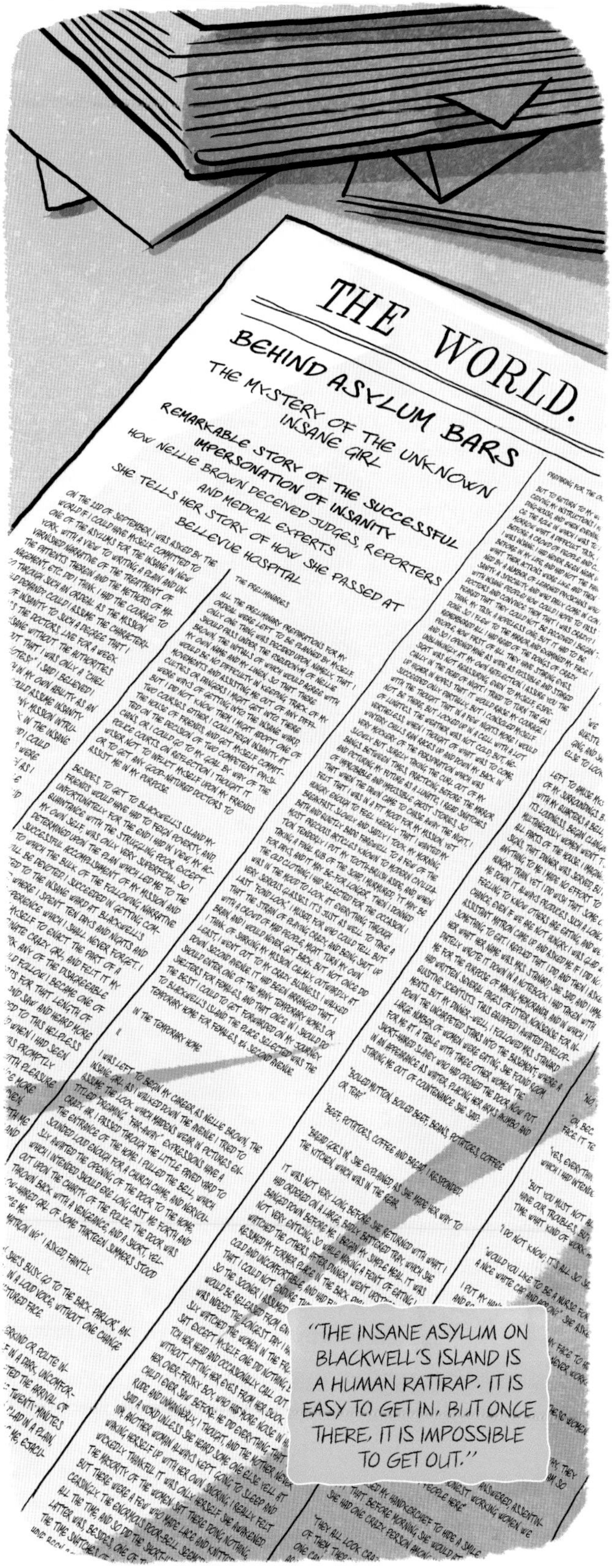
THE WORLD.
BEHIND ASYLUM BARS
THE MYSTERY OF THE UNKNOWN INSANE GIRL
REMARKABLE STORY OF THE SUCCESSFUL IMPERSONATION OF INSANITY
HOW NELLIE BROWN DECEIVED JUDGES, REPORTERS AND MEDICAL EXPERTS
SHE TELLS HER STORY OF HOW SHE PASSED AT BELLEVUE HOSPITAL
"THE INSANE ASYLUM ON BLACKWELL'S ISLAND IS A HUMAN RATTRAP. IT IS EASY TO GET IN, BUT ONCE THERE, IT IS IMPOSSIBLE TO GET OUT."

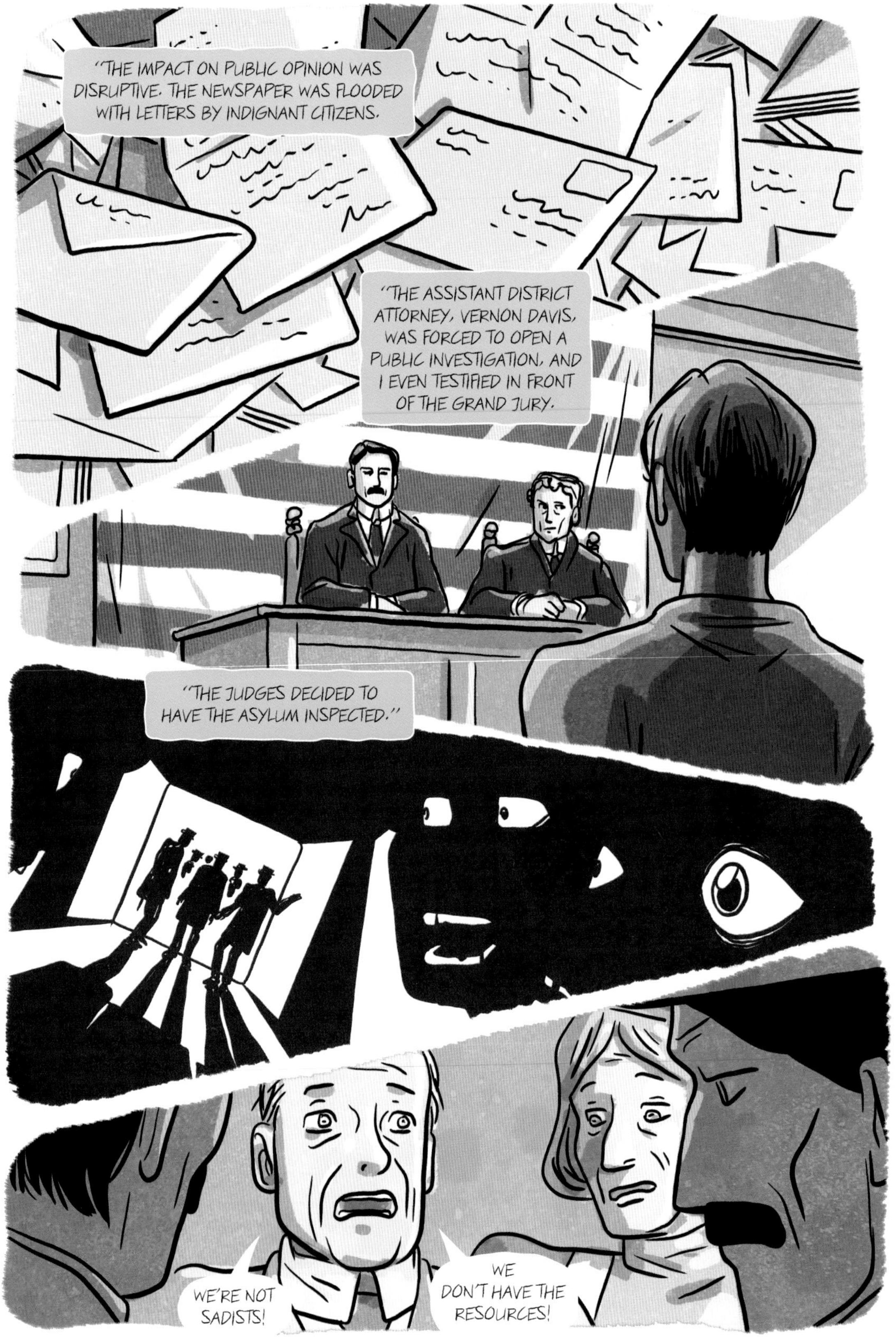
"THE IMPACT ON PUBLIC OPINION WAS DISRUPTIVE. THE NEWSPAPER WAS FLOODED WITH LETTERS BY INDIGNANT CITIZENS.
"THE ASSISTANT DISTRICT ATTORNEY, VERNON DAVIS, WAS FORCED TO OPEN A PUBLIC INVESTIGATION, AND I EVEN TESTIFIED IN FRONT OF THE GRAND JURY.
"THE JUDGES DECIDED TO HAVE THE ASYLUM INSPECTED."
WE'RE NOT SADISTS!
WE DON'T HAVE THE RESOURCES!

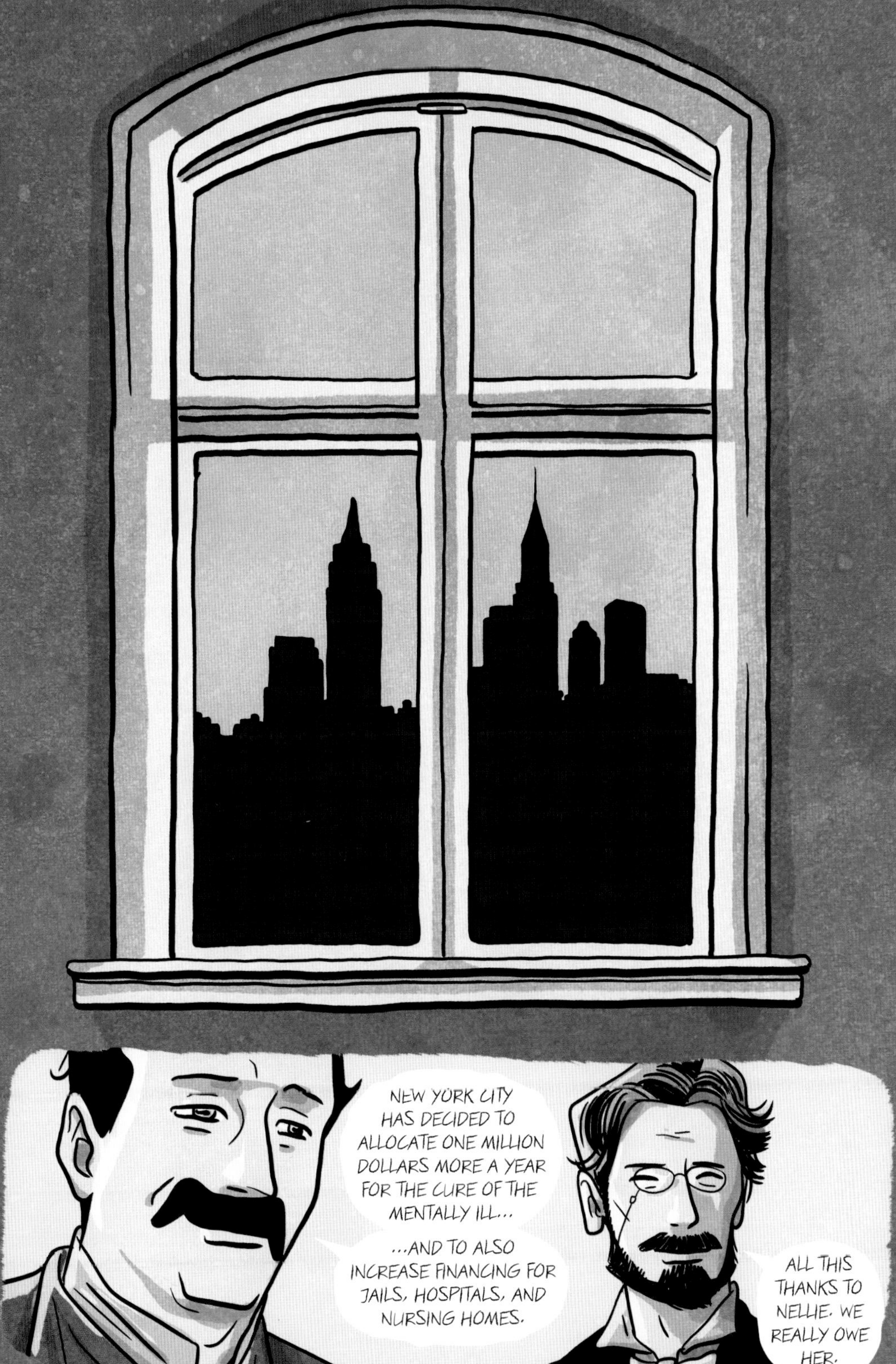
NEW YORK CITY HAS DECIDED TO ALLOCATE ONE MILLION DOLLARS MORE A YEAR FOR THE CURE OF THE MENTALLY ILL...
...AND TO ALSO INCREASE FINANCING FOR JAILS, HOSPITALS, AND NURSING HOMES.
ALL THIS THANKS TO NELLIE. WE REALLY OWE HER.

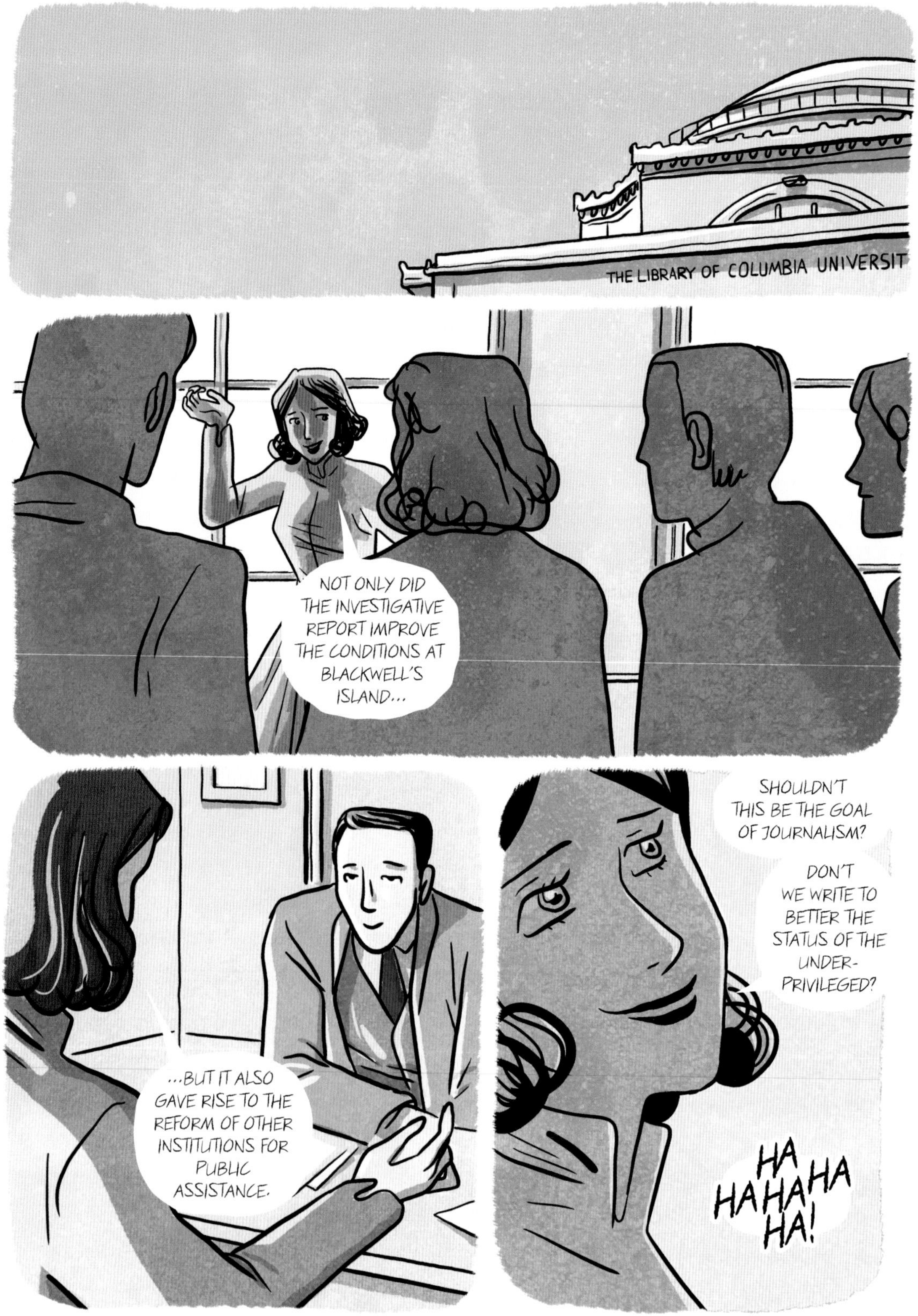
THE LIBRARY OF COLUMBIA UNIVERSIT
NOT ONLY DID THE INVESTIGATIVE REPORT IMPROVE THE CONDITIONS AT BLACKWELL'S ISLAND...
...BUT IT ALSO GAVE RISE TO THE REFORM OF OTHER INSTITUTIONS FOR PUBLIC ASSISTANCE.
SHOULDN'T THIS BE THE GOAL OF JOURNALISM?
DON'T WE WRITE TO BETTER THE STATUS OF THE UNDER-PRIVILEGED?
HA HAHAHA HA!

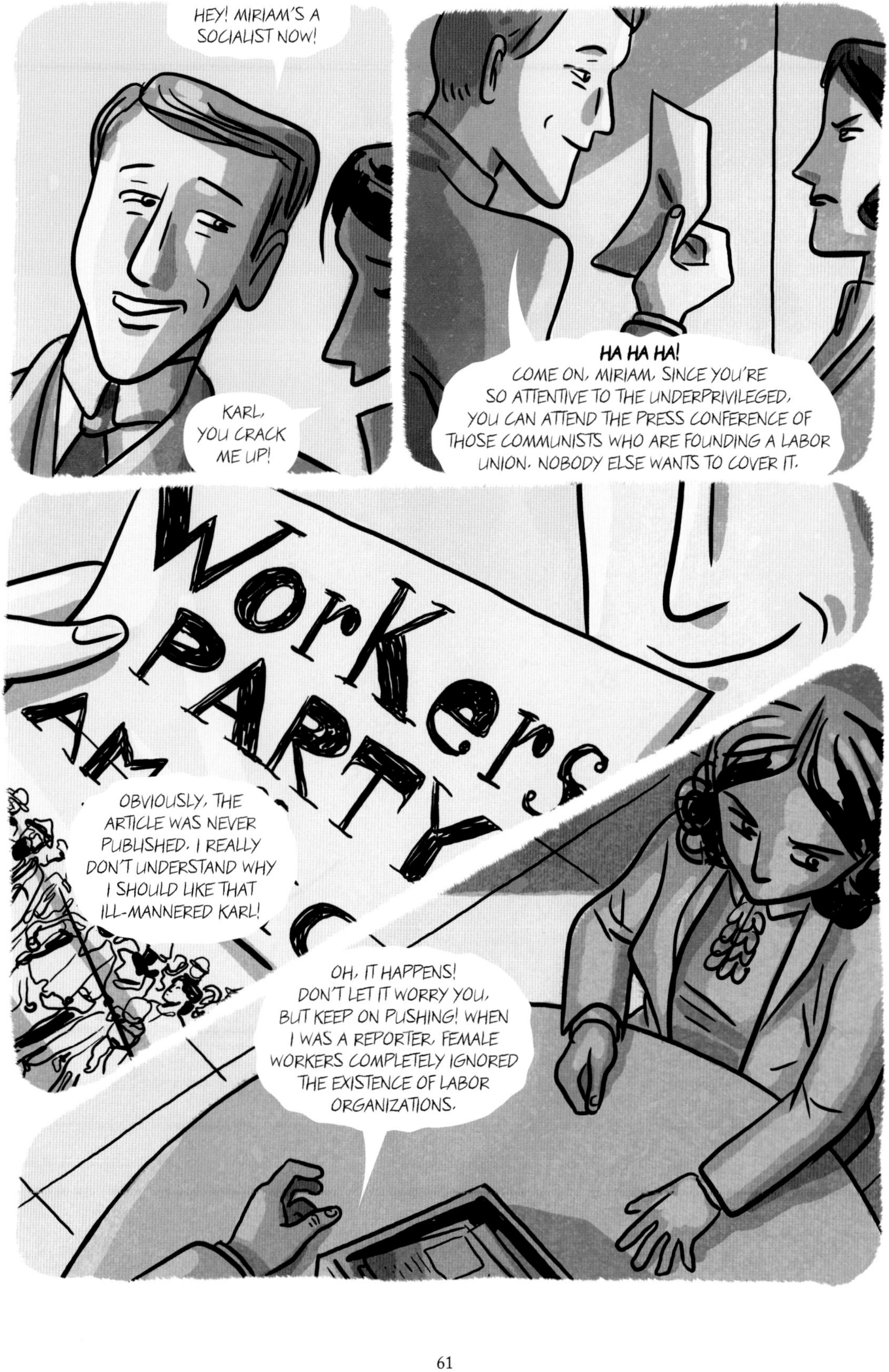
HEY! MIRIAM'S A SOCIALIST NOW!
KARL, YOU CRACK ME UP!
HA HA HA!
COME ON, MIRIAM, SINCE YOU'RE SO ATTENTIVE TO THE UNDERPRIVILEGED, YOU CAN ATTEND THE PRESS CONFERENCE OF THOSE COMMUNISTS WHO ARE FOUNDING A LABOR UNION. NOBODY ELSE WANTS TO COVER IT.
WorKers PARTY
OBVIOUSLY, THE ARTICLE WAS NEVER PUBLISHED. I REALLY DON'T UNDERSTAND WHY I SHOULD LIKE THAT ILL-MANNERED KARL!
OH, IT HAPPENS! DON'T LET IT WORRY YOU, BUT KEEP ON PUSHING! WHEN I WAS A REPORTER, FEMALE WORKERS COMPLETELY IGNORED THE EXISTENCE OF LABOR ORGANIZATIONS.

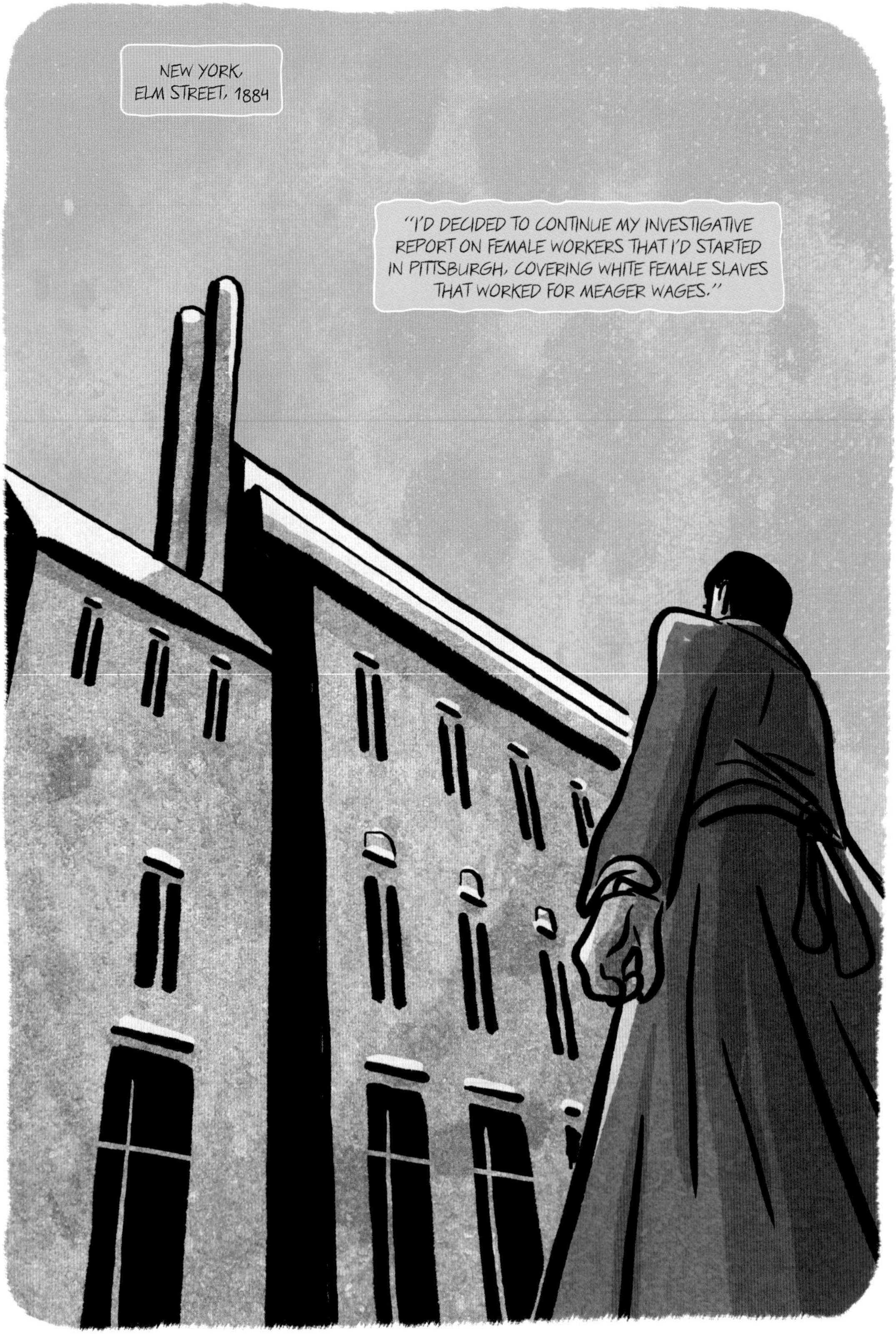
NEW YORK,
ELM STREET, 1884
"I'D DECIDED TO CONTINUE MY INVESTIGATIVE REPORT ON FEMALE WORKERS THAT I'D STARTED IN PITTSBURGH, COVERING WHITE FEMALE SLAVES THAT WORKED FOR MEAGER WAGES."

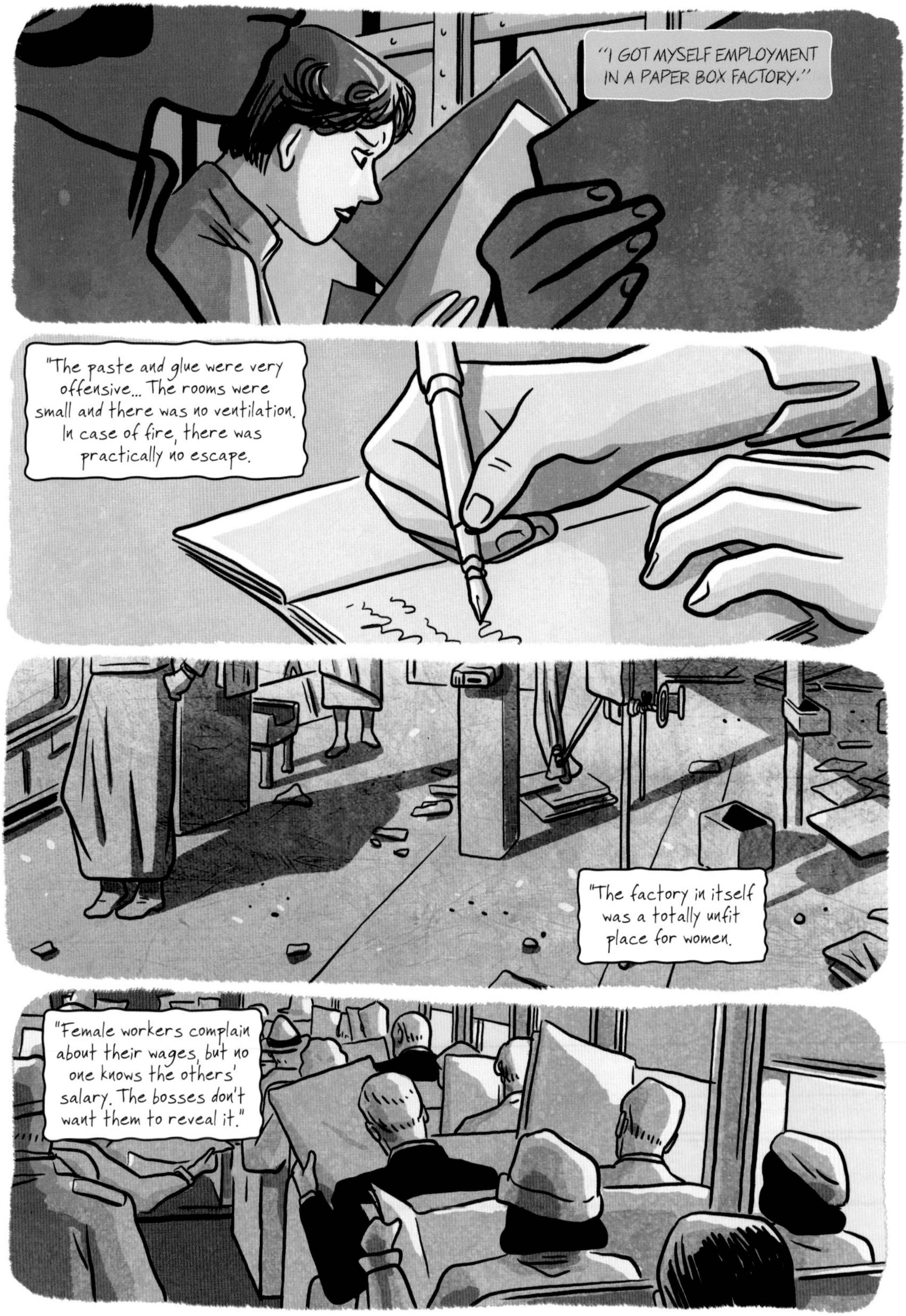
"I GOT MYSELF EMPLOYMENT IN A PAPER BOX FACTORY."
"The paste and glue were very offensive... The rooms were small and there was no ventilation. In case of fire, there was practically no escape.
"The factory in itself was a totally unfit place for women.
"Female workers complain about their wages, but no one knows the others' salary. The bosses don't want them to reveal it."

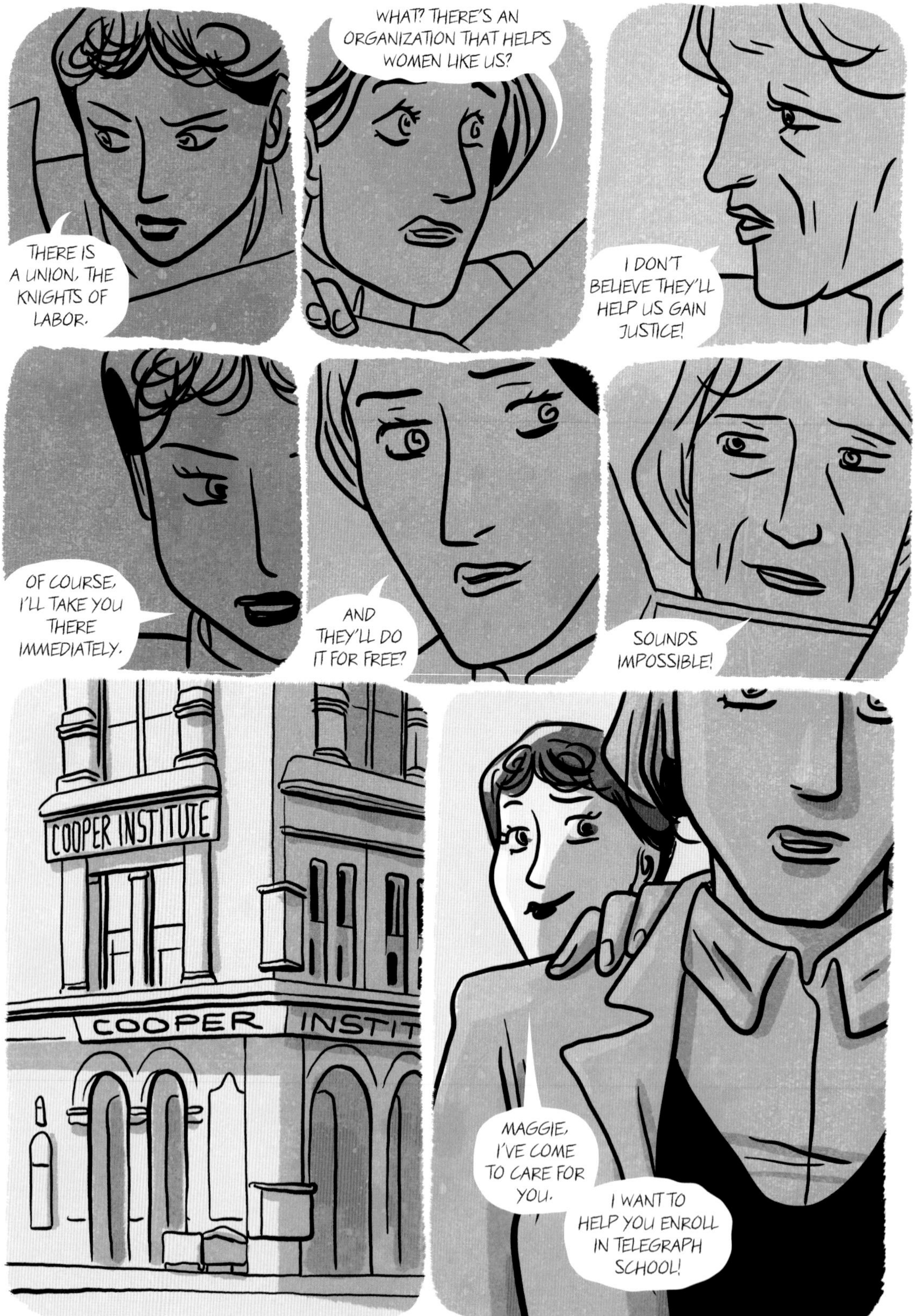

THERE IS A UNION, THE KNIGHTS OF LABOR.
WHAT? THERE'S AN ORGANIZATION THAT HELPS WOMEN LIKE US?
I DON'T BELIEVE THEY'LL HELP US GAIN JUSTICE!
OF COURSE, I'LL TAKE YOU THERE IMMEDIATELY.
AND THEY'LL DO IT FOR FREE?
SOUNDS IMPOSSIBLE!
COOPER INSTITUTE
COOPER INSTIT
MAGGIE, I'VE COME TO CARE FOR YOU.
I WANT TO HELP YOU ENROLL IN TELEGRAPH SCHOOL!

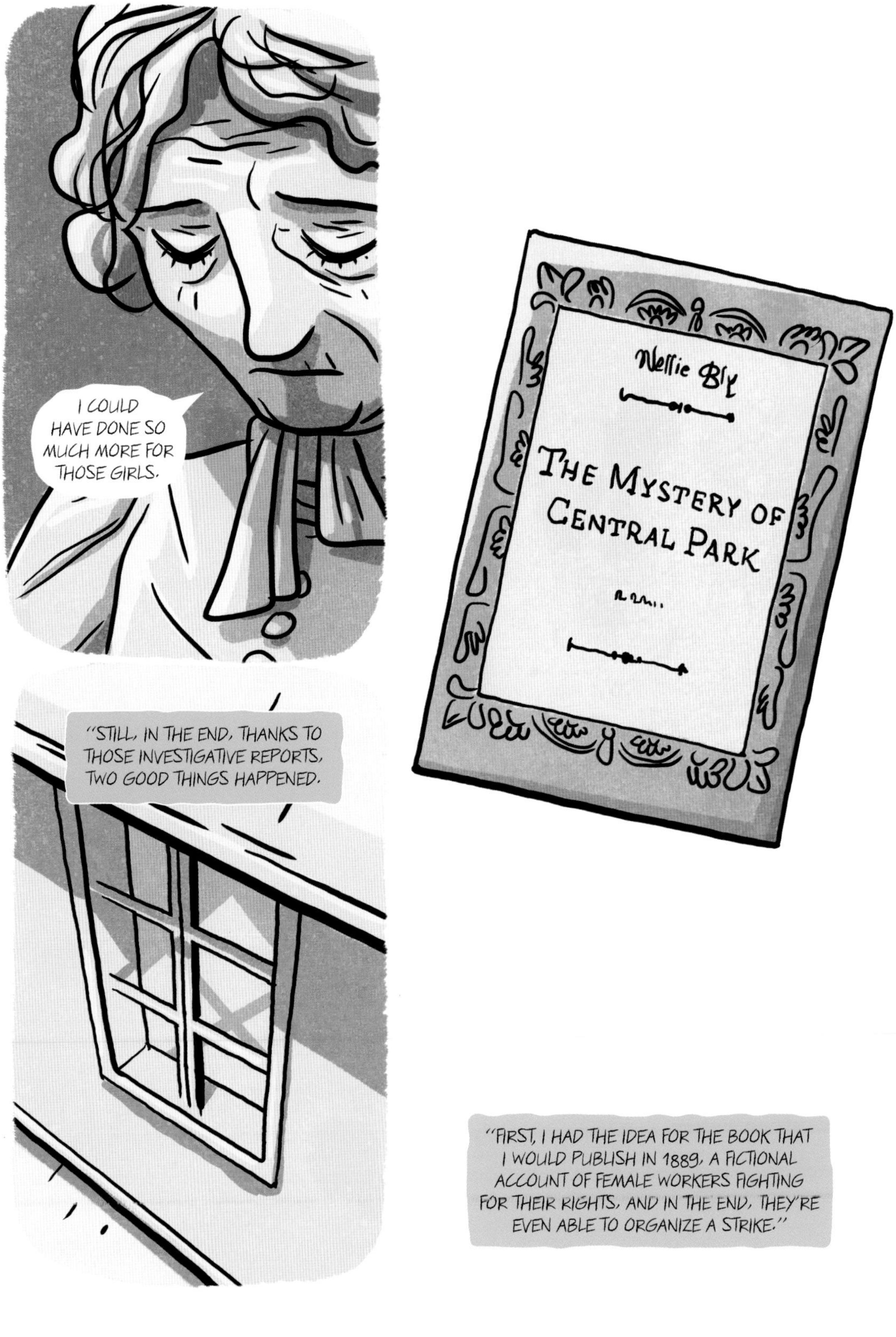
I COULD HAVE DONE SO MUCH MORE FOR THOSE GIRLS.
"STILL, IN THE END, THANKS TO THOSE INVESTIGATIVE REPORTS, TWO GOOD THINGS HAPPENED.
Nellie Bly
THE MYSTERY OF CENTRAL PARK
"FIRST, I HAD THE IDEA FOR THE BOOK THAT I WOULD PUBLISH IN 1889, A FICTIONAL ACCOUNT OF FEMALE WORKERS FIGHTING FOR THEIR RIGHTS, AND IN THE END, THEY'RE EVEN ABLE TO ORGANIZE A STRIKE."

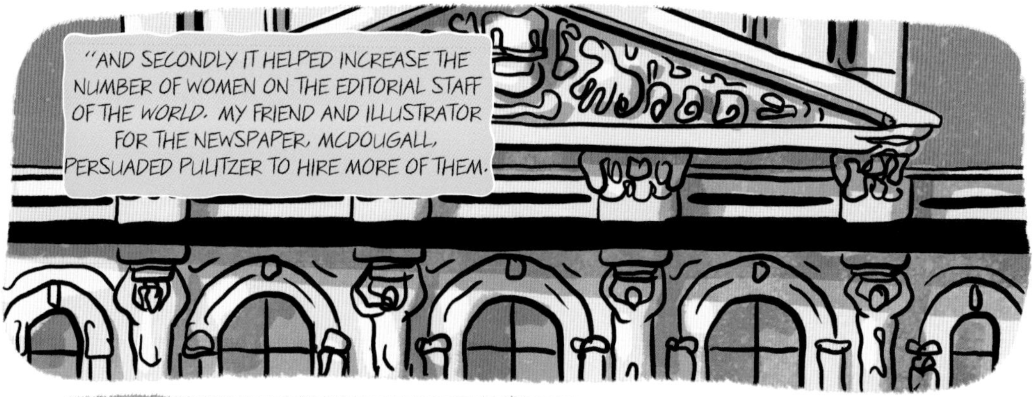
"AND SECONDLY IT HELPED INCREASE THE NUMBER OF WOMEN ON THE EDITORIAL STAFF OF THE *WORLD*. MY FRIEND AND ILLUSTRATOR FOR THE NEWSPAPER, MCDOUGALL, PERSUADED PULITZER TO HIRE MORE OF THEM.

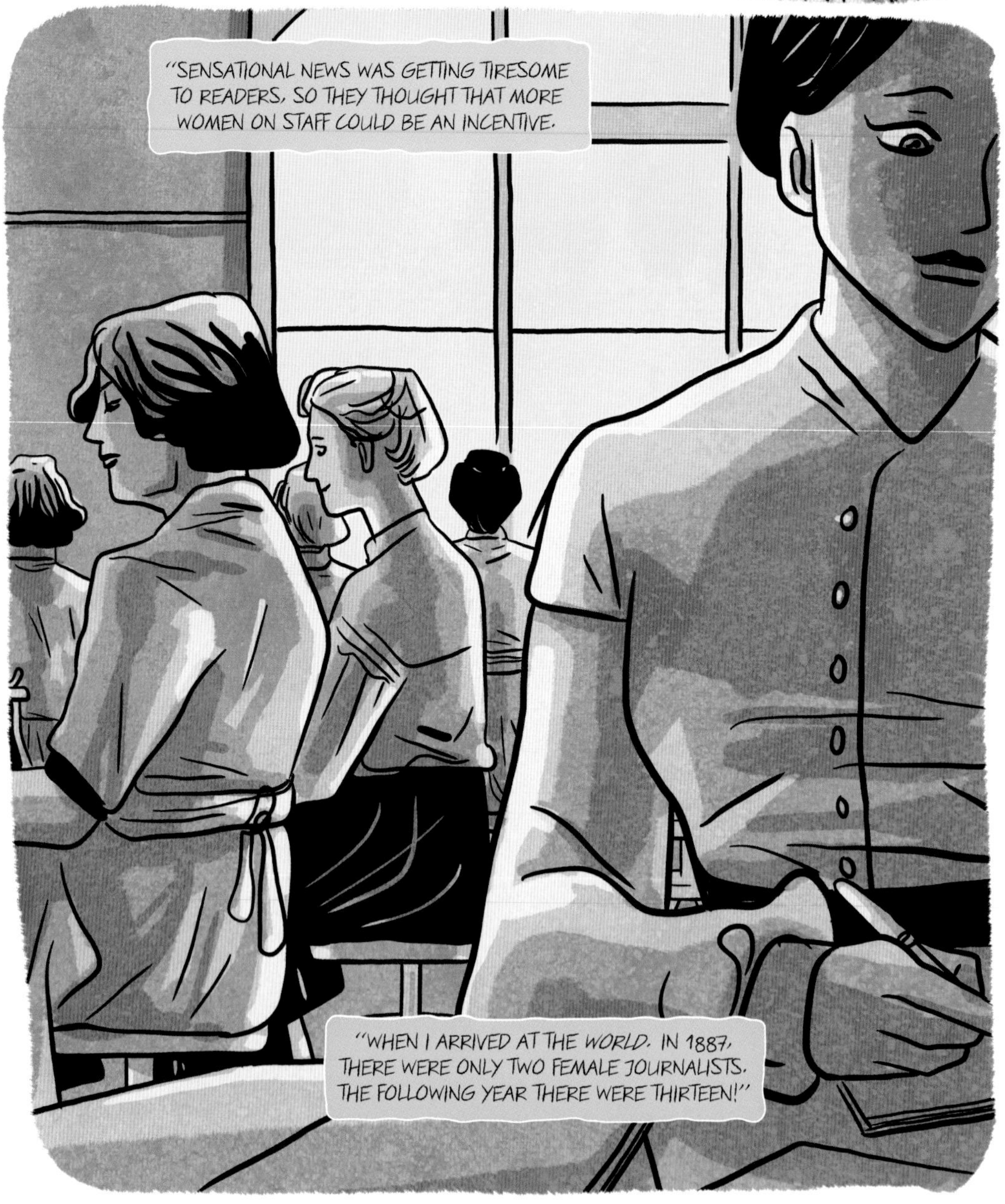
"SENSATIONAL NEWS WAS GETTING TIRESOME TO READERS, SO THEY THOUGHT THAT MORE WOMEN ON STAFF COULD BE AN INCENTIVE.
"WHEN I ARRIVED AT THE *WORLD*, IN 1887, THERE WERE ONLY TWO FEMALE JOURNALISTS. THE FOLLOWING YEAR THERE WERE THIRTEEN!"

"ALTHOUGH THEY HAD GOOD INTENTIONS, THEY WERE MIDDLE-CLASS AND WEREN'T ABLE TO DESCRIBE FEMALE WORKERS AS ANYTHING OTHER THAN CLICHÉD VICTIMS WHO WERE AT THE EMPLOYER'S MERCY. THESE STORIES HAD A MORALIZING VIEW.

"NEVERTHELESS, UNTIL THE 1890S, WOMEN, WITH ME AS AN EXCEPTION, WERE CONFINED TO COSTUME AND FASHION PAGES, OR COVERING FRIVOLOUS TOPICS LIKE SOCIAL LIFE AND RECIPES. THEY WERE EDUCATED, WEALTHY WOMEN.

"I, ON THE OTHER HAND, HAD ACTUALLY BEEN POOR, AND I IDENTIFIED WITH THOSE LESS-EDUCATED WOMEN.

"I DIDN'T FIND THEM WEAK. I THOUGHT THAT, IF THEY ORGANIZED THEMSELVES, THEY COULD BE THE PROTAGONISTS OF THEIR OWN REDEMPTION."

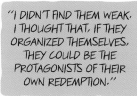

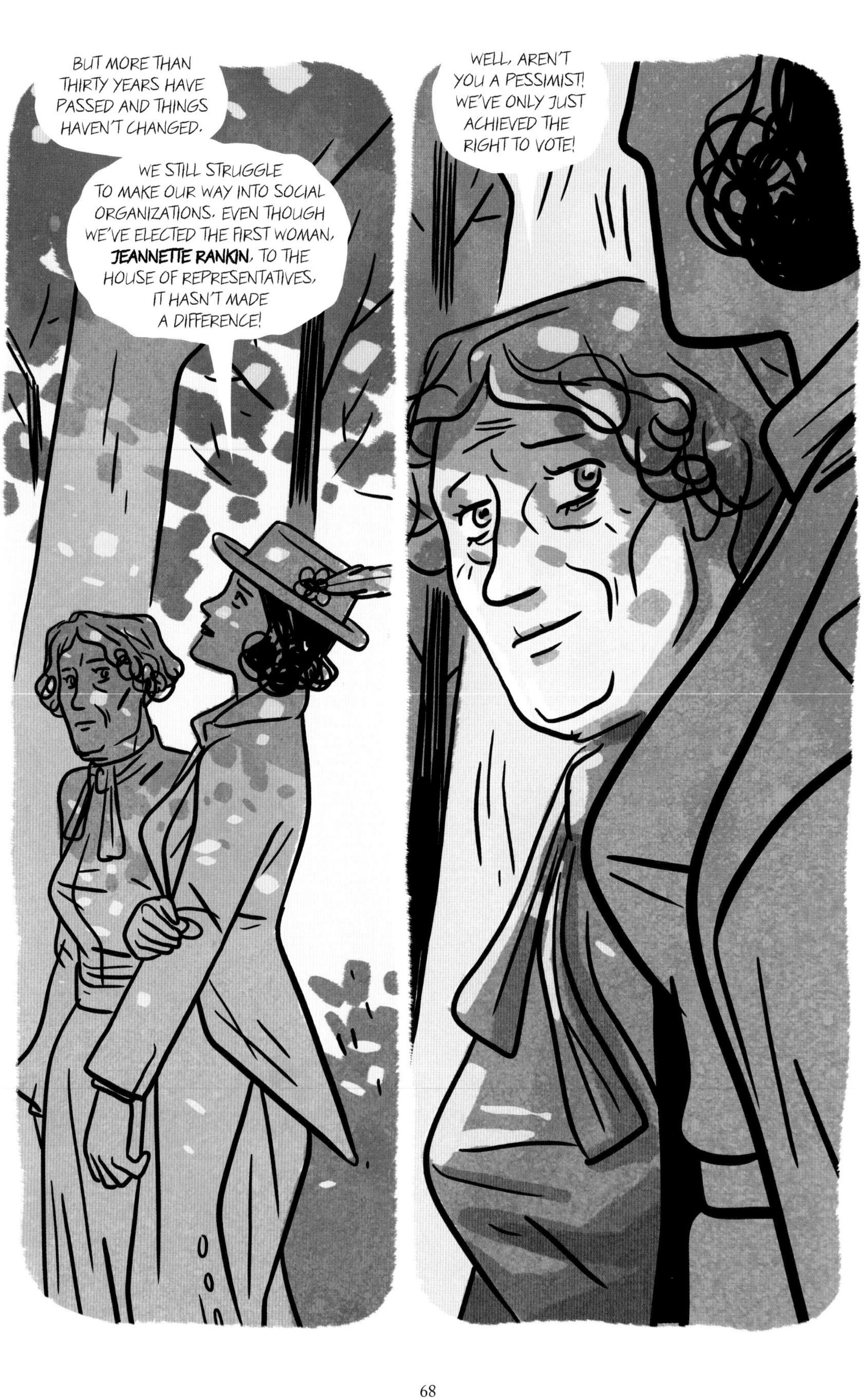
BUT MORE THAN THIRTY YEARS HAVE PASSED AND THINGS HAVEN'T CHANGED.
WE STILL STRUGGLE TO MAKE OUR WAY INTO SOCIAL ORGANIZATIONS. EVEN THOUGH WE'VE ELECTED THE FIRST WOMAN, **JEANNETTE RANKIN**, TO THE HOUSE OF REPRESENTATIVES, IT HASN'T MADE A DIFFERENCE!
WELL, AREN'T YOU A PESSIMIST! WE'VE ONLY JUST ACHIEVED THE RIGHT TO VOTE!

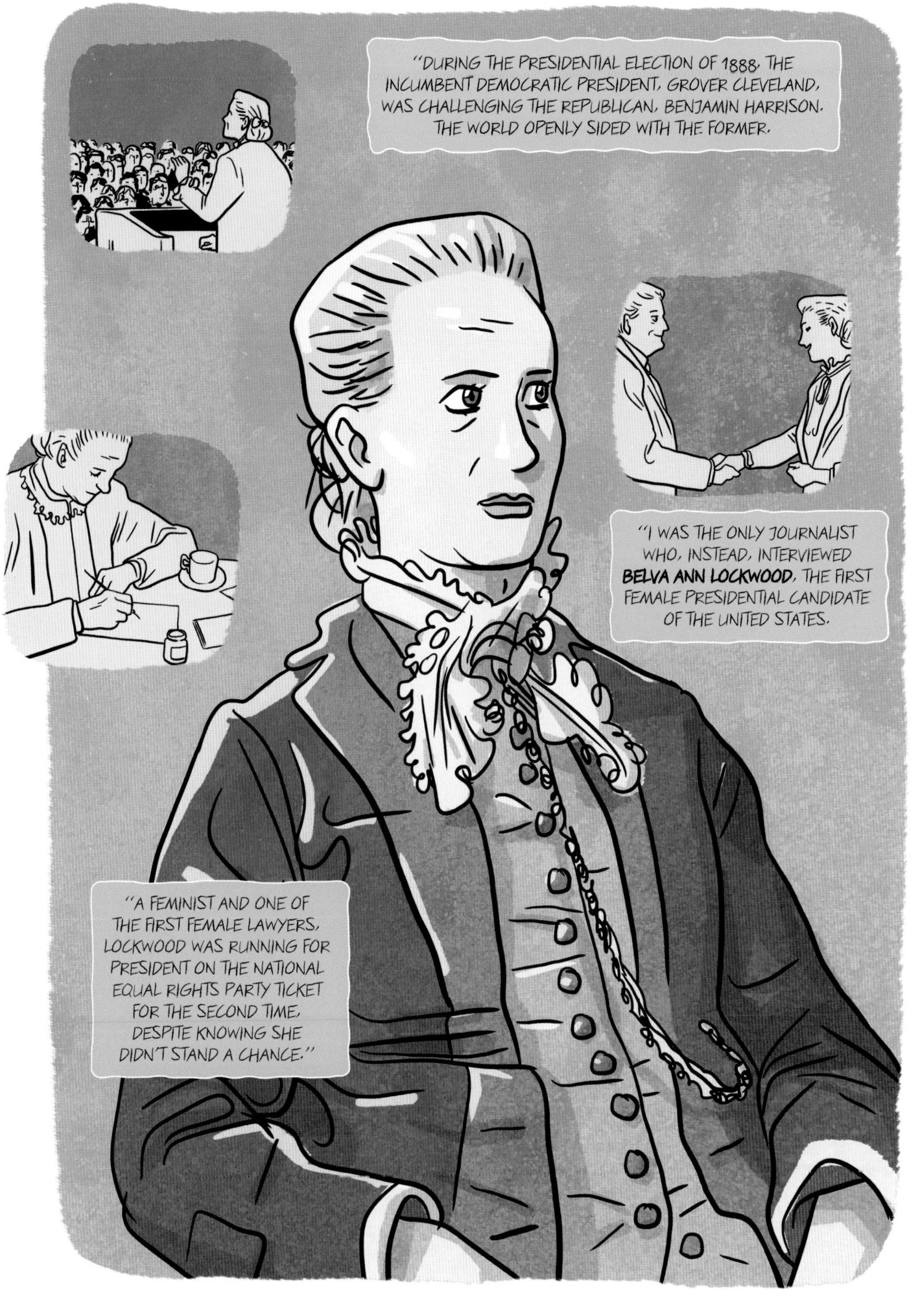
"DURING THE PRESIDENTIAL ELECTION OF 1888, THE INCUMBENT DEMOCRATIC PRESIDENT, GROVER CLEVELAND, WAS CHALLENGING THE REPUBLICAN, BENJAMIN HARRISON. THE WORLD OPENLY SIDED WITH THE FORMER.
"I WAS THE ONLY JOURNALIST WHO, INSTEAD, INTERVIEWED **BELVA ANN LOCKWOOD**, THE FIRST FEMALE PRESIDENTIAL CANDIDATE OF THE UNITED STATES.
"A FEMINIST AND ONE OF THE FIRST FEMALE LAWYERS, LOCKWOOD WAS RUNNING FOR PRESIDENT ON THE NATIONAL EQUAL RIGHTS PARTY TICKET FOR THE SECOND TIME, DESPITE KNOWING SHE DIDN'T STAND A CHANCE."

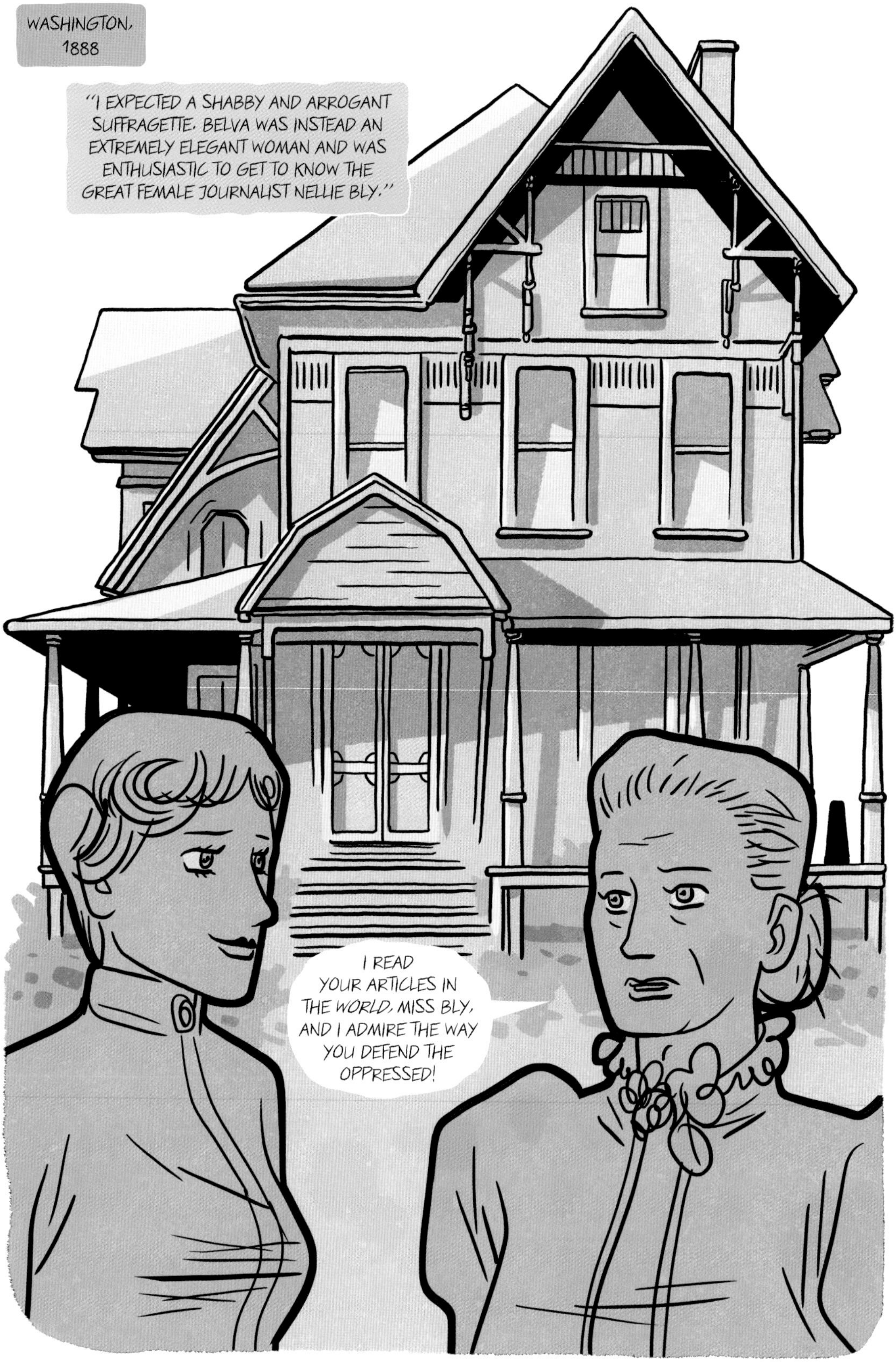
WASHINGTON, 1888
"I EXPECTED A SHABBY AND ARROGANT SUFFRAGETTE. BELVA WAS INSTEAD AN EXTREMELY ELEGANT WOMAN AND WAS ENTHUSIASTIC TO GET TO KNOW THE GREAT FEMALE JOURNALIST NELLIE BLY."
I READ YOUR ARTICLES IN THE *WORLD*, MISS BLY, AND I ADMIRE THE WAY YOU DEFEND THE OPPRESSED!

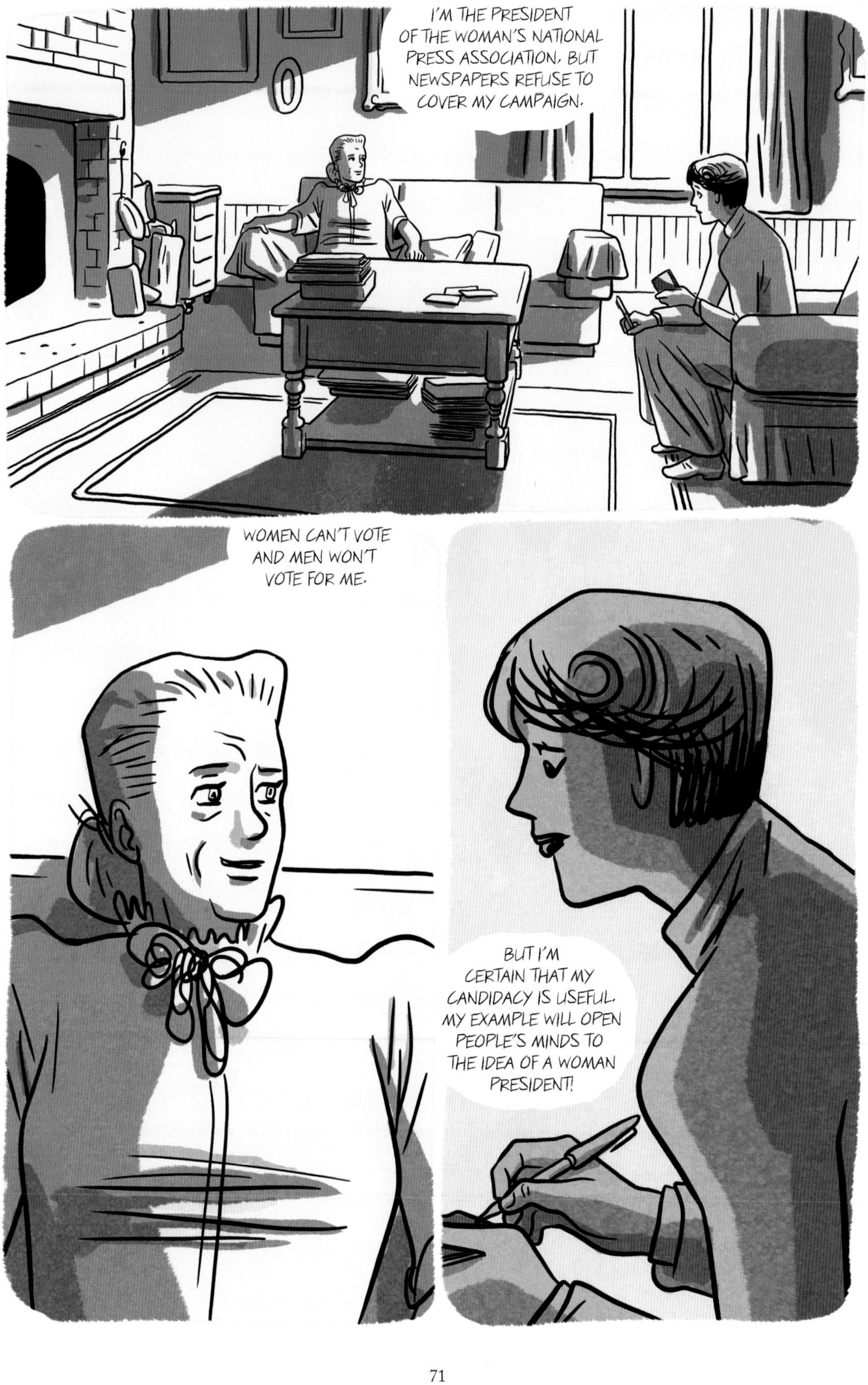
I'M THE PRESIDENT OF THE WOMAN'S NATIONAL PRESS ASSOCIATION, BUT NEWSPAPERS REFUSE TO COVER MY CAMPAIGN.
WOMEN CAN'T VOTE AND MEN WON'T VOTE FOR ME.
BUT I'M CERTAIN THAT MY CANDIDACY IS USEFUL. MY EXAMPLE WILL OPEN PEOPLE'S MINDS TO THE IDEA OF A WOMAN PRESIDENT!

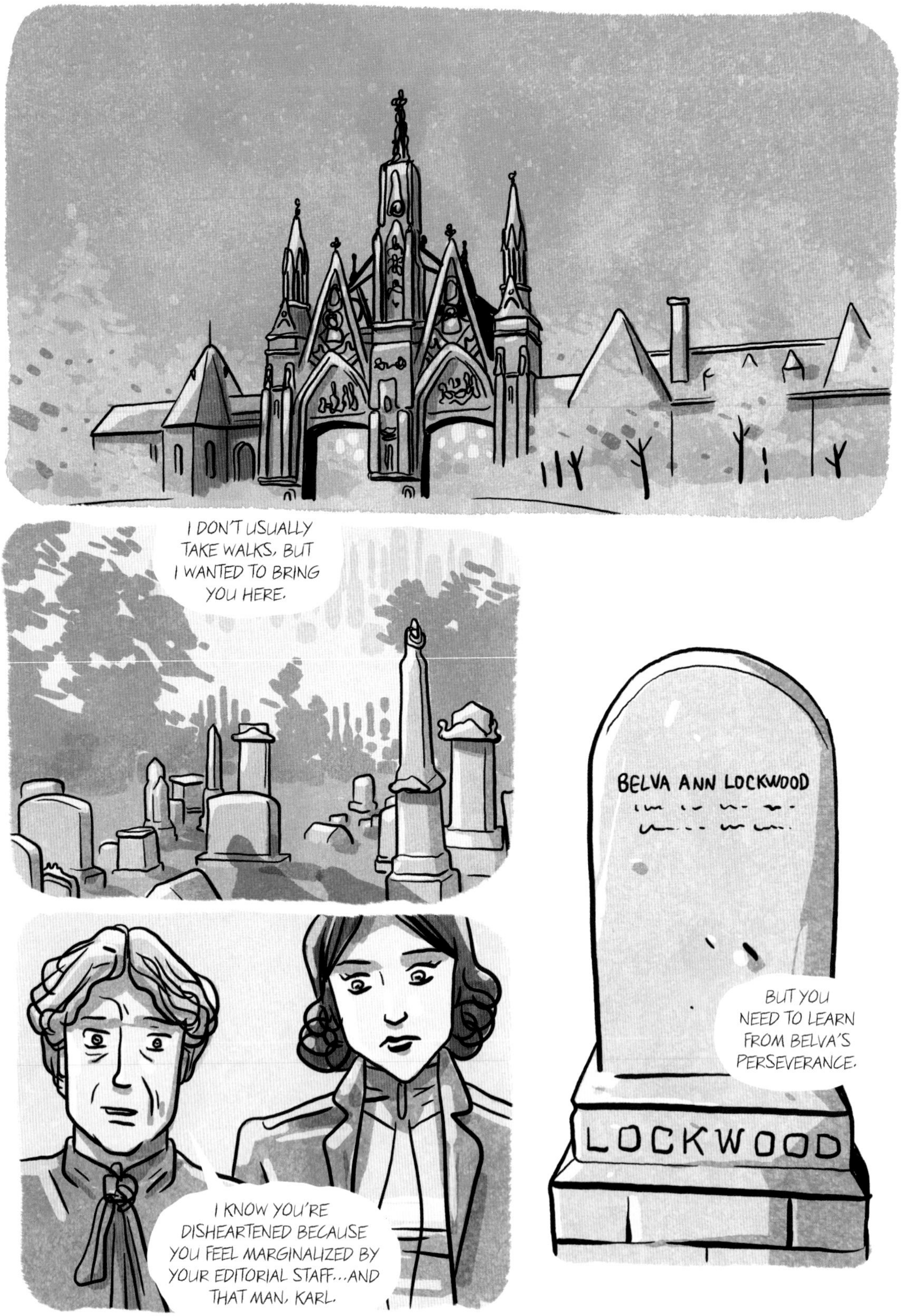
I DON'T USUALLY TAKE WALKS, BUT I WANTED TO BRING YOU HERE.
I KNOW YOU'RE DISHEARTENED BECAUSE YOU FEEL MARGINALIZED BY YOUR EDITORIAL STAFF...AND THAT MAN, KARL.
BELVA ANN LOCKWOOD
LOCKWOOD
BUT YOU NEED TO LEARN FROM BELVA'S PERSEVERANCE.

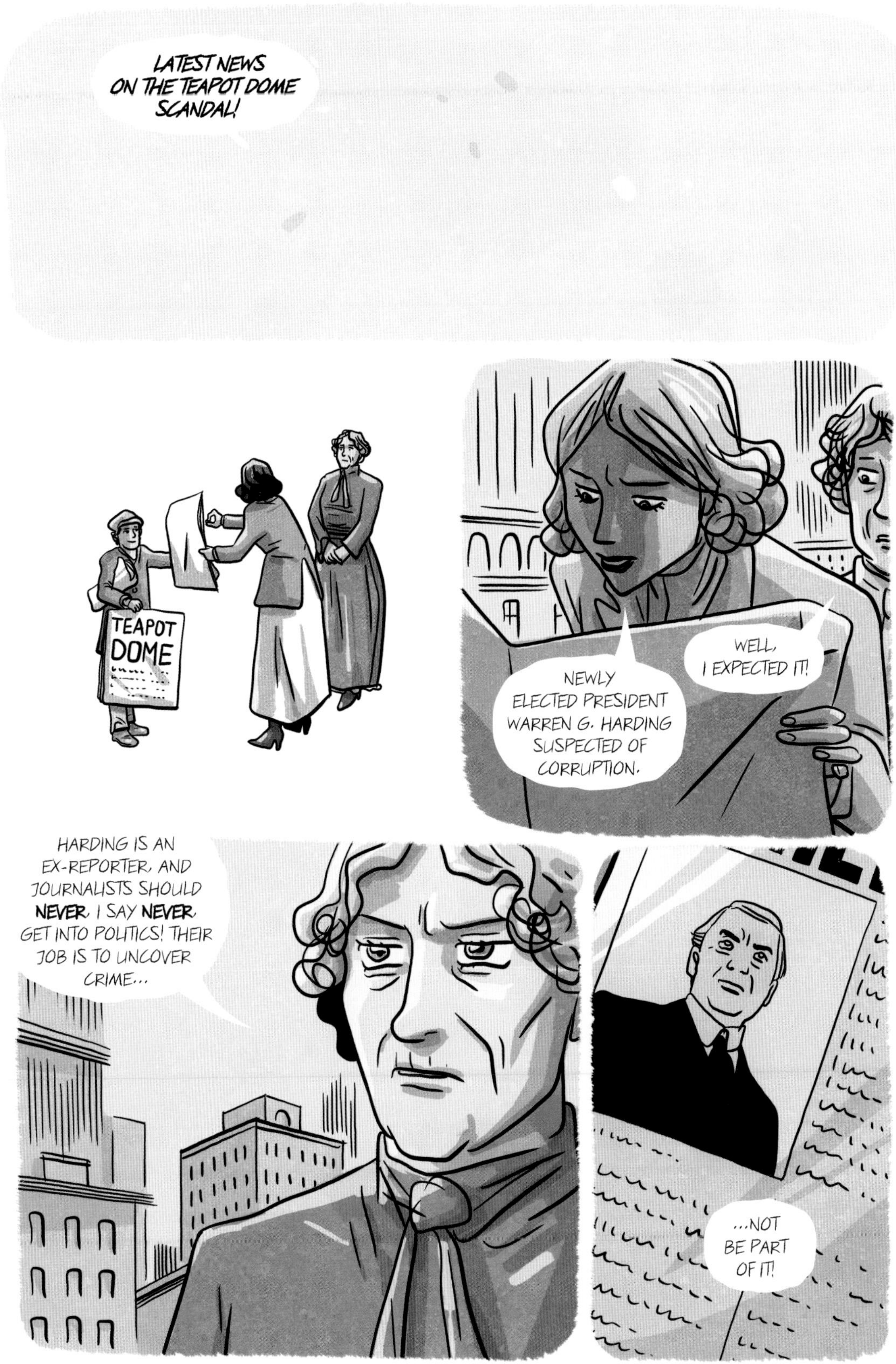
LATEST NEWS ON THE TEAPOT DOME SCANDAL!
TEAPOT DOME
NEWLY ELECTED PRESIDENT WARREN G. HARDING SUSPECTED OF CORRUPTION.
WELL, I EXPECTED IT!
HARDING IS AN EX-REPORTER, AND JOURNALISTS SHOULD **NEVER**, I SAY **NEVER**, GET INTO POLITICS! THEIR JOB IS TO UNCOVER CRIME...
...NOT BE PART OF IT!

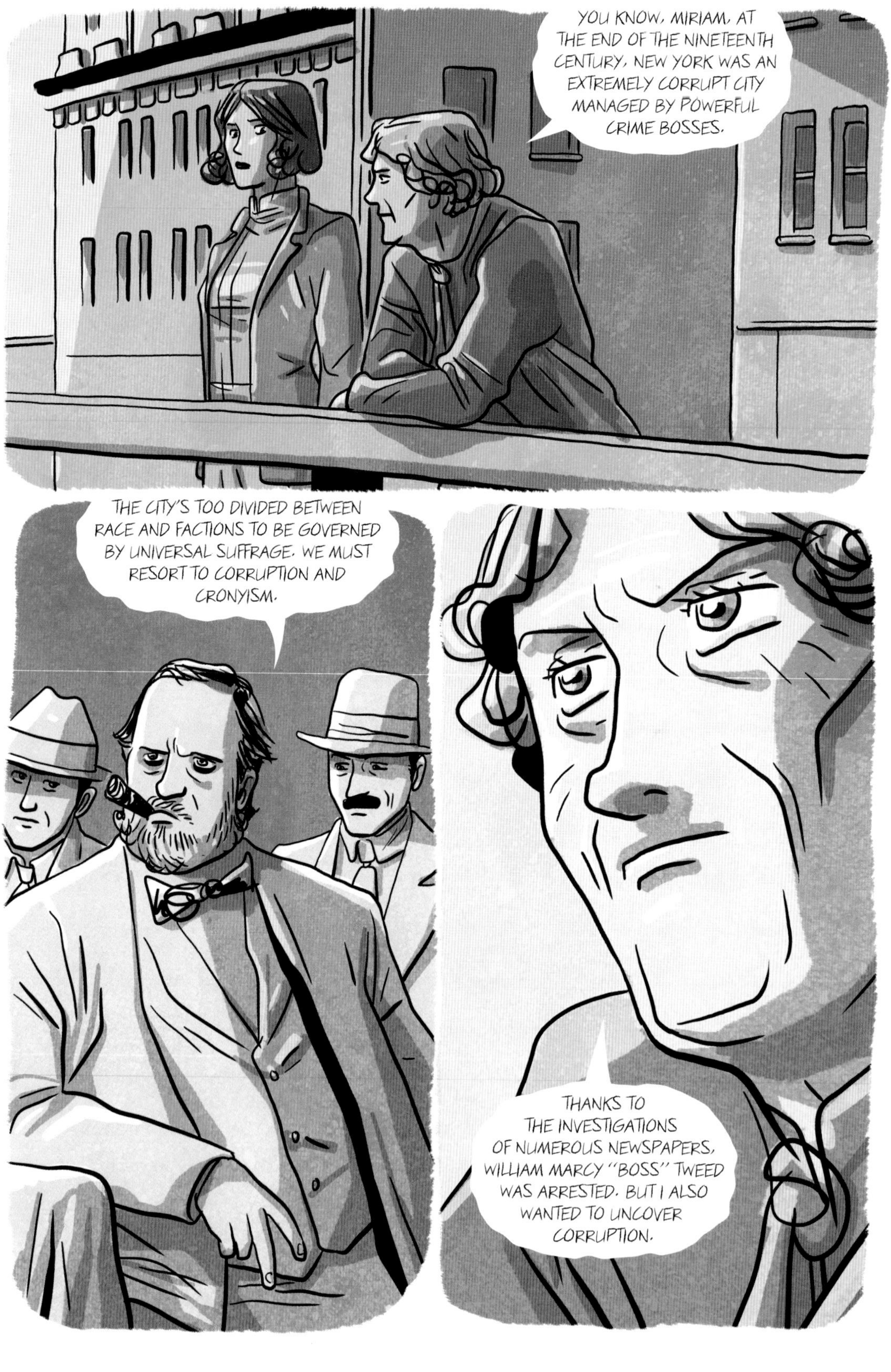
YOU KNOW, MIRIAM, AT THE END OF THE NINETEENTH CENTURY, NEW YORK WAS AN EXTREMELY CORRUPT CITY MANAGED BY POWERFUL CRIME BOSSES.
THE CITY'S TOO DIVIDED BETWEEN RACE AND FACTIONS TO BE GOVERNED BY UNIVERSAL SUFFRAGE. WE MUST RESORT TO CORRUPTION AND CRONYISM.
THANKS TO THE INVESTIGATIONS OF NUMEROUS NEWSPAPERS, WILLIAM MARCY "BOSS" TWEED WAS ARRESTED. BUT I ALSO WANTED TO UNCOVER CORRUPTION.

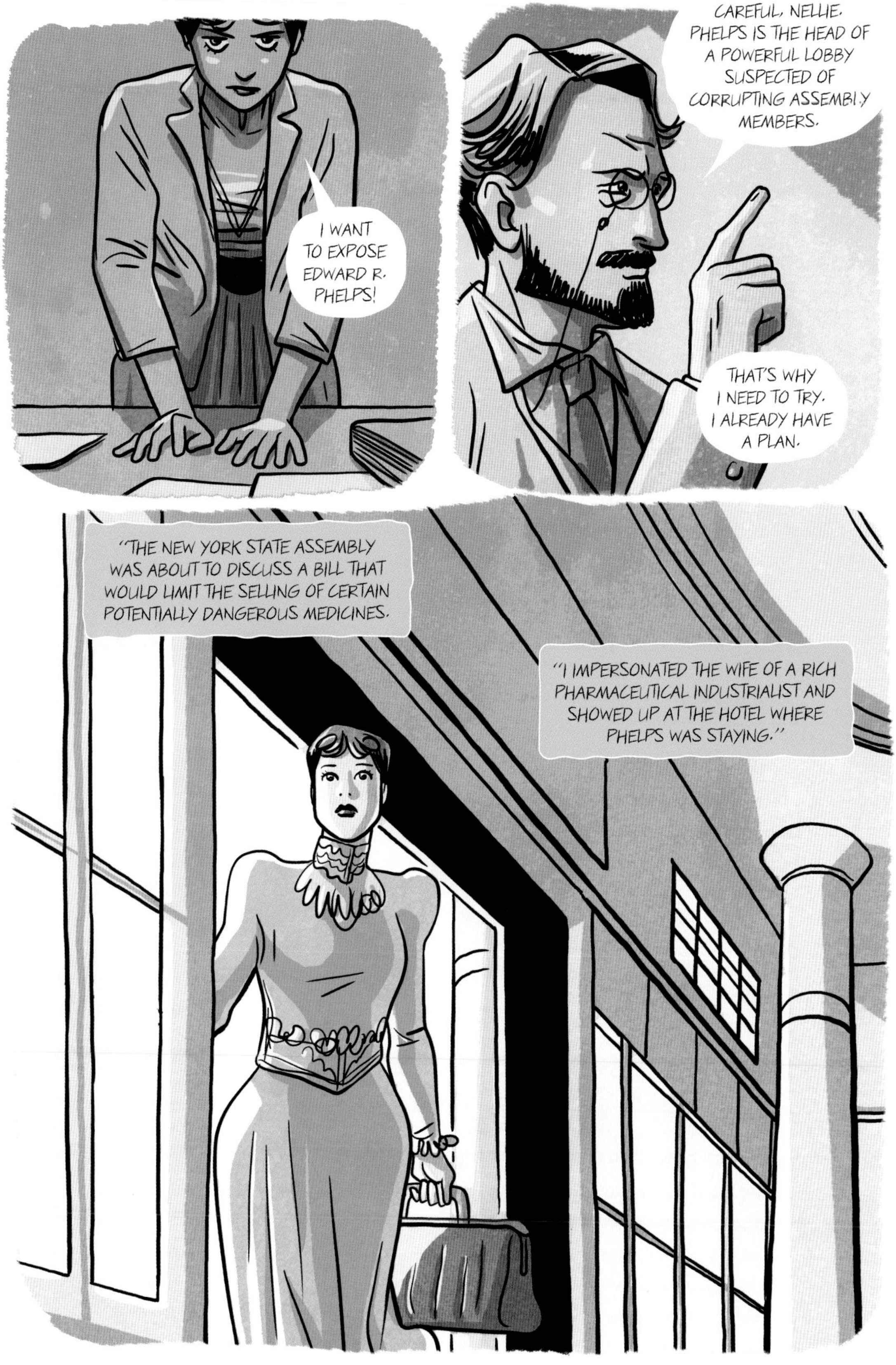
I WANT TO EXPOSE EDWARD R. PHELPS!
CAREFUL, NELLIE. PHELPS IS THE HEAD OF A POWERFUL LOBBY SUSPECTED OF CORRUPTING ASSEMBLY MEMBERS.
THAT'S WHY I NEED TO TRY. I ALREADY HAVE A PLAN.
"THE NEW YORK STATE ASSEMBLY WAS ABOUT TO DISCUSS A BILL THAT WOULD LIMIT THE SELLING OF CERTAIN POTENTIALLY DANGEROUS MEDICINES.
"I IMPERSONATED THE WIFE OF A RICH PHARMACEUTICAL INDUSTRIALIST AND SHOWED UP AT THE HOTEL WHERE PHELPS WAS STAYING."

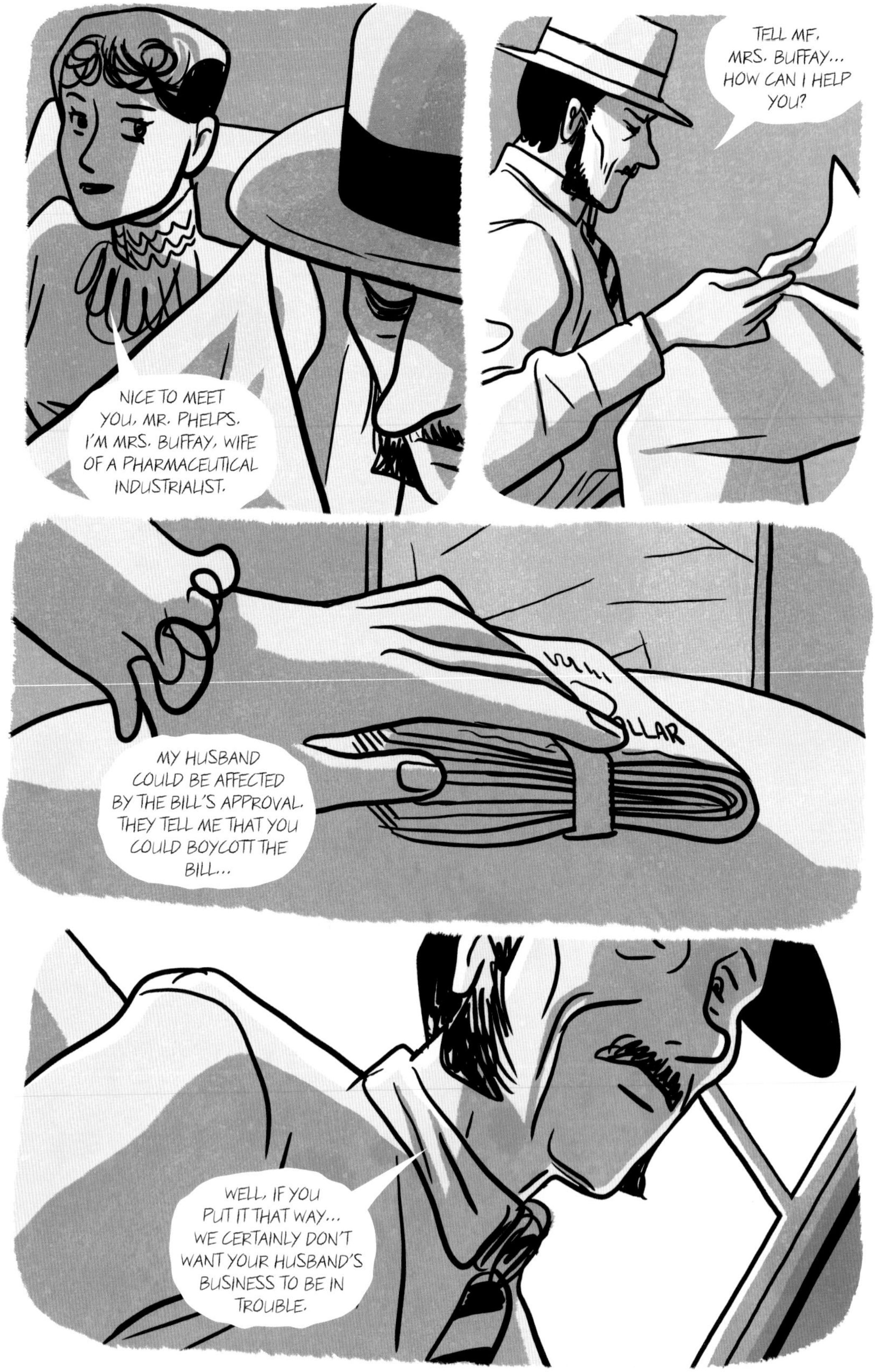
NICE TO MEET YOU, MR. PHELPS. I'M MRS. BUFFAY, WIFE OF A PHARMACEUTICAL INDUSTRIALIST.
TELL ME. MRS. BUFFAY... HOW CAN I HELP YOU?
ILLAR
MY HUSBAND COULD BE AFFECTED BY THE BILL'S APPROVAL. THEY TELL ME THAT YOU COULD BOYCOTT THE BILL...
WELL, IF YOU PUT IT THAT WAY... WE CERTAINLY DON'T WANT YOUR HUSBAND'S BUSINESS TO BE IN TROUBLE.

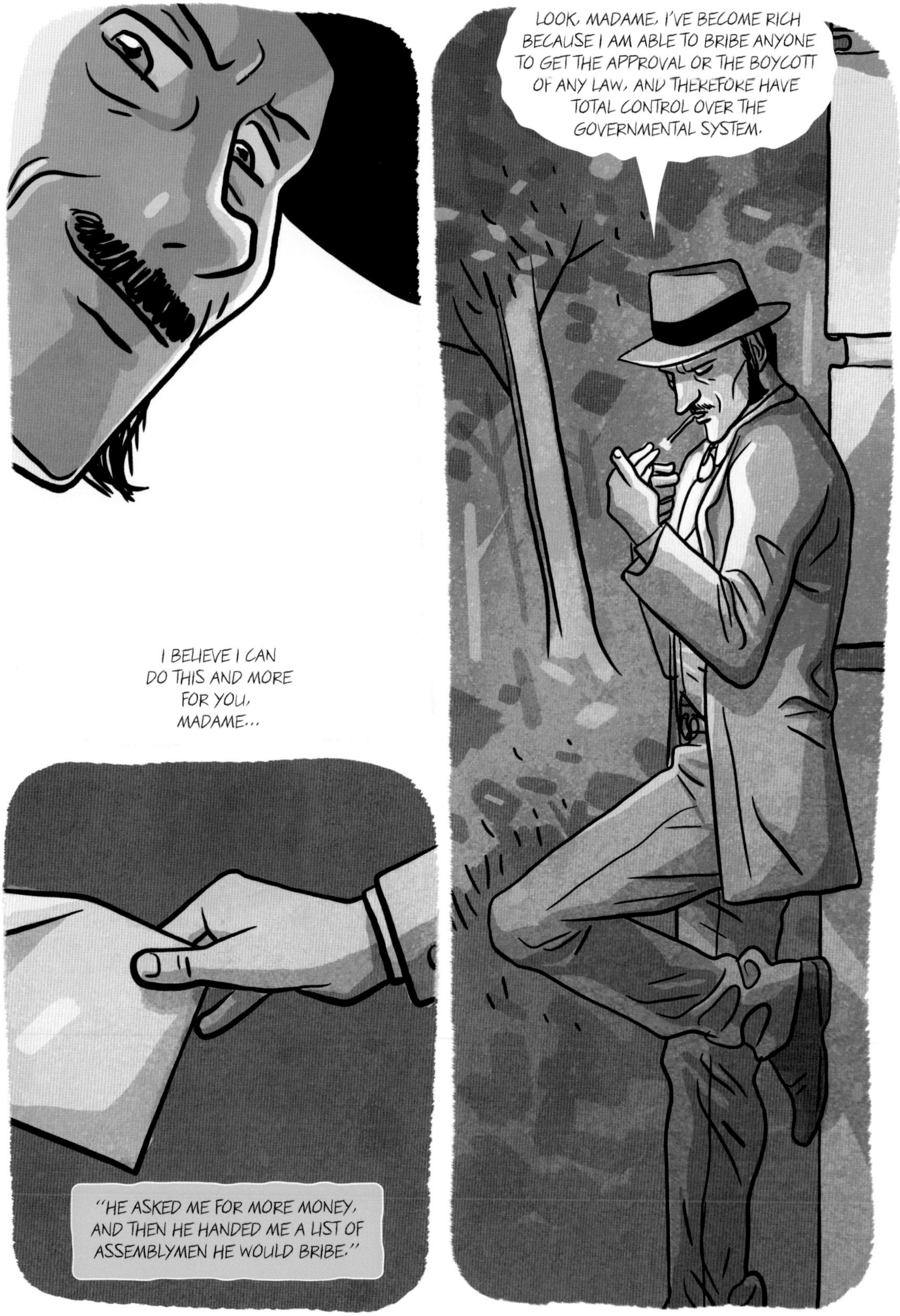
I BELIEVE I CAN DO THIS AND MORE FOR YOU, MADAME...
"HE ASKED ME FOR MORE MONEY, AND THEN HE HANDED ME A LIST OF ASSEMBLYMEN HE WOULD BRIBE."
LOOK, MADAME, I'VE BECOME RICH BECAUSE I AM ABLE TO BRIBE ANYONE TO GET THE APPROVAL OR THE BOYCOTT OF ANY LAW, AND THEREFORE HAVE TOTAL CONTROL OVER THE GOVERNMENTAL SYSTEM.

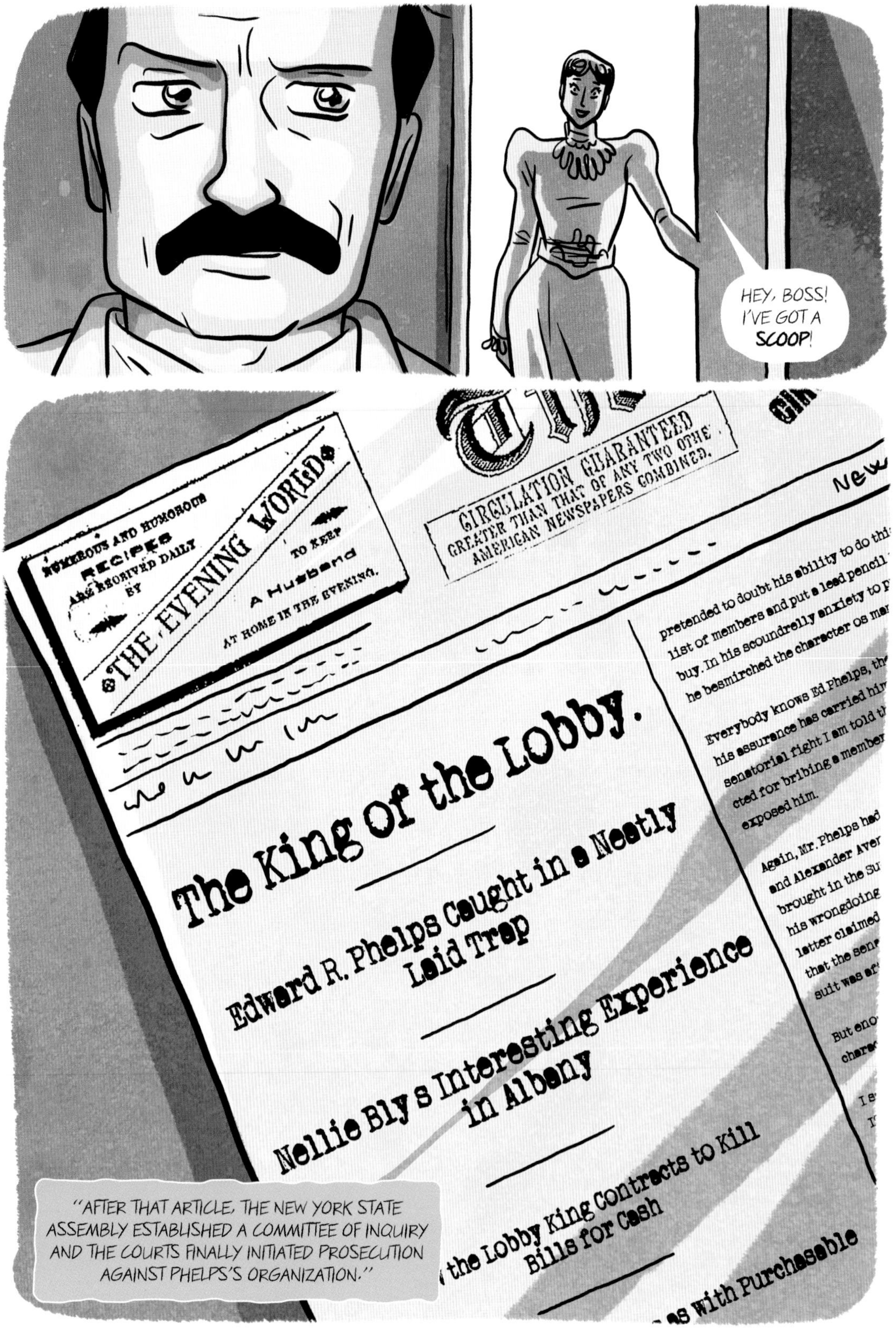
HEY, BOSS! I'VE GOT A SCOOP!
NUMEROUS AND HUMOROUS RECIPES ARE RECEIVED DAILY BY THE EVENING WORLD TO KEEP A Husband AT HOME IN THE EVENING.
CIRCULATION GUARANTEED GREATER THAN THAT OF ANY TWO OTHE AMERICAN NEWSPAPERS COMBINED.
The King of the Lobby.
Edward R. Phelps Caught in a Neatly Laid Trap
Nellie Bly s Interesting Experience in Albany
the Lobby King Contracts to Kill Bills for Cash
"AFTER THAT ARTICLE, THE NEW YORK STATE ASSEMBLY ESTABLISHED A COMMITTEE OF INQUIRY AND THE COURTS FINALLY INITIATED PROSECUTION AGAINST PHELPS'S ORGANIZATION."

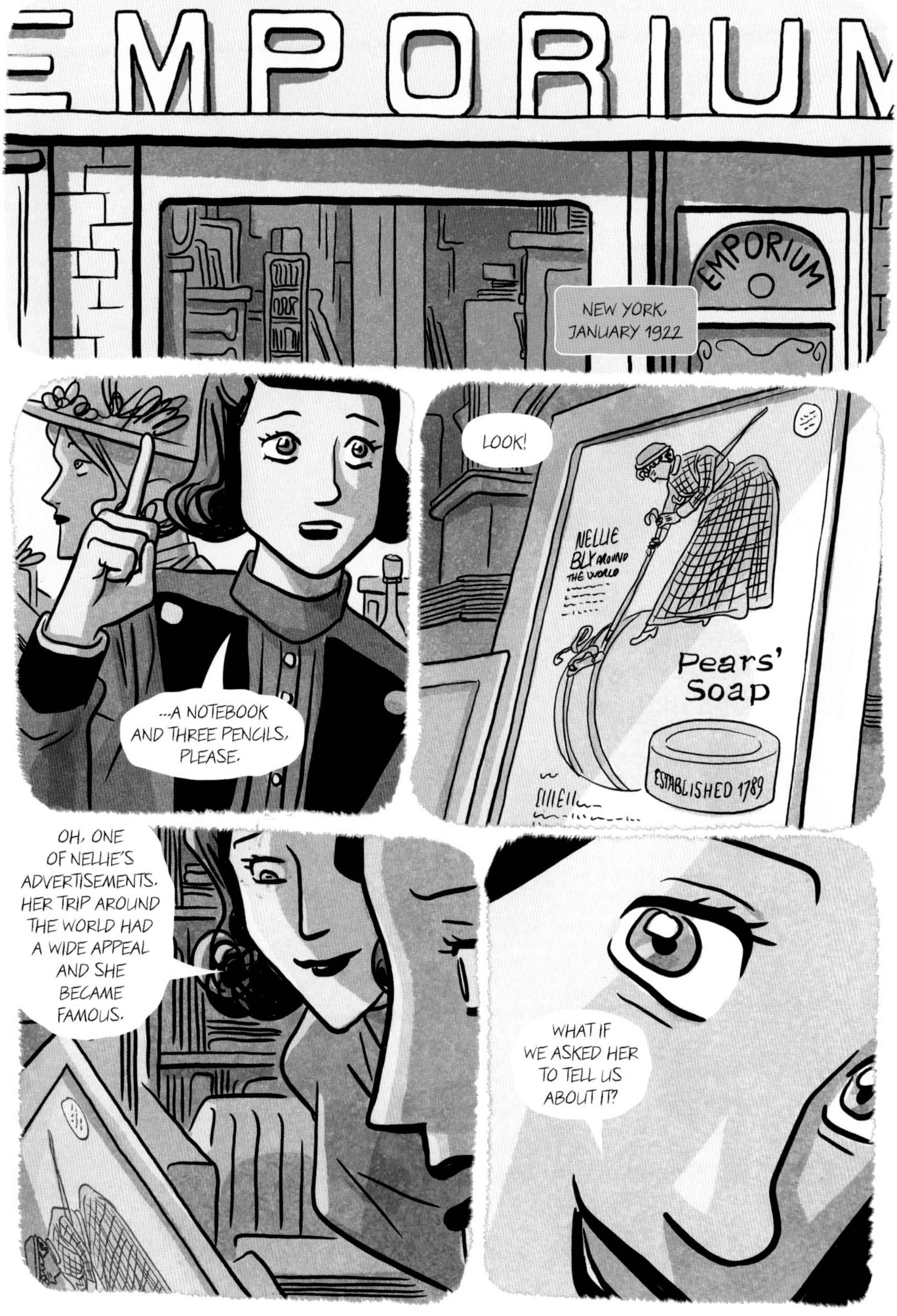
EMPORIUM
EMPORIUM
NEW YORK, JANUARY 1922
...A NOTEBOOK AND THREE PENCILS, PLEASE.
LOOK!
NELLIE BLY AROUND THE WORLD
Pears' Soap
ESTABLISHED 1789
OH, ONE OF NELLIE'S ADVERTISEMENTS. HER TRIP AROUND THE WORLD HAD A WIDE APPEAL AND SHE BECAME FAMOUS.
WHAT IF WE ASKED HER TO TELL US ABOUT IT?

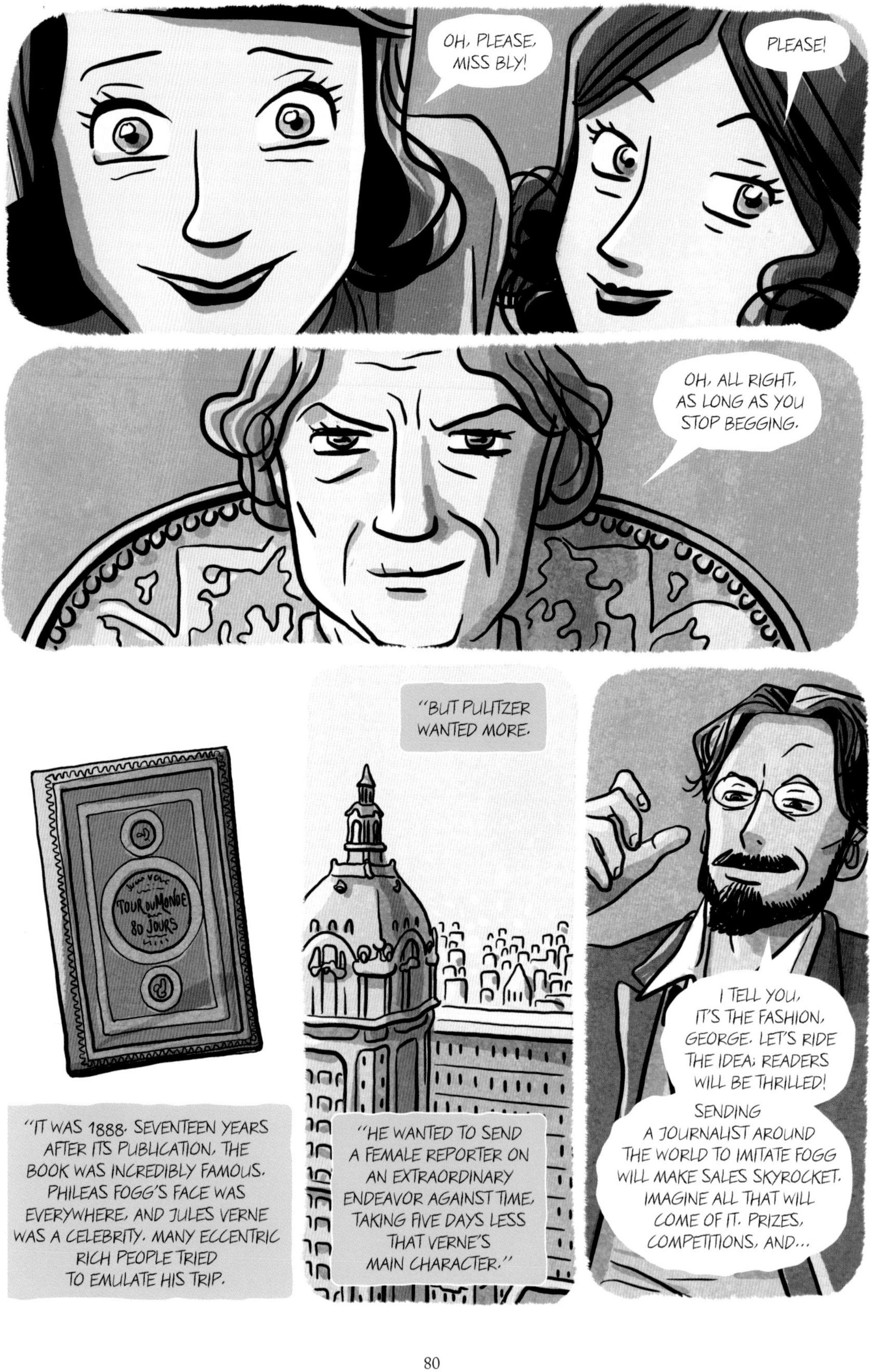
OH, PLEASE, MISS BLY!
PLEASE!
OH, ALL RIGHT, AS LONG AS YOU STOP BEGGING.
TOUR DU MONDE 80 JOURS
"IT WAS 1888. SEVENTEEN YEARS AFTER ITS PUBLICATION, THE BOOK WAS INCREDIBLY FAMOUS. PHILEAS FOGG'S FACE WAS EVERYWHERE, AND JULES VERNE WAS A CELEBRITY. MANY ECCENTRIC RICH PEOPLE TRIED TO EMULATE HIS TRIP.
"BUT PULITZER WANTED MORE.
"HE WANTED TO SEND A FEMALE REPORTER ON AN EXTRAORDINARY ENDEAVOR AGAINST TIME, TAKING FIVE DAYS LESS THAT VERNE'S MAIN CHARACTER."
I TELL YOU, IT'S THE FASHION, GEORGE. LET'S RIDE THE IDEA; READERS WILL BE THRILLED!
SENDING A JOURNALIST AROUND THE WORLD TO IMITATE FOGG WILL MAKE SALES SKYROCKET. IMAGINE ALL THAT WILL COME OF IT. PRIZES, COMPETITIONS, AND...

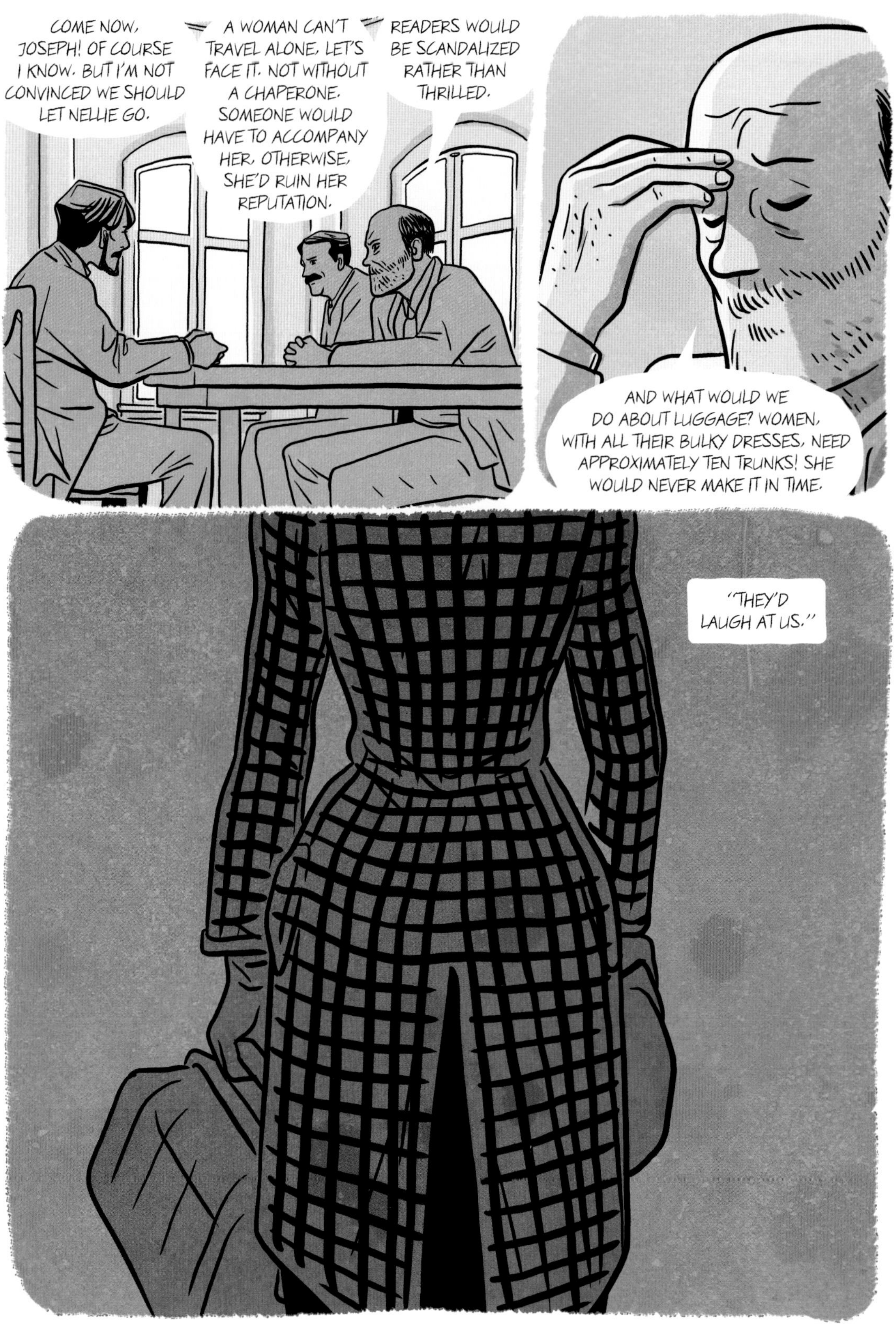
COME NOW, JOSEPH! OF COURSE I KNOW. BUT I'M NOT CONVINCED WE SHOULD LET NELLIE GO.
A WOMAN CAN'T TRAVEL ALONE, LET'S FACE IT. NOT WITHOUT A CHAPERONE. SOMEONE WOULD HAVE TO ACCOMPANY HER. OTHERWISE, SHE'D RUIN HER REPUTATION.
READERS WOULD BE SCANDALIZED RATHER THAN THRILLED.
AND WHAT WOULD WE DO ABOUT LUGGAGE? WOMEN, WITH ALL THEIR BULKY DRESSES, NEED APPROXIMATELY TEN TRUNKS! SHE WOULD NEVER MAKE IT IN TIME.
"THEY'D LAUGH AT US."

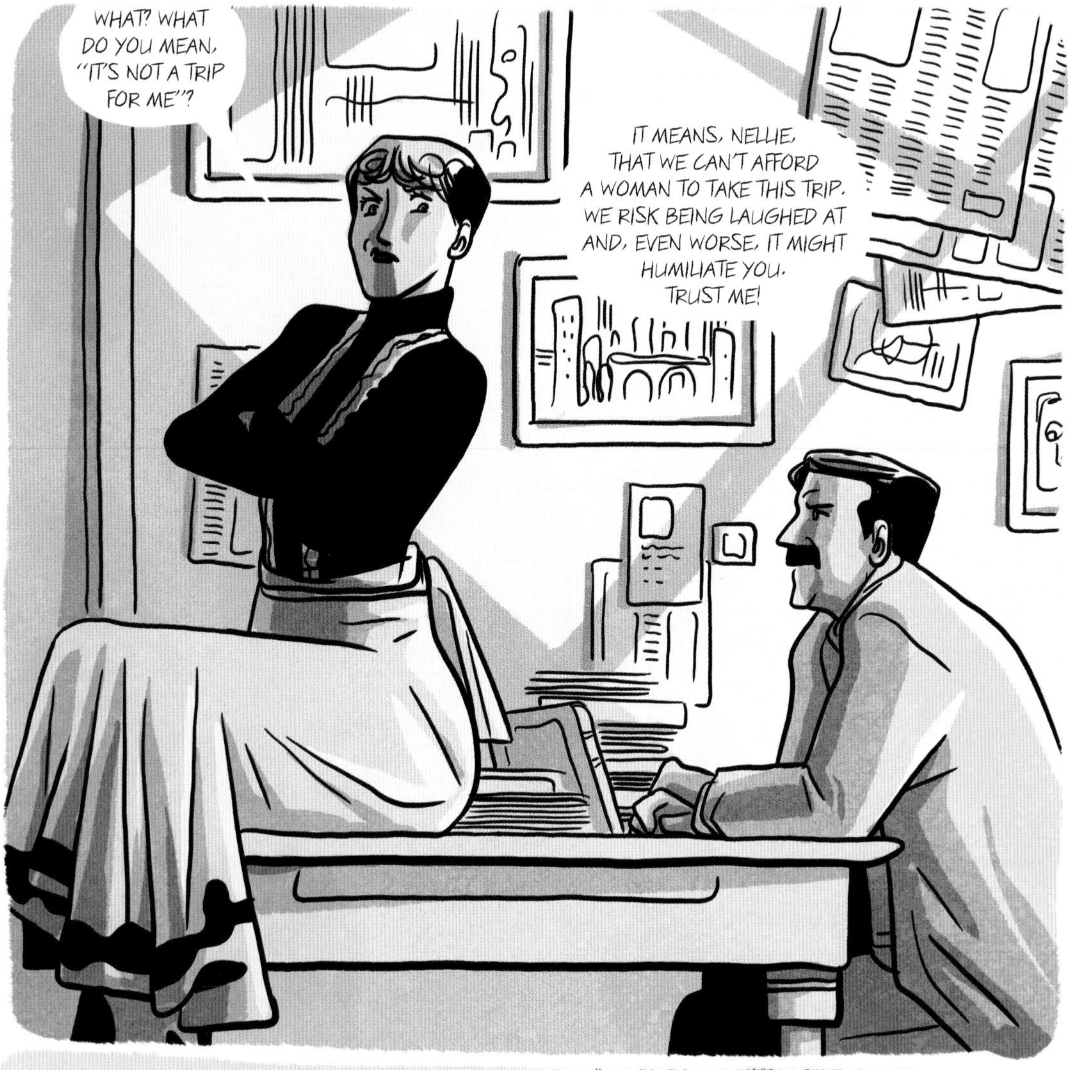
WHAT? WHAT DO YOU MEAN, "IT'S NOT A TRIP FOR ME"?
IT MEANS, NELLIE, THAT WE CAN'T AFFORD A WOMAN TO TAKE THIS TRIP. WE RISK BEING LAUGHED AT AND, EVEN WORSE, IT MIGHT HUMILIATE YOU. TRUST ME!

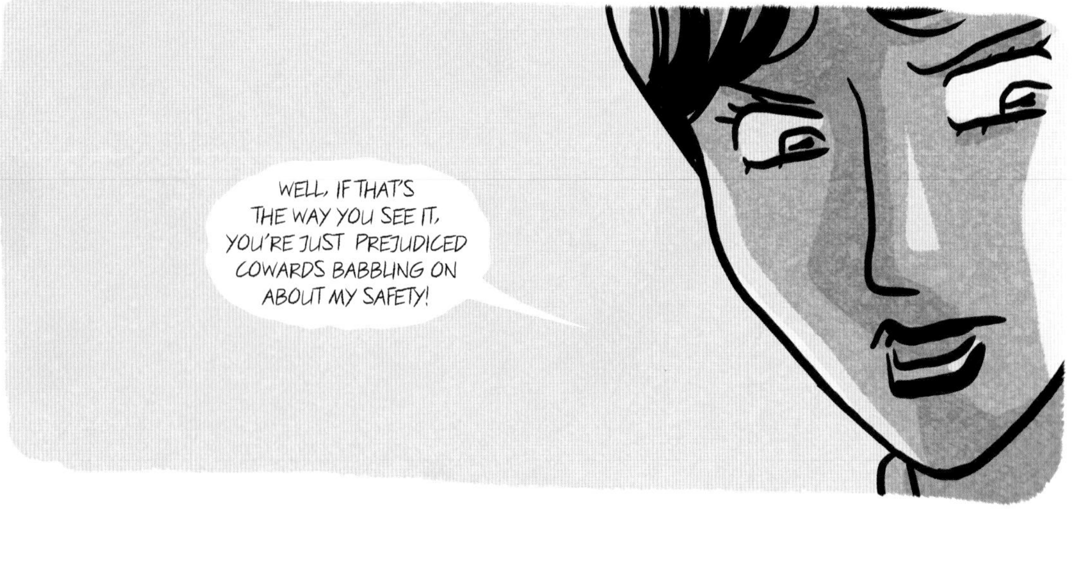
WELL, IF THAT'S THE WAY YOU SEE IT, YOU'RE JUST PREJUDICED COWARDS BABBLING ON ABOUT MY SAFETY!

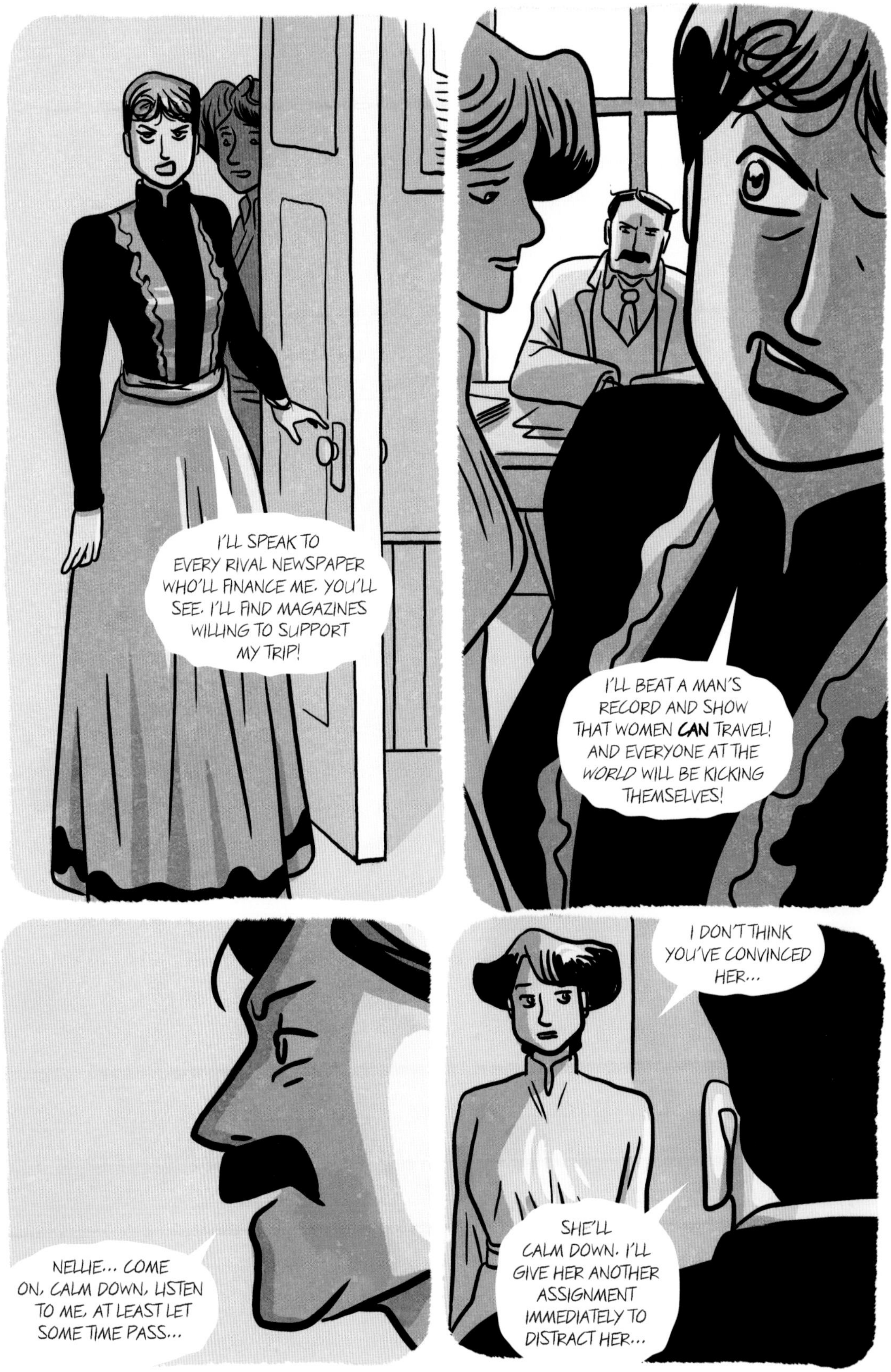
I'LL SPEAK TO EVERY RIVAL NEWSPAPER WHO'LL FINANCE ME. YOU'LL SEE. I'LL FIND MAGAZINES WILLING TO SUPPORT MY TRIP!
I'LL BEAT A MAN'S RECORD AND SHOW THAT WOMEN CAN TRAVEL! AND EVERYONE AT THE WORLD WILL BE KICKING THEMSELVES!
NELLIE... COME ON, CALM DOWN, LISTEN TO ME, AT LEAST LET SOME TIME PASS...
I DON'T THINK YOU'VE CONVINCED HER...
SHE'LL CALM DOWN. I'LL GIVE HER ANOTHER ASSIGNMENT IMMEDIATELY TO DISTRACT HER...

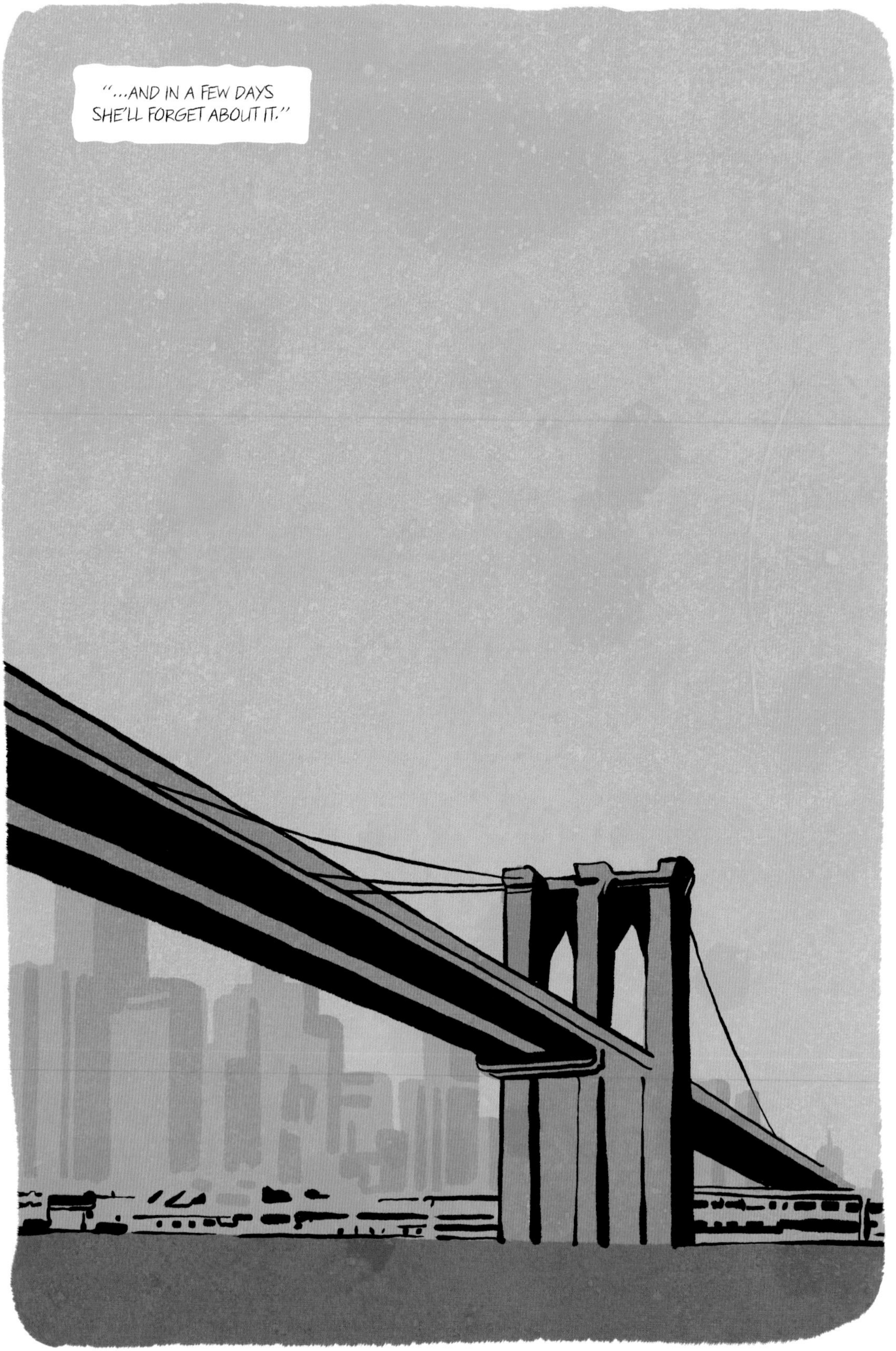
"...AND IN A FEW DAYS
SHE'LL FORGET ABOUT IT."

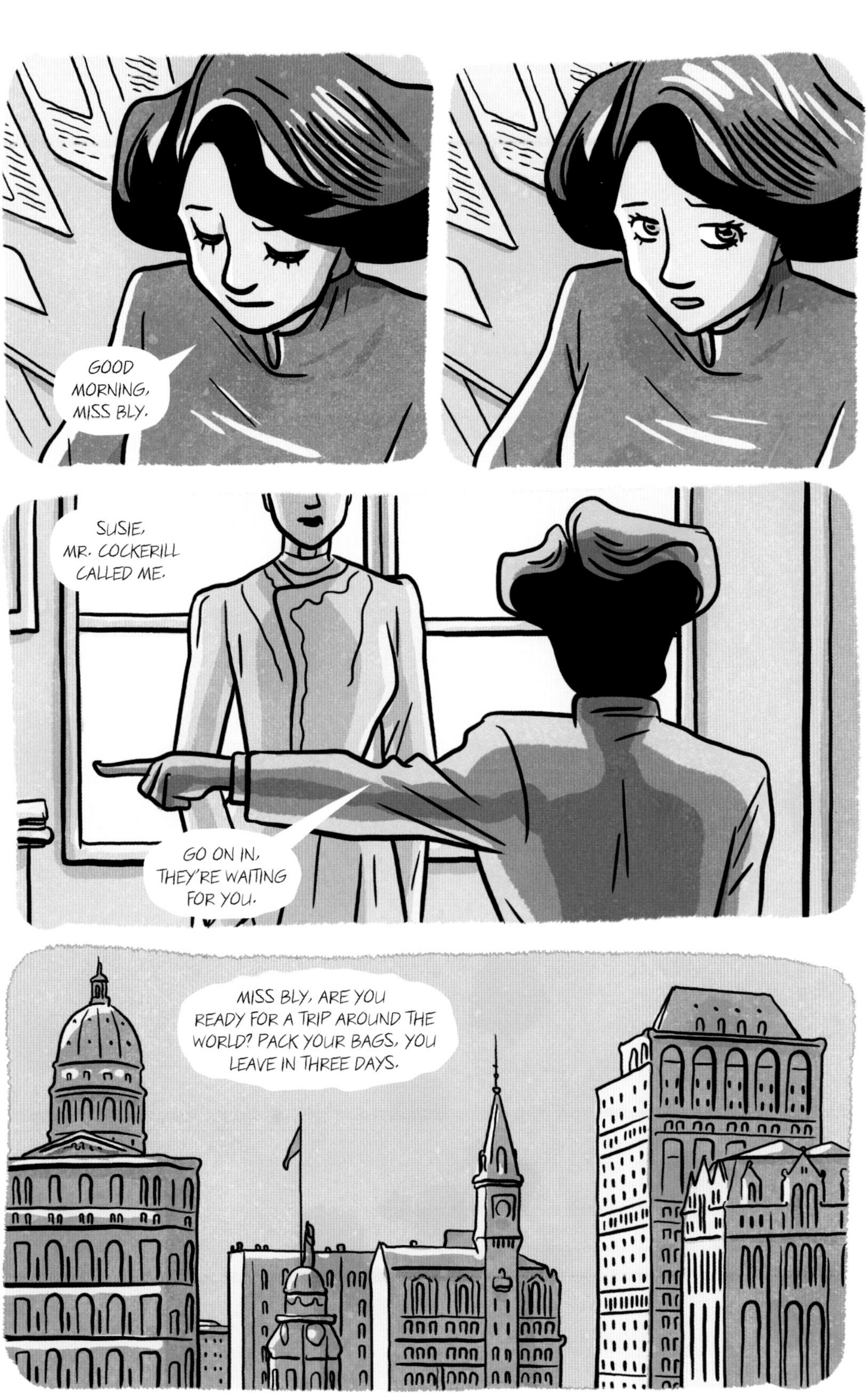
GOOD MORNING, MISS BLY.
SUSIE, MR. COCKERILL CALLED ME.
GO ON IN, THEY'RE WAITING FOR YOU.
MISS BLY, ARE YOU READY FOR A TRIP AROUND THE WORLD? PACK YOUR BAGS, YOU LEAVE IN THREE DAYS.

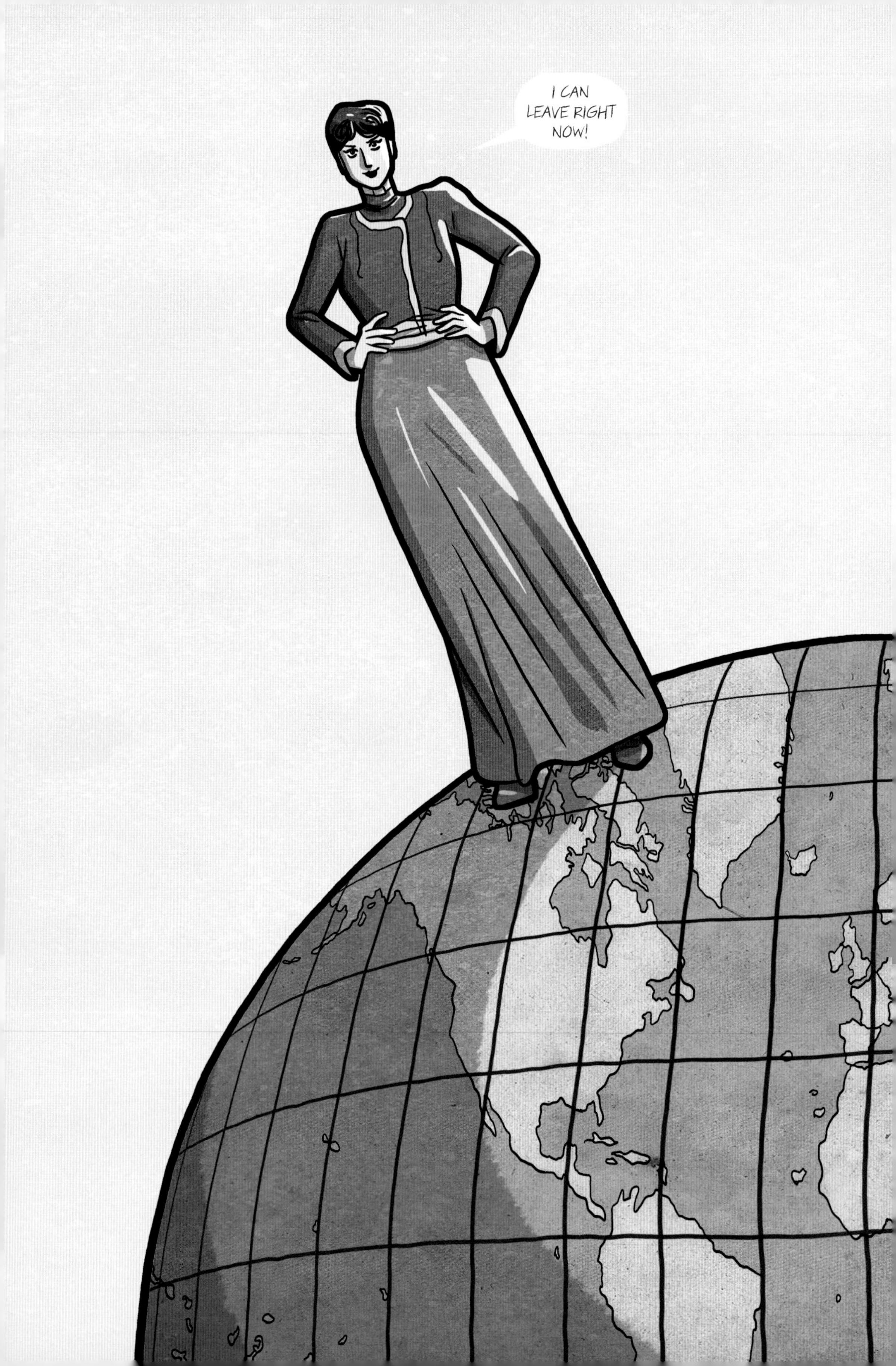
I CAN LEAVE RIGHT NOW!

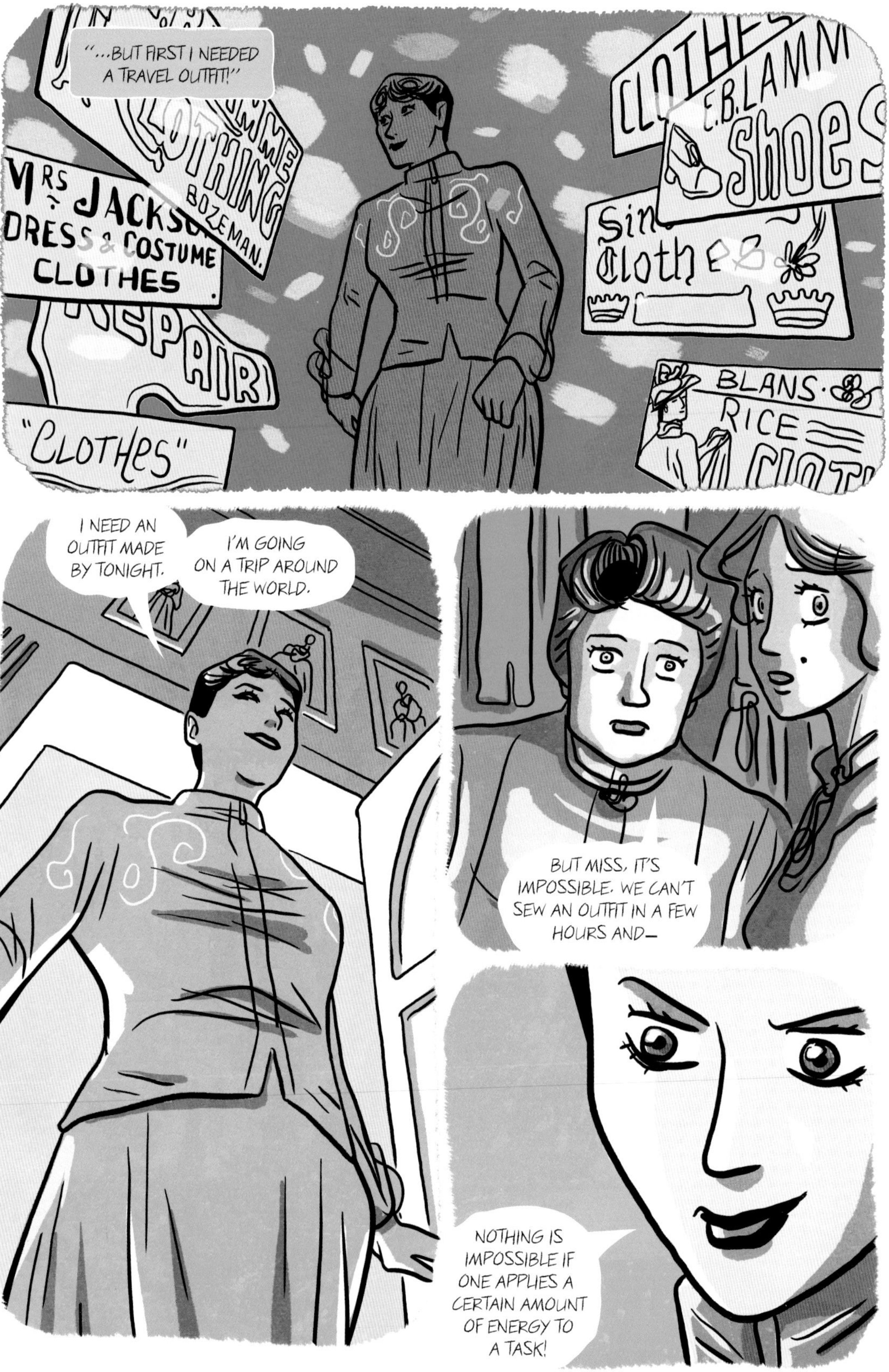
"...BUT FIRST I NEEDED A TRAVEL OUTFIT!"
CLOTHING
BOZEMAN.
DRESS & COSTUME
CLOTHES
E.B.LAMM
Shoes
BLANS.
RICE
"CLOTHES"
I NEED AN OUTFIT MADE BY TONIGHT.
I'M GOING ON A TRIP AROUND THE WORLD.
BUT MISS, IT'S IMPOSSIBLE. WE CAN'T SEW AN OUTFIT IN A FEW HOURS AND—
NOTHING IS IMPOSSIBLE IF ONE APPLIES A CERTAIN AMOUNT OF ENERGY TO A TASK!

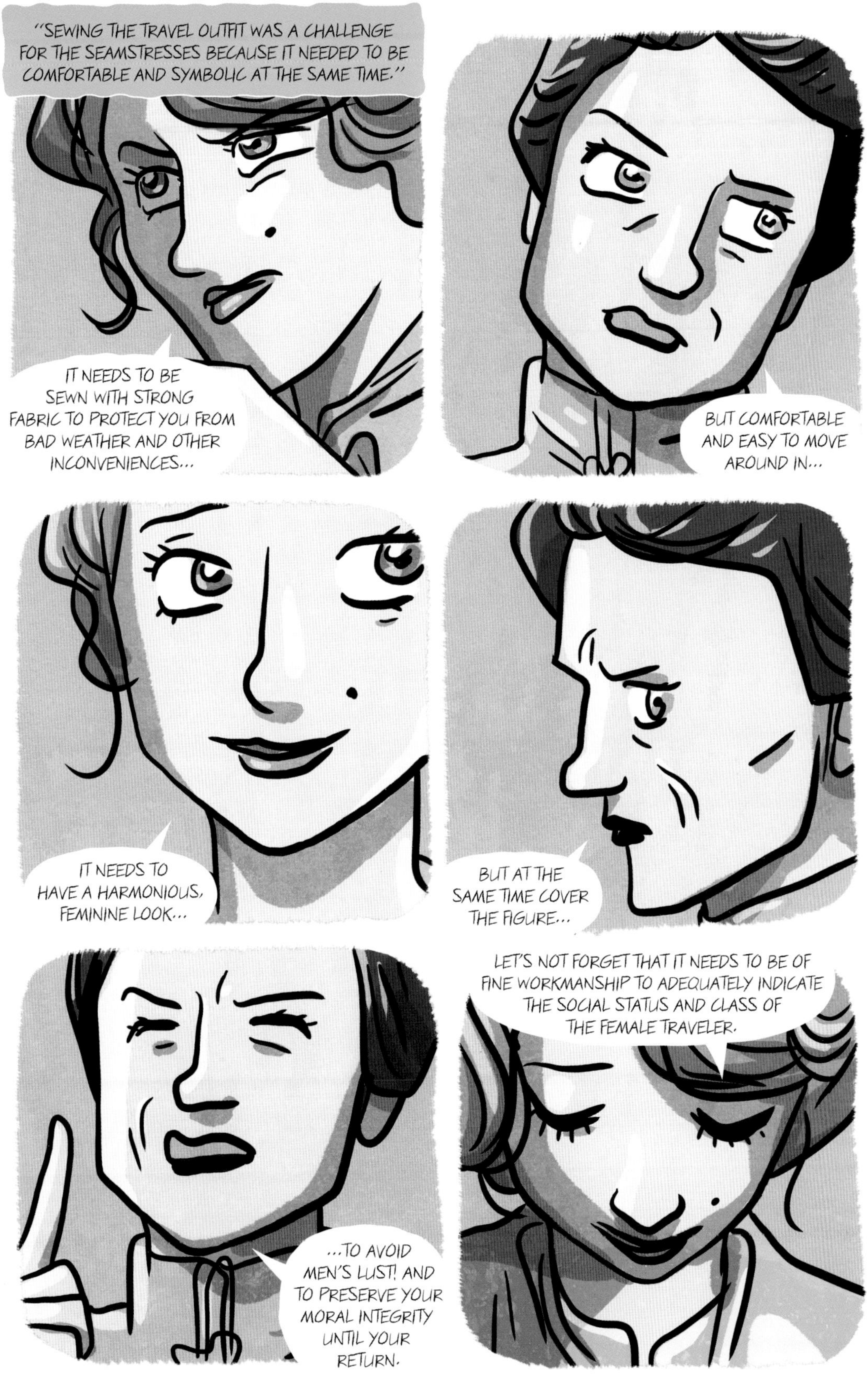
"SEWING THE TRAVEL OUTFIT WAS A CHALLENGE FOR THE SEAMSTRESSES BECAUSE IT NEEDED TO BE COMFORTABLE AND SYMBOLIC AT THE SAME TIME."
IT NEEDS TO BE SEWN WITH STRONG FABRIC TO PROTECT YOU FROM BAD WEATHER AND OTHER INCONVENIENCES...
BUT COMFORTABLE AND EASY TO MOVE AROUND IN...
IT NEEDS TO HAVE A HARMONIOUS, FEMININE LOOK...
BUT AT THE SAME TIME COVER THE FIGURE...
...TO AVOID MEN'S LUST! AND TO PRESERVE YOUR MORAL INTEGRITY UNTIL YOUR RETURN.
LET'S NOT FORGET THAT IT NEEDS TO BE OF FINE WORKMANSHIP TO ADEQUATELY INDICATE THE SOCIAL STATUS AND CLASS OF THE FEMALE TRAVELER.

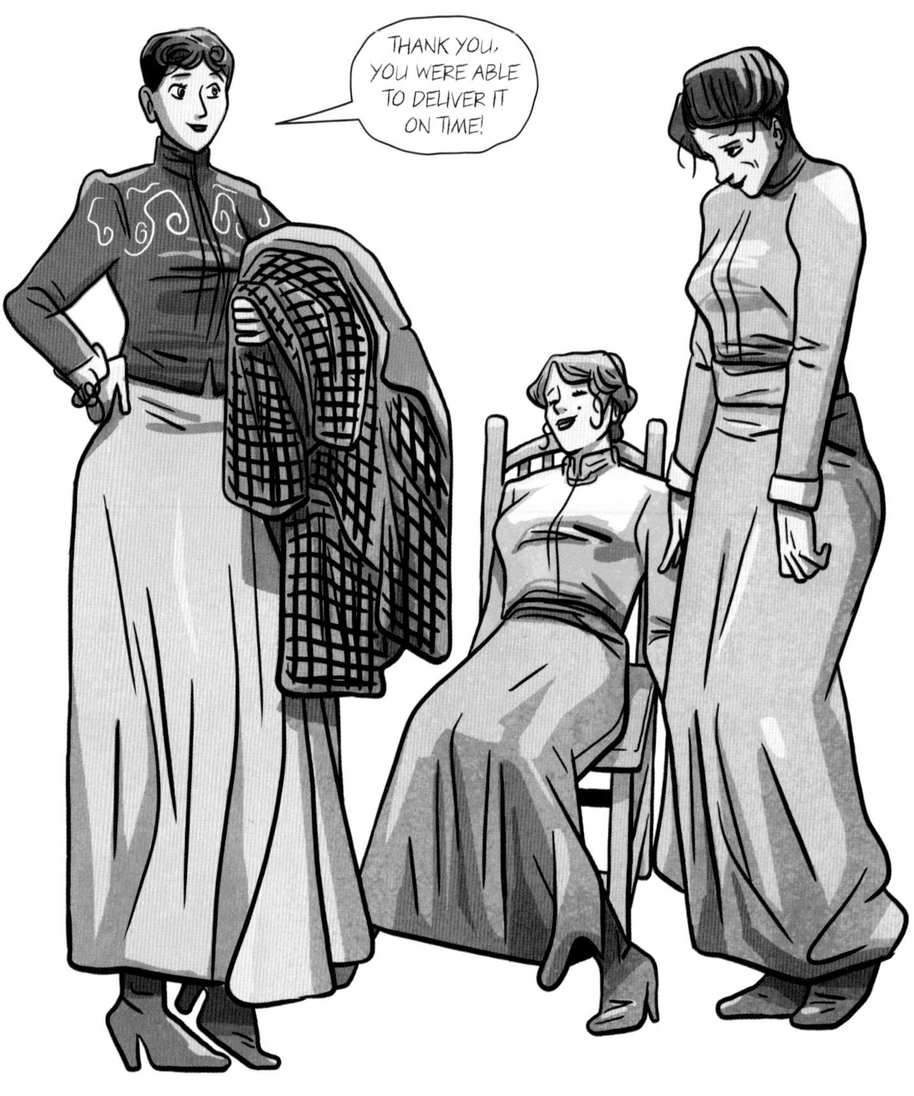
THANK YOU, YOU WERE ABLE TO DELIVER IT ON TIME!

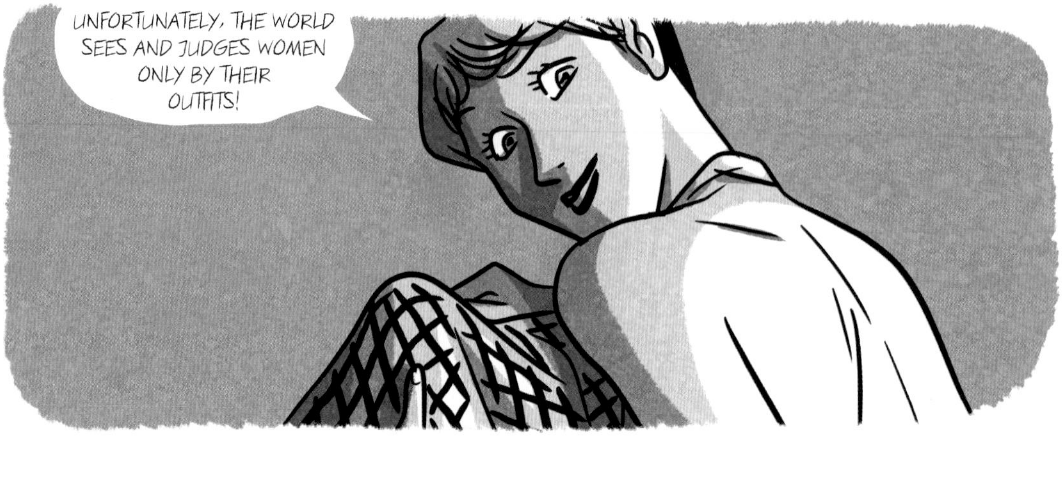
UNFORTUNATELY, THE WORLD SEES AND JUDGES WOMEN ONLY BY THEIR OUTFITS!

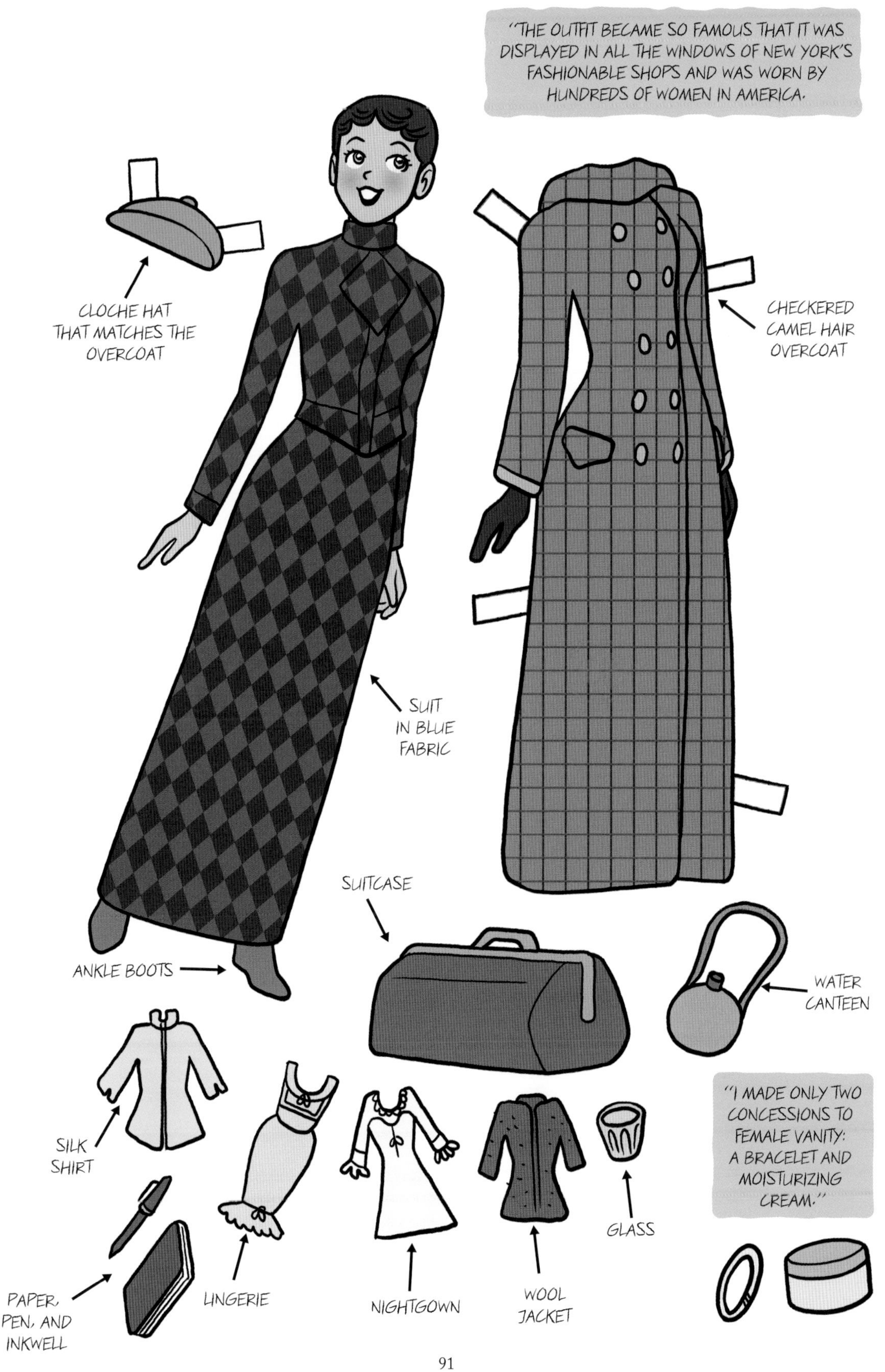
"THE OUTFIT BECAME SO FAMOUS THAT IT WAS DISPLAYED IN ALL THE WINDOWS OF NEW YORK'S FASHIONABLE SHOPS AND WAS WORN BY HUNDREDS OF WOMEN IN AMERICA.
CLOCHE HAT THAT MATCHES THE OVERCOAT
CHECKERED CAMEL HAIR OVERCOAT
SUIT IN BLUE FABRIC
SUITCASE
ANKLE BOOTS
WATER CANTEEN
"I MADE ONLY TWO CONCESSIONS TO FEMALE VANITY: A BRACELET AND MOISTURIZING CREAM."
SILK SHIRT
GLASS
PAPER, PEN, AND INKWELL
LINGERIE
NIGHTGOWN
WOOL JACKET

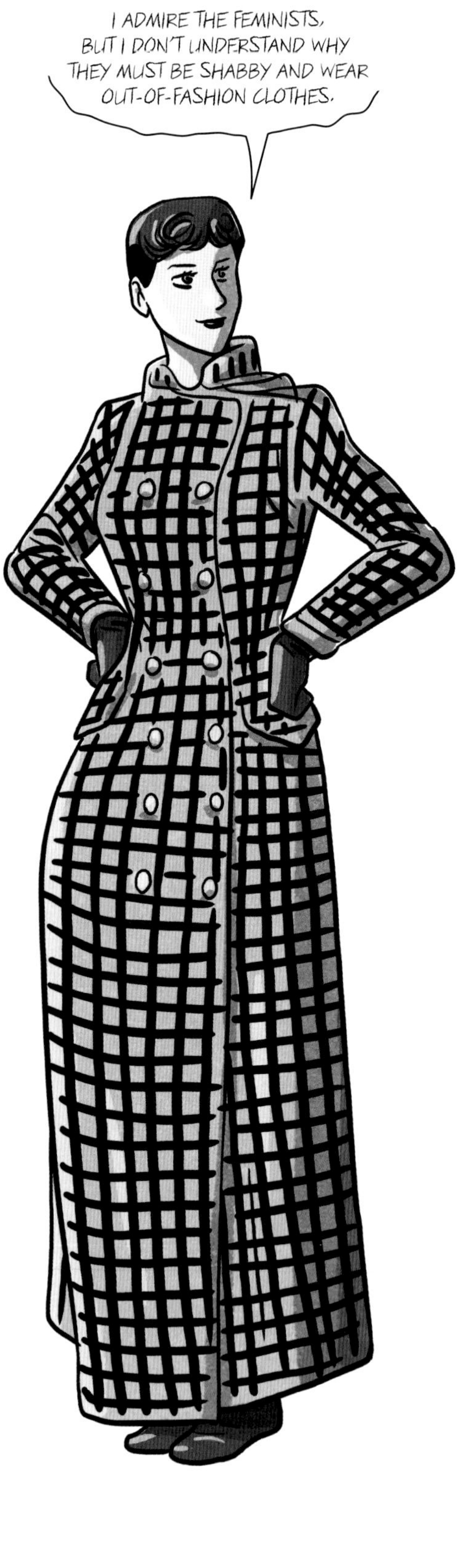
I ADMIRE THE FEMINISTS, BUT I DON'T UNDERSTAND WHY THEY MUST BE SHABBY AND WEAR OUT-OF-FASHION CLOTHES.

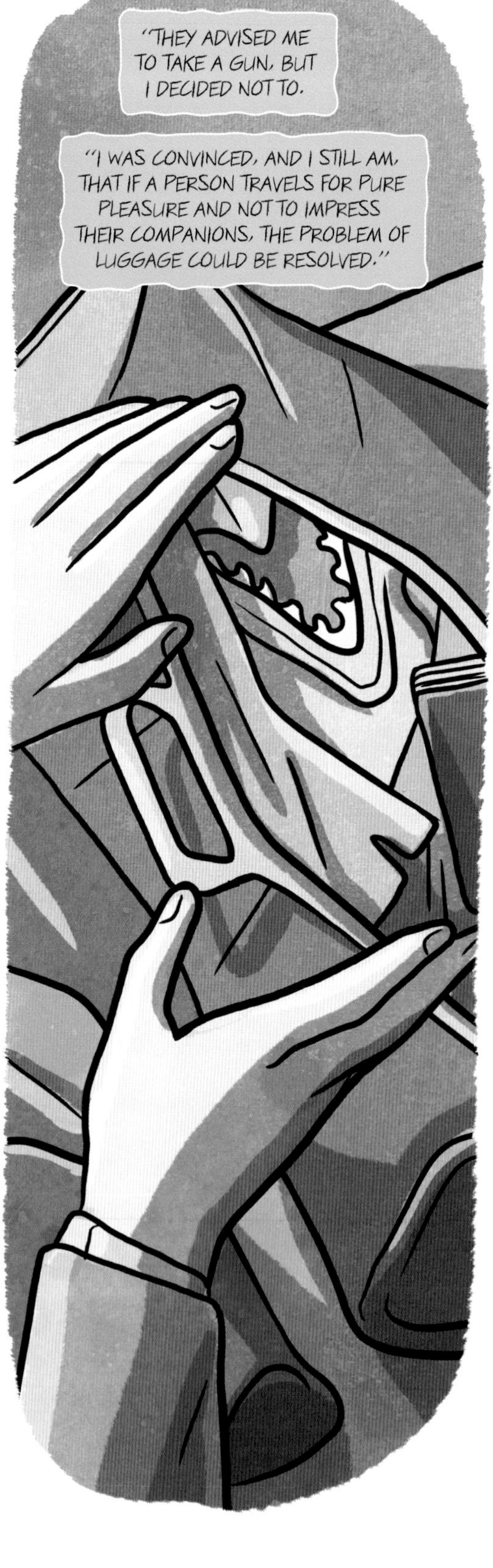
"THEY ADVISED ME TO TAKE A GUN, BUT I DECIDED NOT TO.
"I WAS CONVINCED, AND I STILL AM, THAT IF A PERSON TRAVELS FOR PURE PLEASURE AND NOT TO IMPRESS THEIR COMPANIONS, THE PROBLEM OF LUGGAGE COULD BE RESOLVED."

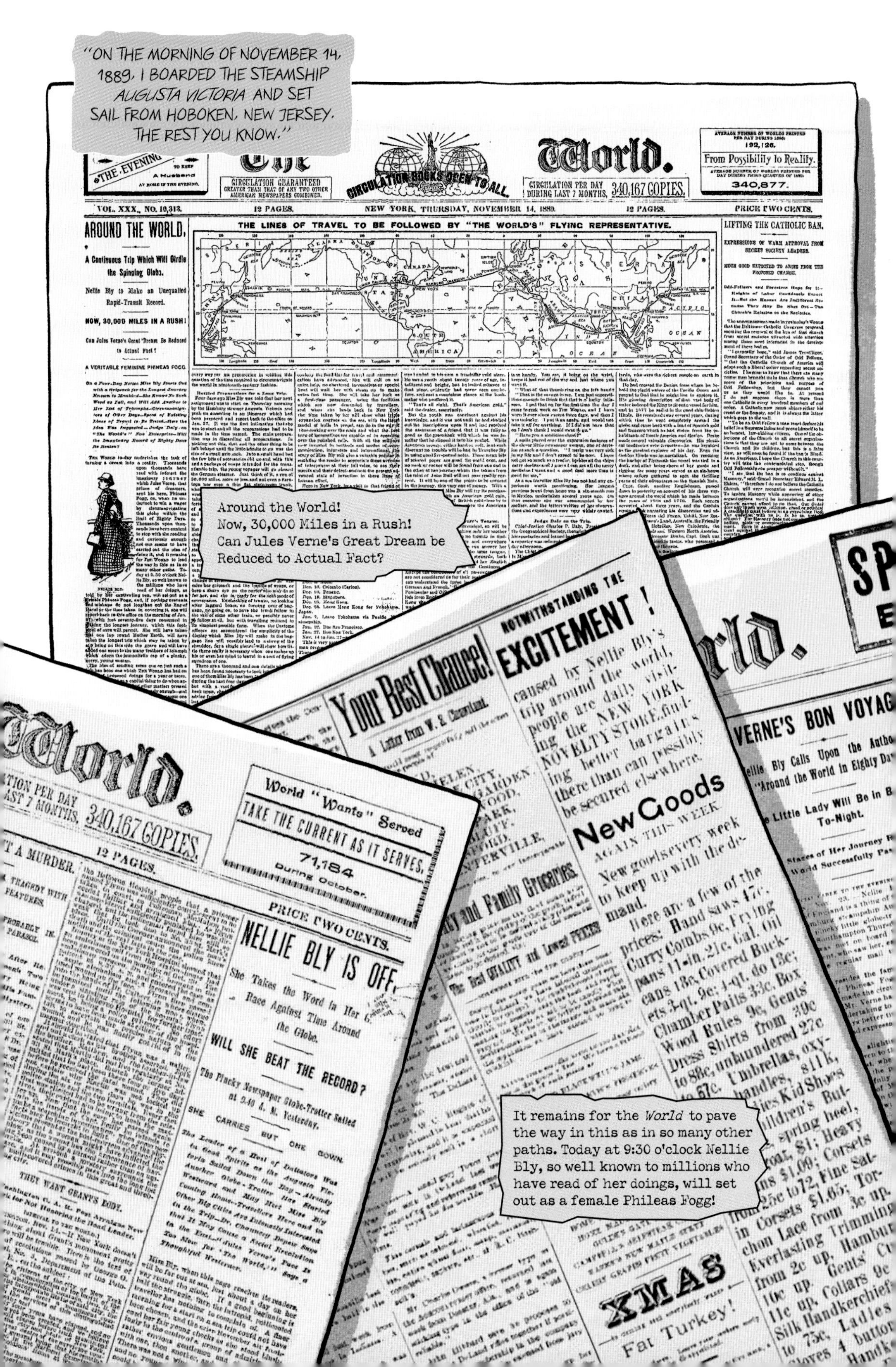
"ON THE MORNING OF NOVEMBER 14, 1889, I BOARDED THE STEAMSHIP *AUGUSTA VICTORIA* AND SET SAIL FROM HOBOKEN, NEW JERSEY. THE REST YOU KNOW."
The World.
NEW YORK, THURSDAY, NOVEMBER 14, 1889.
PRICE TWO CENTS.
THE LINES OF TRAVEL TO BE FOLLOWED BY "THE WORLD'S" FLYING REPRESENTATIVE.
AROUND THE WORLD.
A Continuous Trip Which Will Girdle the Spinning Globe.
Nellie Bly to Make an Unequalled Rapid-Transit Record.
NOW, 30,000 MILES IN A RUSH!
A VERITABLE FEMININE PHINEAS FOGG.
LIFTING THE CATHOLIC BAN.
Around the World! Now, 30,000 Miles in a Rush! Can Jules Verne's Great Dream be Reduced to Actual Fact?
Your Best Chance!
NOTWITHSTANDING THE EXCITEMENT!
caused by Nellie Bly's trip around the world, people are daily visiting the NEW YORK NOVELTY STORE, finding better bargains there than can possibly be secured elsewhere.
New Goods AGAIN THIS WEEK
XMAS
Fat Turkey!
VERNE'S BON VOYAG
World "Wants" Served
TAKE THE CURRENT AS IT SERVES.
71,184 During October.
PRICE TWO CENTS.
NELLIE BLY IS OFF,
She Takes the Word in Her Race Against Time Around the Globe.
WILL SHE BEAT THE RECORD?
SHE CARRIES BUT ONE GOWN.
It remains for the *World* to pave the way in this as in so many other paths. Today at 9:30 o'clock Nellie Bly, so well known to millions who have read of her doings, will set out as a female Phileas Fogg!

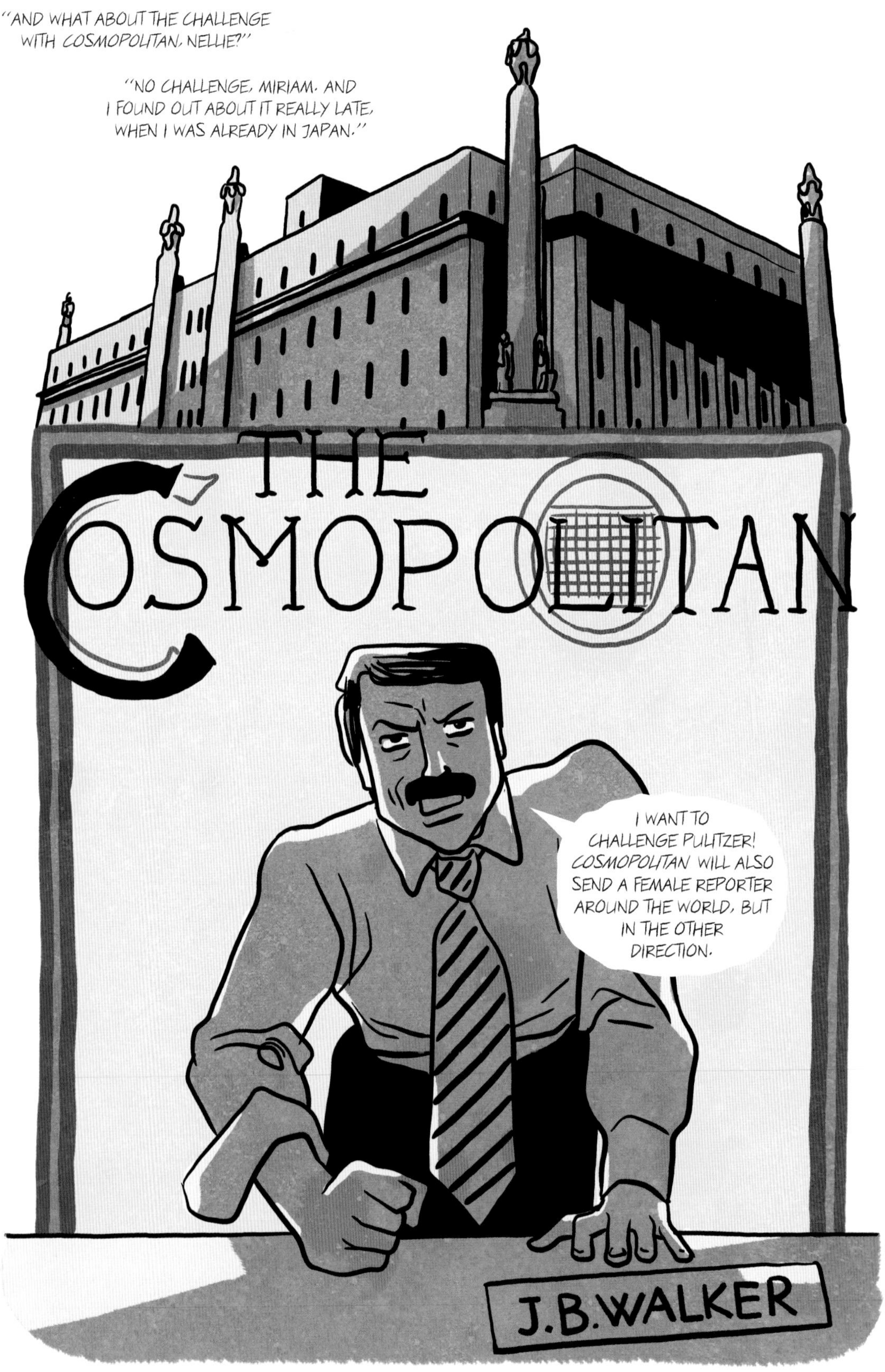
"AND WHAT ABOUT THE CHALLENGE WITH COSMOPOLITAN, NELLIE?"
"NO CHALLENGE, MIRIAM. AND I FOUND OUT ABOUT IT REALLY LATE, WHEN I WAS ALREADY IN JAPAN."
THE COSMOPOLITAN
I WANT TO CHALLENGE PULITZER! COSMOPOLITAN WILL ALSO SEND A FEMALE REPORTER AROUND THE WORLD, BUT IN THE OTHER DIRECTION.
J.B.WALKER

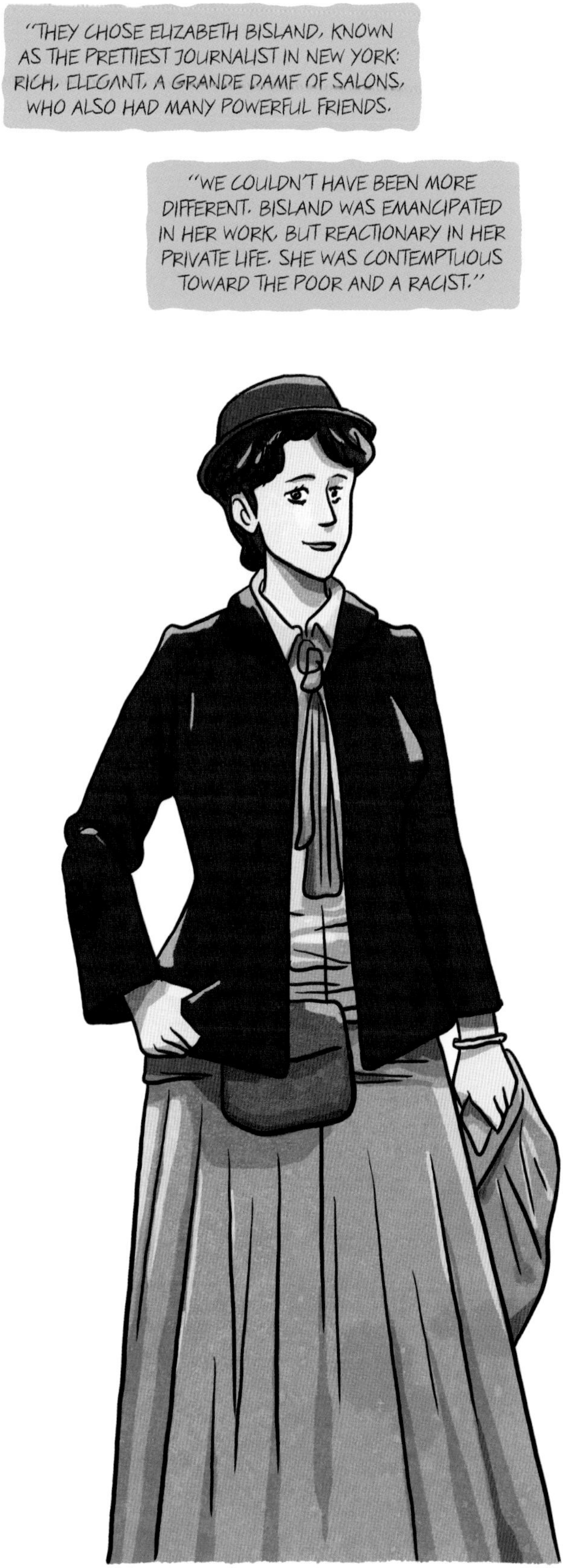
"THEY CHOSE ELIZABETH BISLAND, KNOWN AS THE PRETTIEST JOURNALIST IN NEW YORK: RICH, ELEGANT, A GRANDE DAME OF SALONS, WHO ALSO HAD MANY POWERFUL FRIENDS.
"WE COULDN'T HAVE BEEN MORE DIFFERENT. BISLAND WAS EMANCIPATED IN HER WORK, BUT REACTIONARY IN HER PRIVATE LIFE. SHE WAS CONTEMPTUOUS TOWARD THE POOR AND A RACIST."

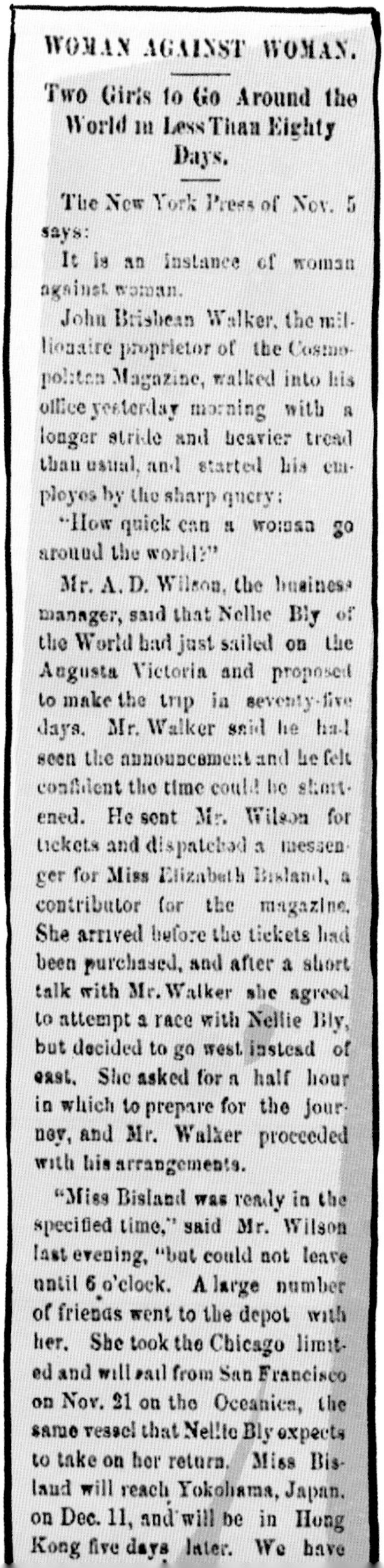

WOMAN AGAINST WOMAN.

Two Girls to Go Around the World in Less Than Eighty Days.

The New York Press of Nov. 5 says:

It is an instance of woman against woman.

John Brisbean Walker, the millionaire proprietor of the Cosmopolitan Magazine, walked into his office yesterday morning with a longer stride and heavier tread than usual, and started his employes by the sharp query:

"How quick can a woman go around the world?"

Mr. A. D. Wilson, the business manager, said that Nellie Bly of the World had just sailed on the Augusta Victoria and proposed to make the trip in seventy-five days. Mr. Walker said he had seen the announcement and he felt confident the time could be shortened. He sent Mr. Wilson for tickets and dispatched a messenger for Miss Elizabeth Bisland, a contributor for the magazine. She arrived before the tickets had been purchased, and after a short talk with Mr. Walker she agreed to attempt a race with Nellie Bly, but decided to go west instead of east. She asked for a half hour in which to prepare for the journey, and Mr. Walker proceeded with his arrangements.

"Miss Bisland was ready in the specified time," said Mr. Wilson last evening, "but could not leave until 6 o'clock. A large number of friends went to the depot with her. She took the Chicago limited and will sail from San Francisco on Nov. 21 on the Oceanica, the same vessel that Nellie Bly expects to take on her return. Miss Bisland will reach Yokohama, Japan, on Dec. 11, and will be in Hong Kong five days later. We have

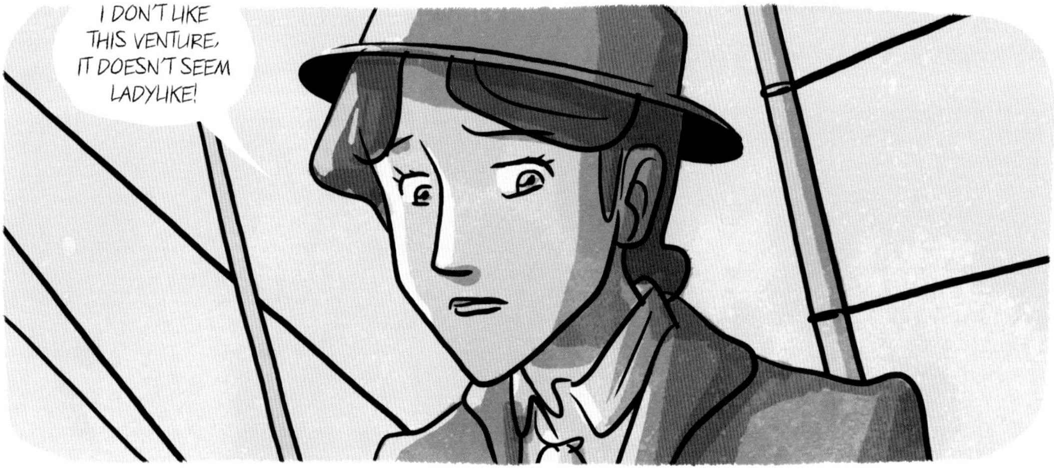
I DON'T LIKE THIS VENTURE, IT DOESN'T SEEM LADYLIKE!

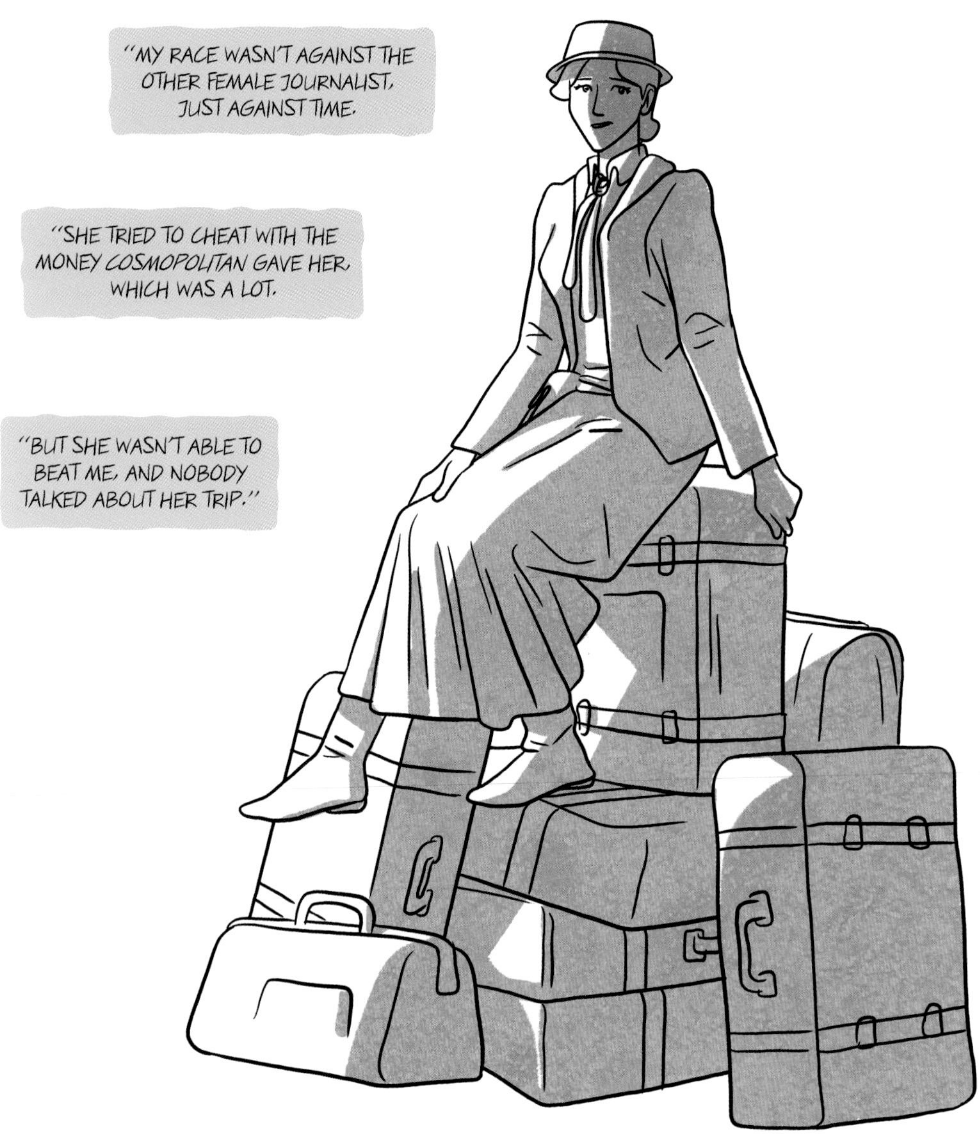
"MY RACE WASN'T AGAINST THE OTHER FEMALE JOURNALIST, JUST AGAINST TIME.
"SHE TRIED TO CHEAT WITH THE MONEY *COSMOPOLITAN* GAVE HER, WHICH WAS A LOT.
"BUT SHE WASN'T ABLE TO BEAT ME, AND NOBODY TALKED ABOUT HER TRIP."

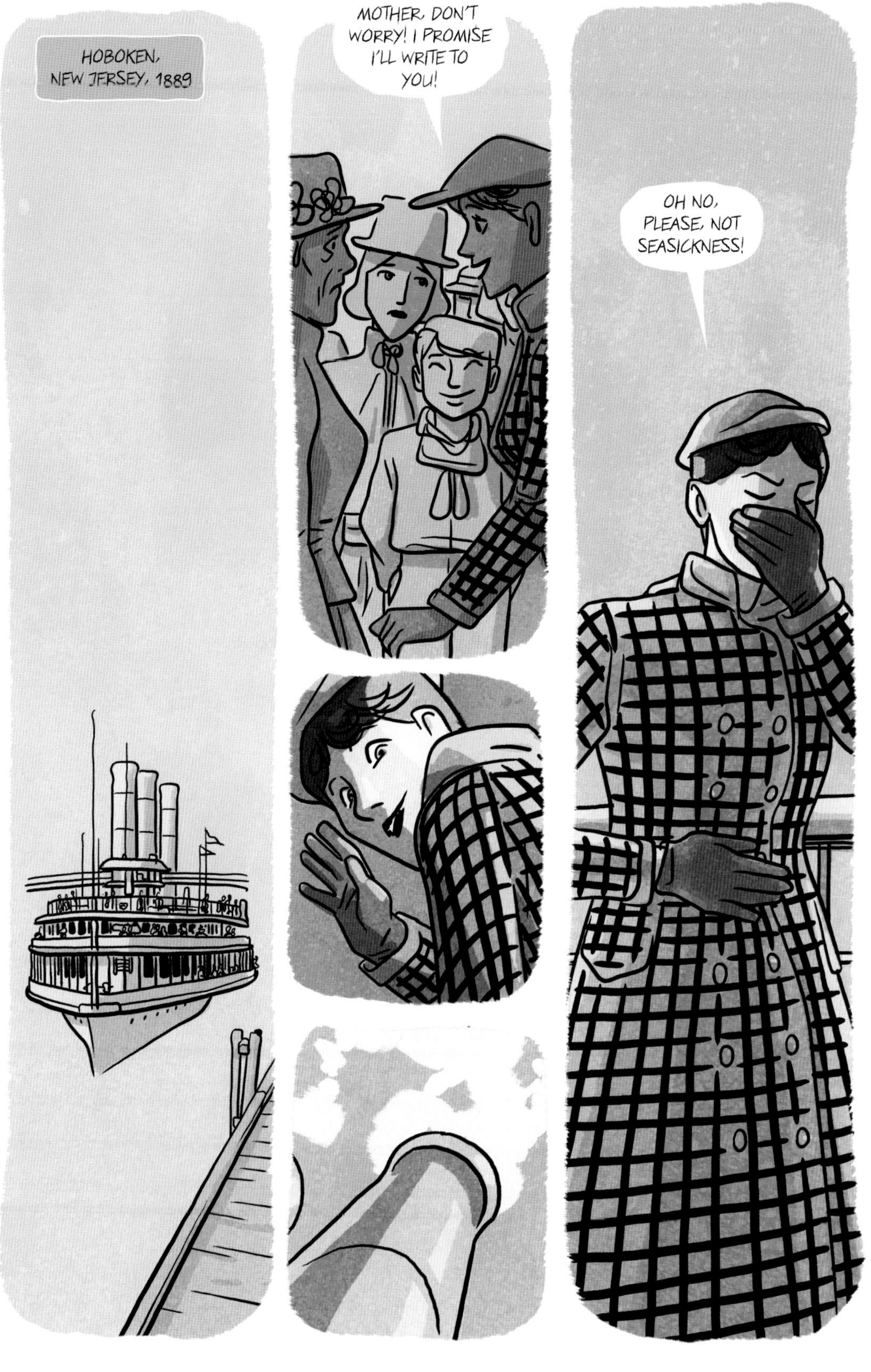
HOBOKEN, NEW JERSEY, 1889
MOTHER, DON'T WORRY! I PROMISE I'LL WRITE TO YOU!
OH NO, PLEASE, NOT SEASICKNESS!

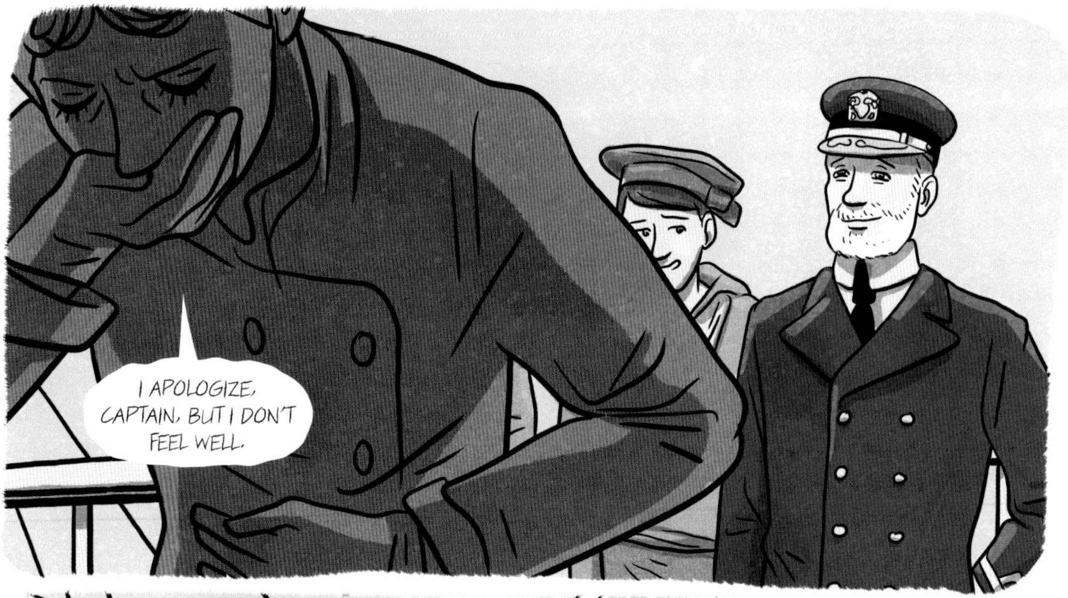
I APOLOGIZE, CAPTAIN, BUT I DON'T FEEL WELL.

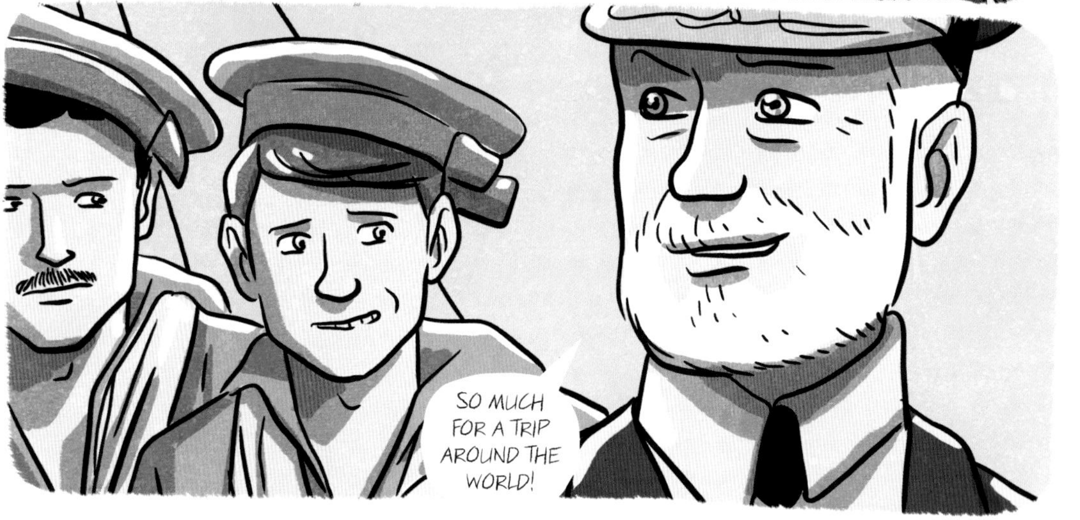
SO MUCH FOR A TRIP AROUND THE WORLD!

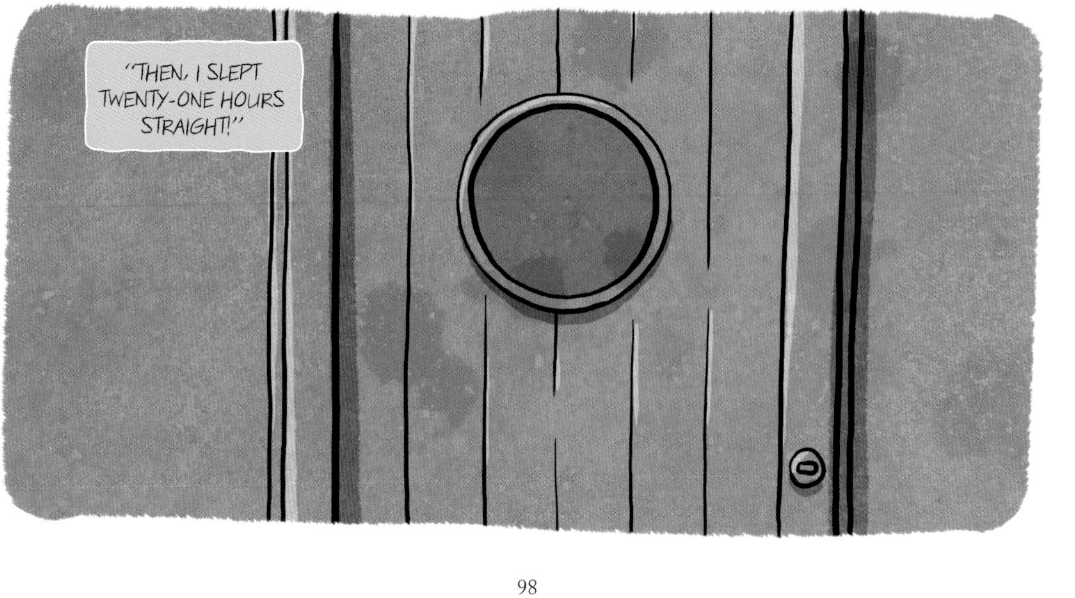
"THEN, I SLEPT TWENTY-ONE HOURS STRAIGHT!"

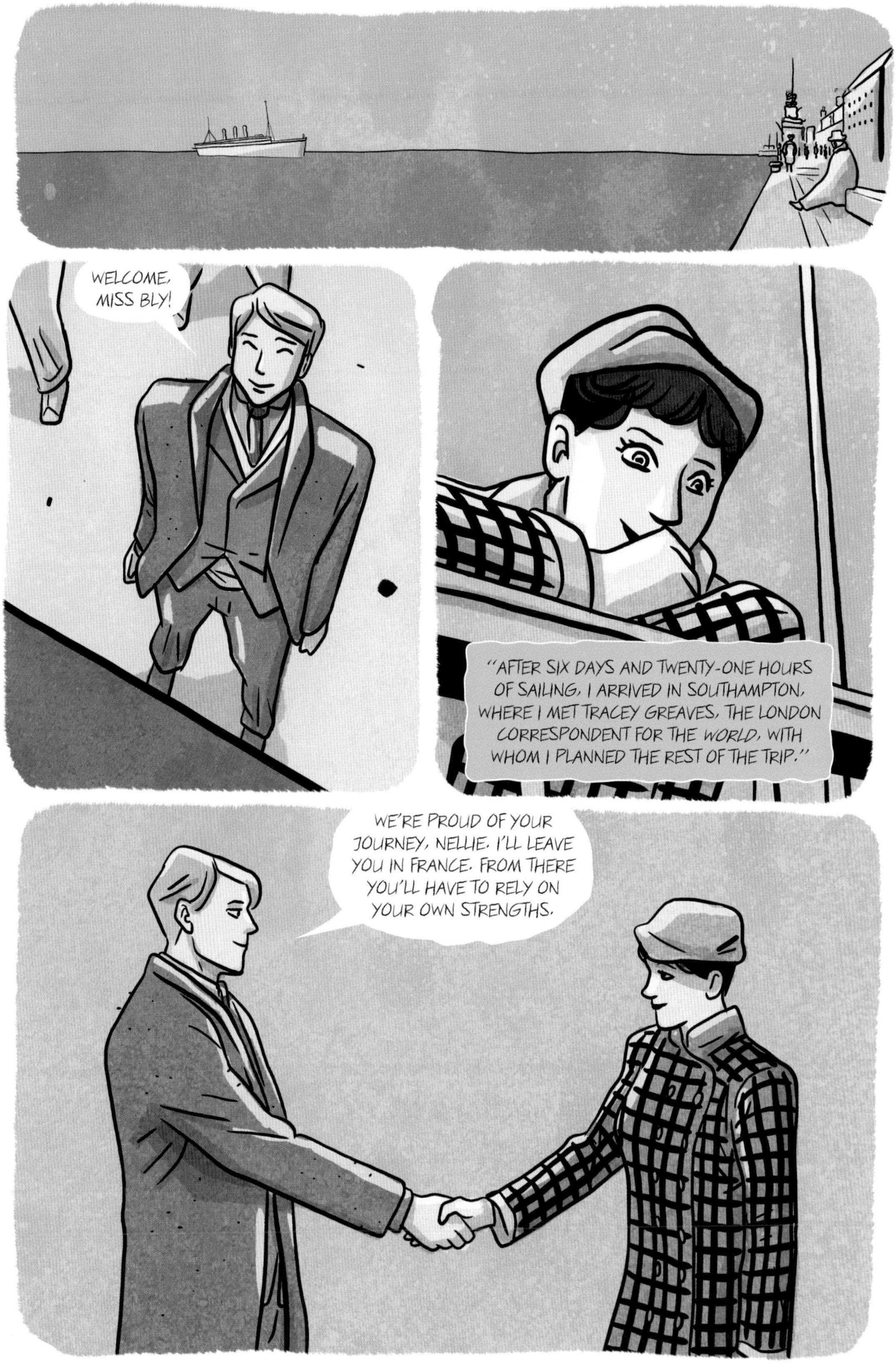
WELCOME, MISS BLY!
"AFTER SIX DAYS AND TWENTY-ONE HOURS OF SAILING, I ARRIVED IN SOUTHAMPTON, WHERE I MET TRACEY GREAVES, THE LONDON CORRESPONDENT FOR THE *WORLD*, WITH WHOM I PLANNED THE REST OF THE TRIP."
WE'RE PROUD OF YOUR JOURNEY, NELLIE. I'LL LEAVE YOU IN FRANCE. FROM THERE YOU'LL HAVE TO RELY ON YOUR OWN STRENGTHS.

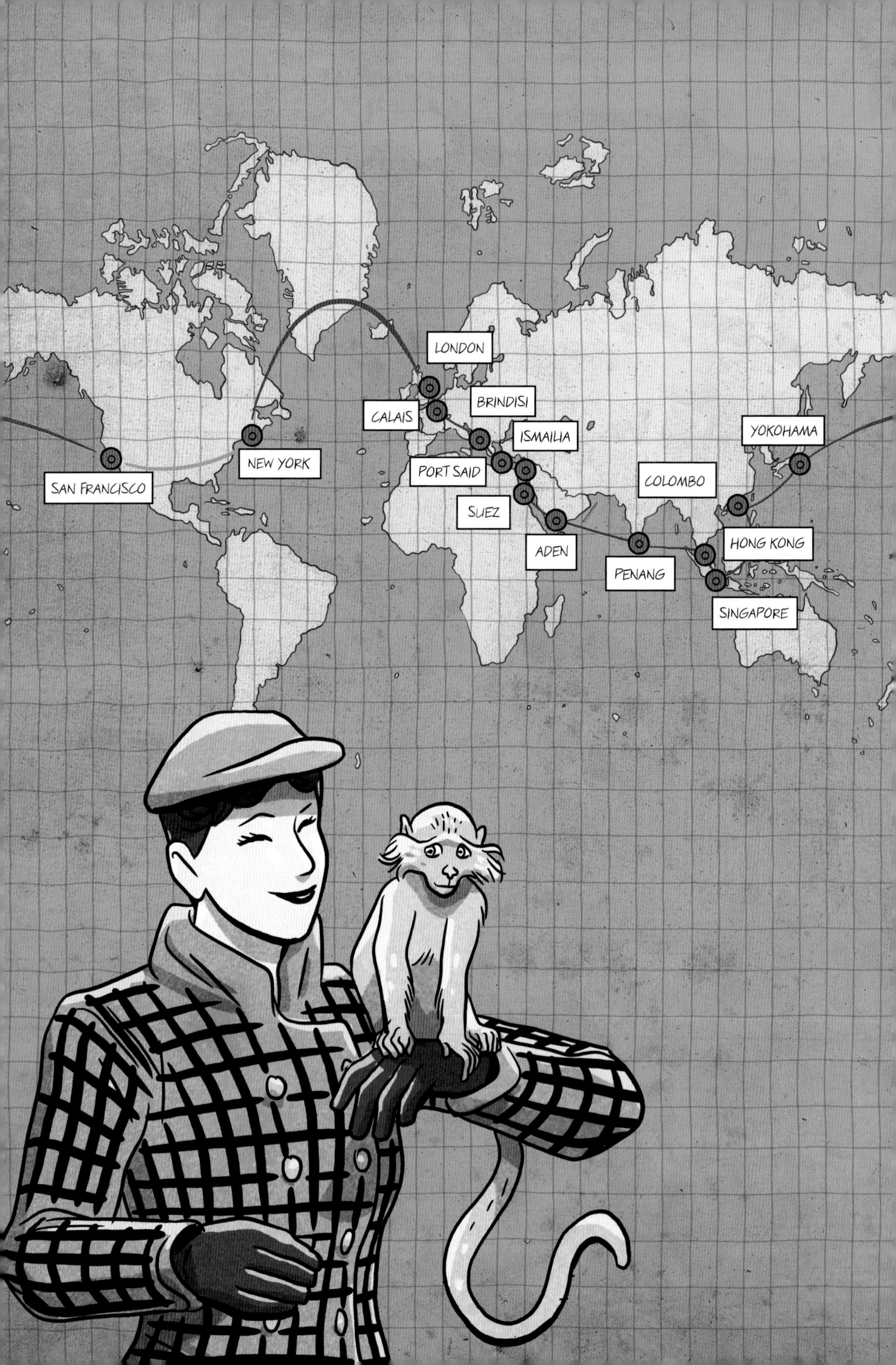
LONDON
BRINDISI
CALAIS
ISMAILIA
YOKOHAMA
SAN FRANCISCO
NEW YORK
PORT SAID
COLOMBO
SUEZ
ADEN
HONG KONG
PENANG
SINGAPORE

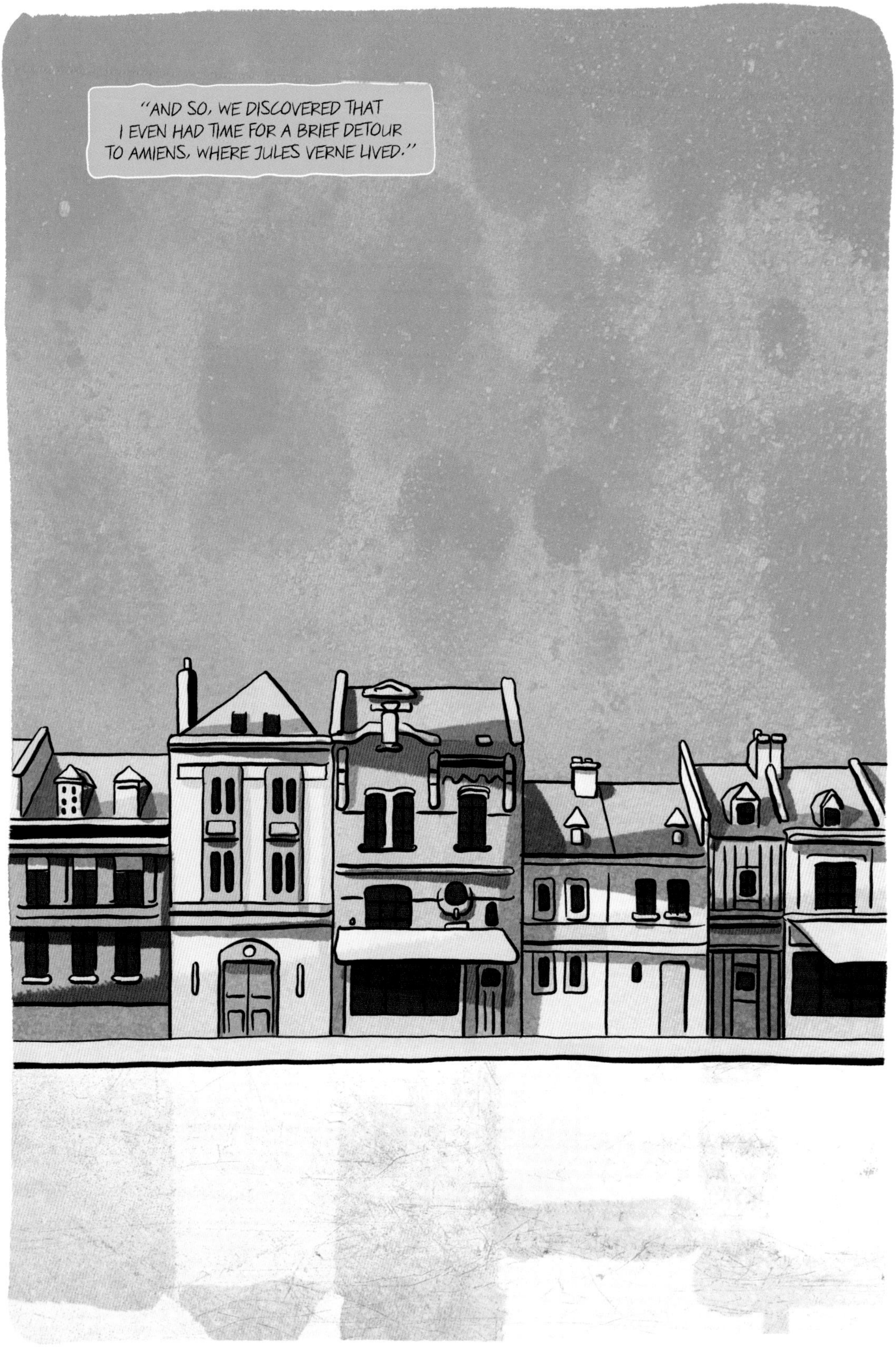
"AND SO, WE DISCOVERED THAT I EVEN HAD TIME FOR A BRIEF DETOUR TO AMIENS, WHERE JULES VERNE LIVED."

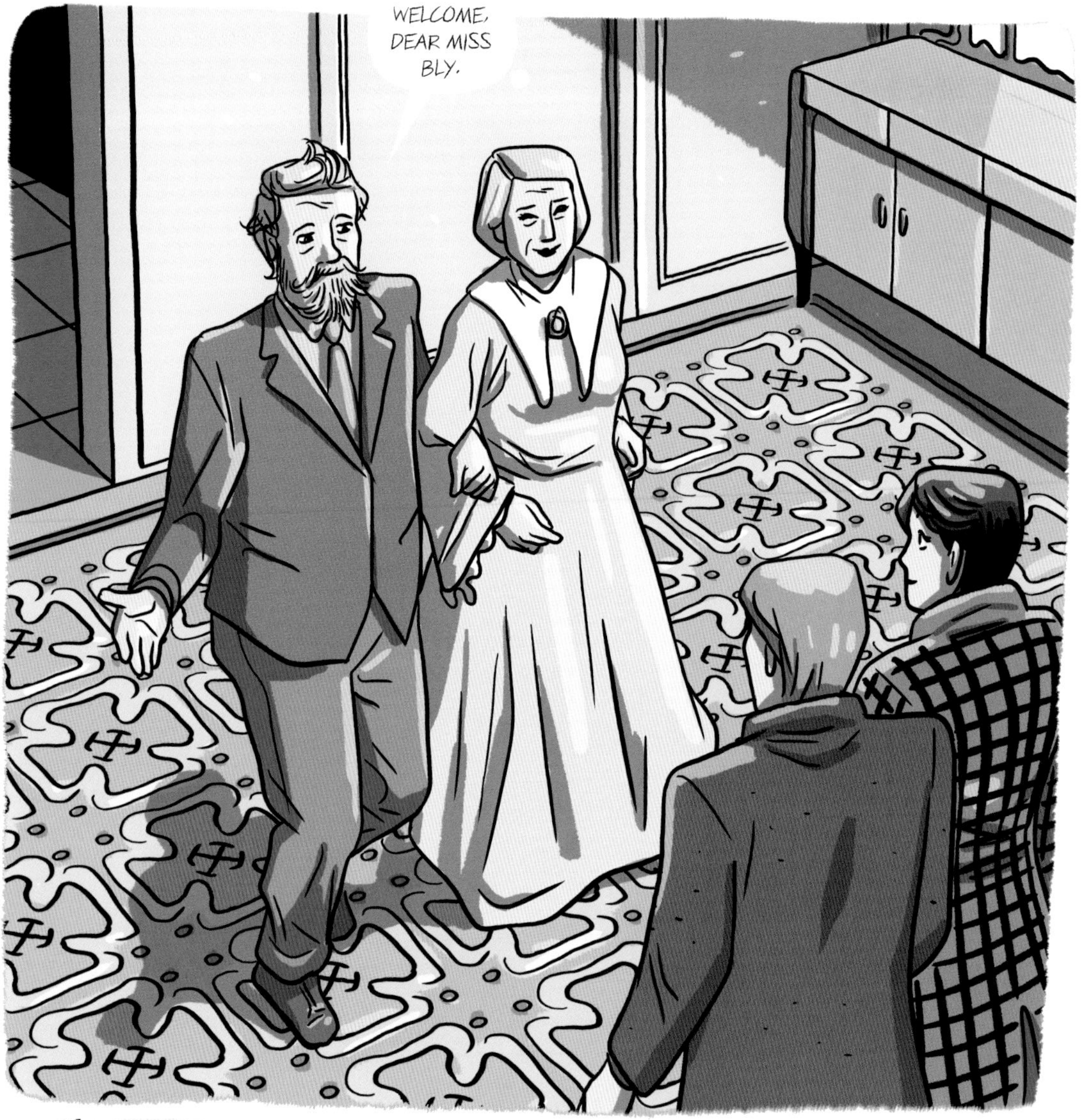
WELCOME, DEAR MISS BLY.

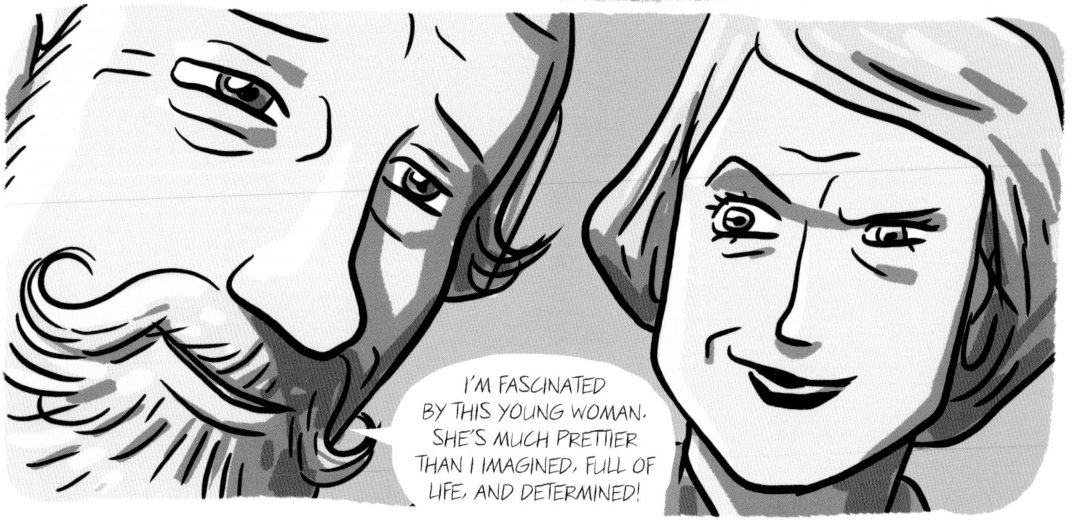
I'M FASCINATED BY THIS YOUNG WOMAN. SHE'S MUCH PRETTIER THAN I IMAGINED, FULL OF LIFE, AND DETERMINED!

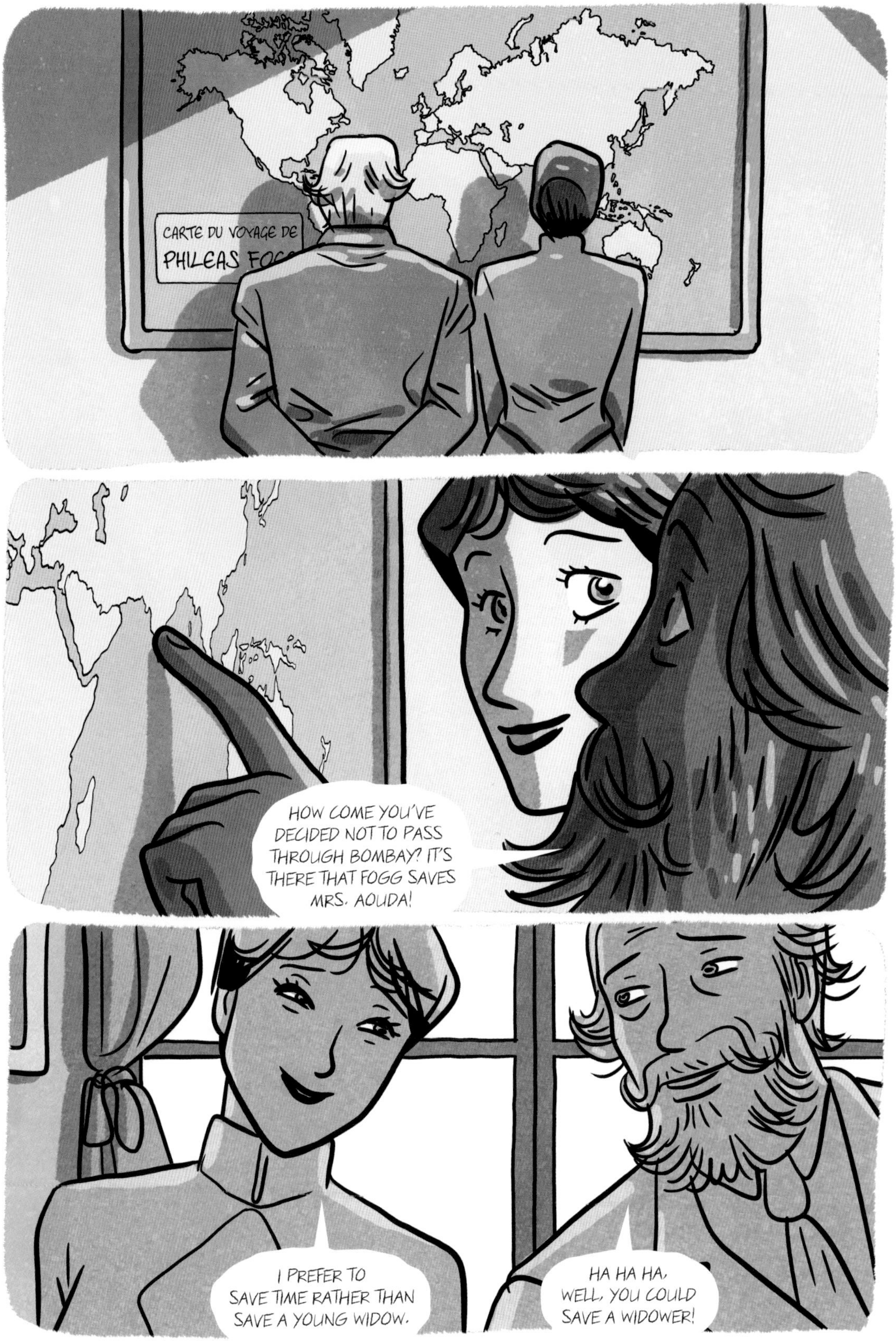
CARTE DU VOYAGE DE
PHILEAS
HOW COME YOU'VE DECIDED NOT TO PASS THROUGH BOMBAY? IT'S THERE THAT FOGG SAVES MRS. AOUDA!
I PREFER TO SAVE TIME RATHER THAN SAVE A YOUNG WIDOW.
HA HA HA, WELL, YOU COULD SAVE A WIDOWER!

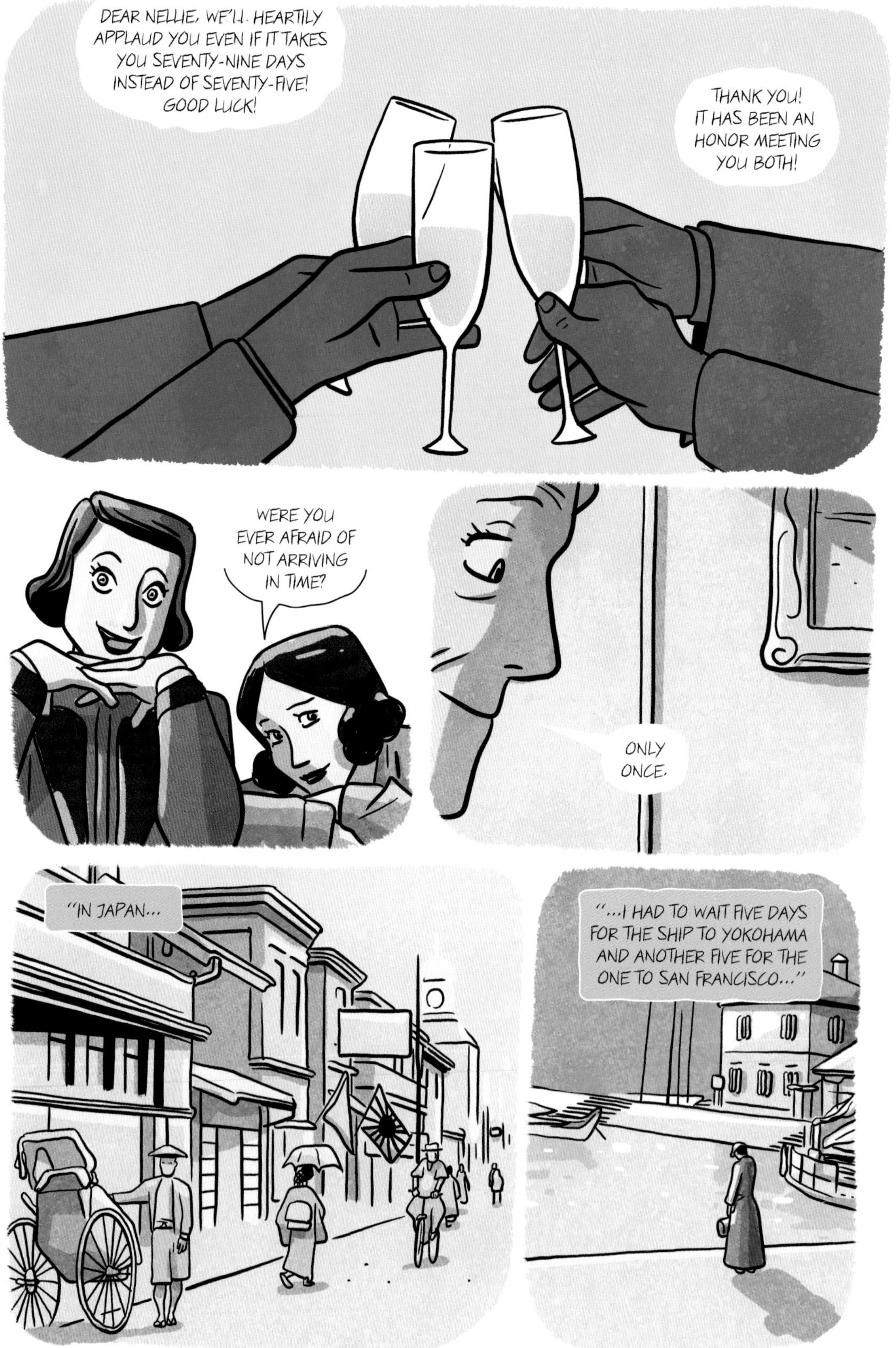
DEAR NELLIE, WE'LL HEARTILY APPLAUD YOU EVEN IF IT TAKES YOU SEVENTY-NINE DAYS INSTEAD OF SEVENTY-FIVE! GOOD LUCK!
THANK YOU! IT HAS BEEN AN HONOR MEETING YOU BOTH!
WERE YOU EVER AFRAID OF NOT ARRIVING IN TIME?
ONLY ONCE.
"IN JAPAN...
"...I HAD TO WAIT FIVE DAYS FOR THE SHIP TO YOKOHAMA AND ANOTHER FIVE FOR THE ONE TO SAN FRANCISCO..."

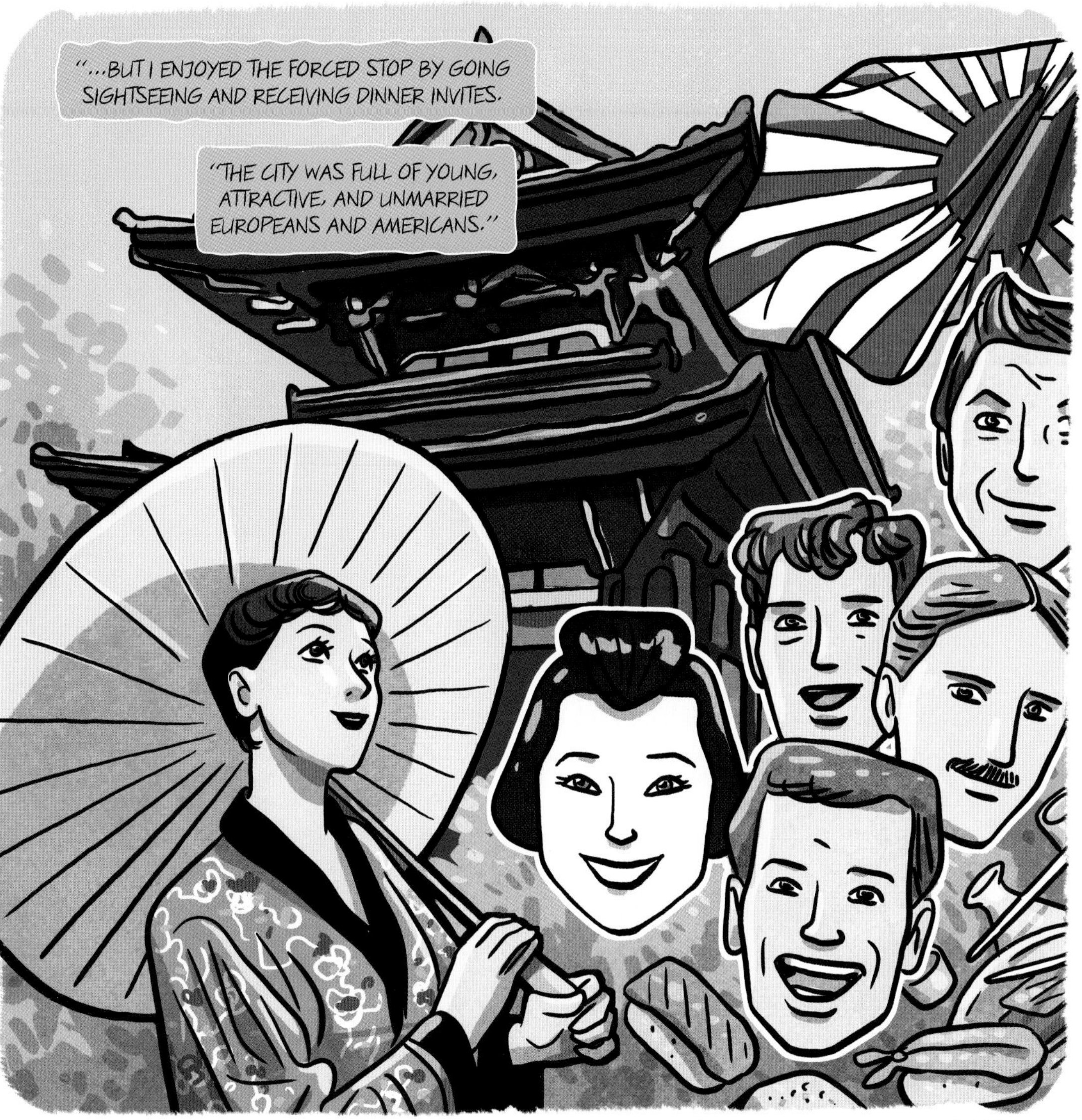
"...BUT I ENJOYED THE FORCED STOP BY GOING SIGHTSEEING AND RECEIVING DINNER INVITES.
"THE CITY WAS FULL OF YOUNG, ATTRACTIVE, AND UNMARRIED EUROPEANS AND AMERICANS."

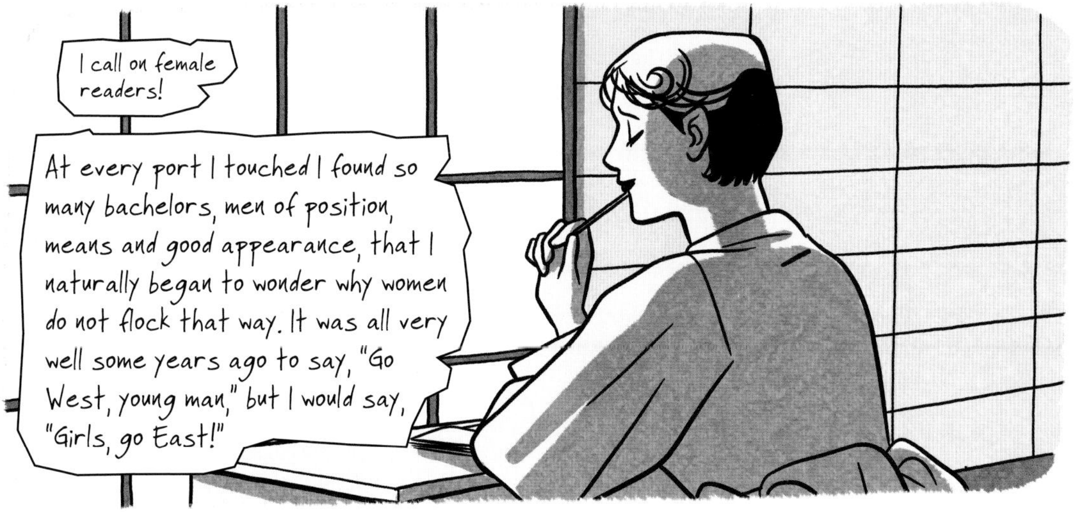
I call on female readers!
At every port I touched I found so many bachelors, men of position, means and good appearance, that I naturally began to wonder why women do not flock that way. It was all very well some years ago to say, "Go West, young man," but I would say, "Girls, go East!"

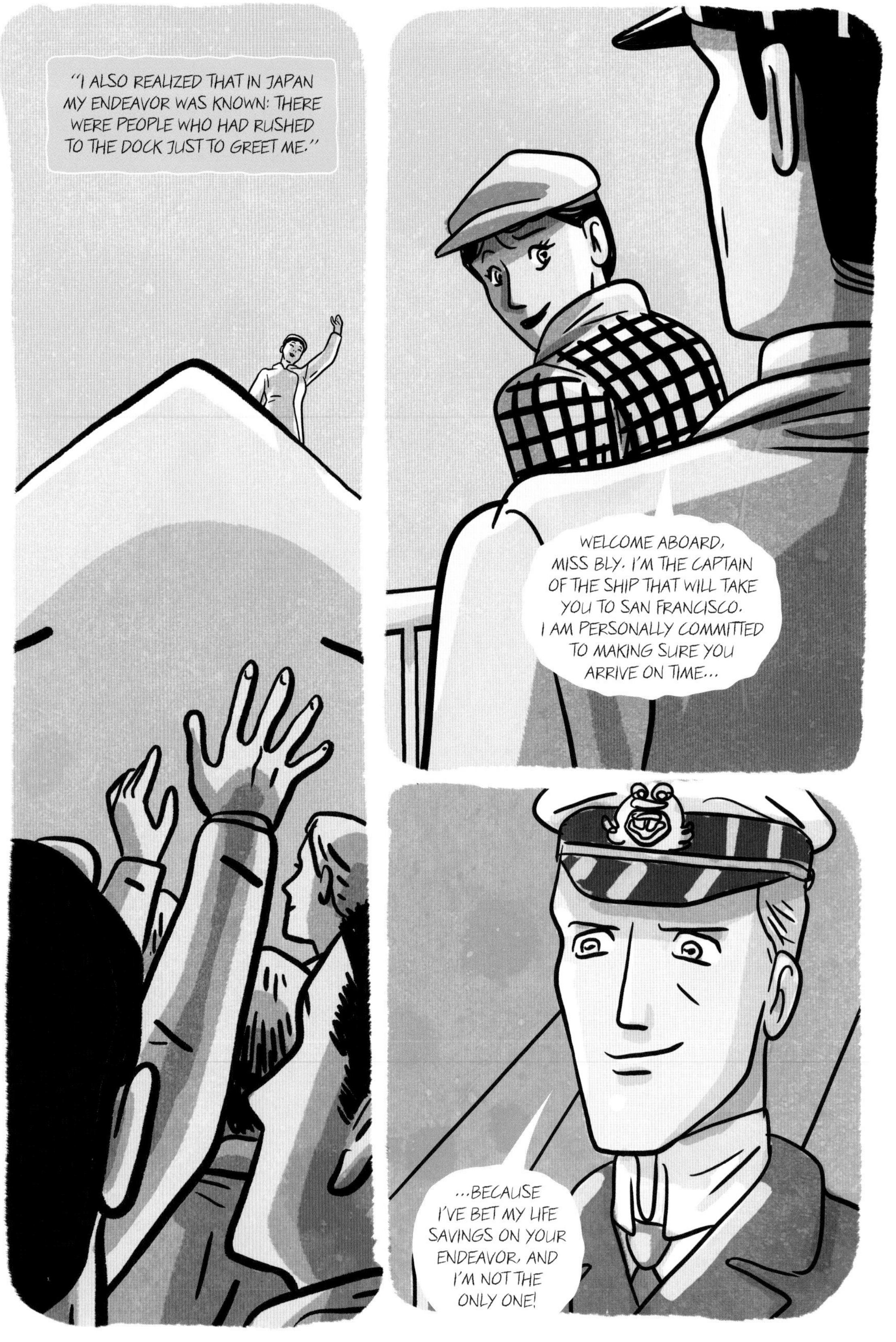
"I ALSO REALIZED THAT IN JAPAN MY ENDEAVOR WAS KNOWN: THERE WERE PEOPLE WHO HAD RUSHED TO THE DOCK JUST TO GREET ME."
WELCOME ABOARD, MISS BLY. I'M THE CAPTAIN OF THE SHIP THAT WILL TAKE YOU TO SAN FRANCISCO. I AM PERSONALLY COMMITTED TO MAKING SURE YOU ARRIVE ON TIME...
...BECAUSE I'VE BET MY LIFE SAVINGS ON YOUR ENDEAVOR, AND I'M NOT THE ONLY ONE!

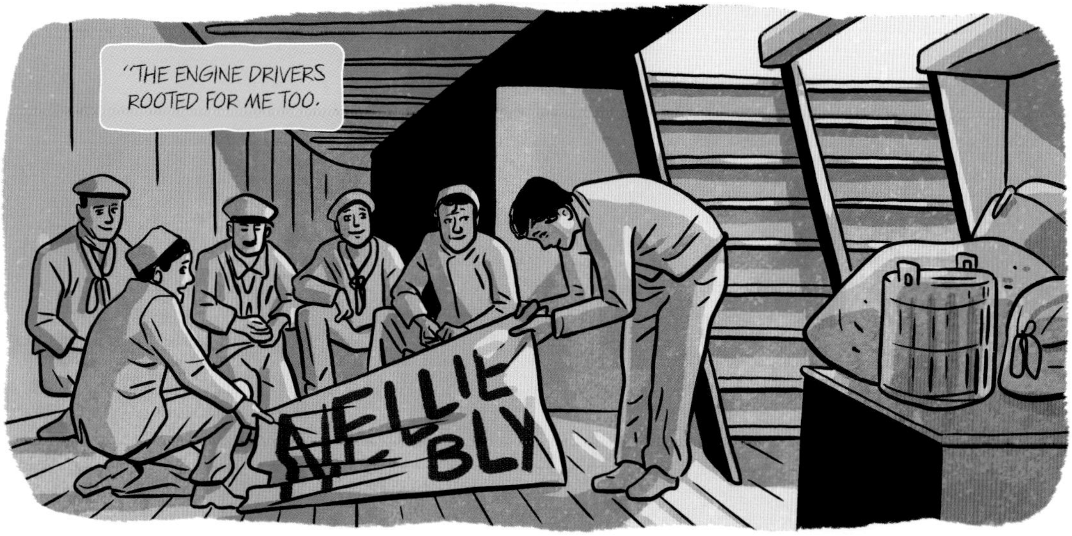
"THE ENGINE DRIVERS ROOTED FOR ME TOO.
NELLIE BLY

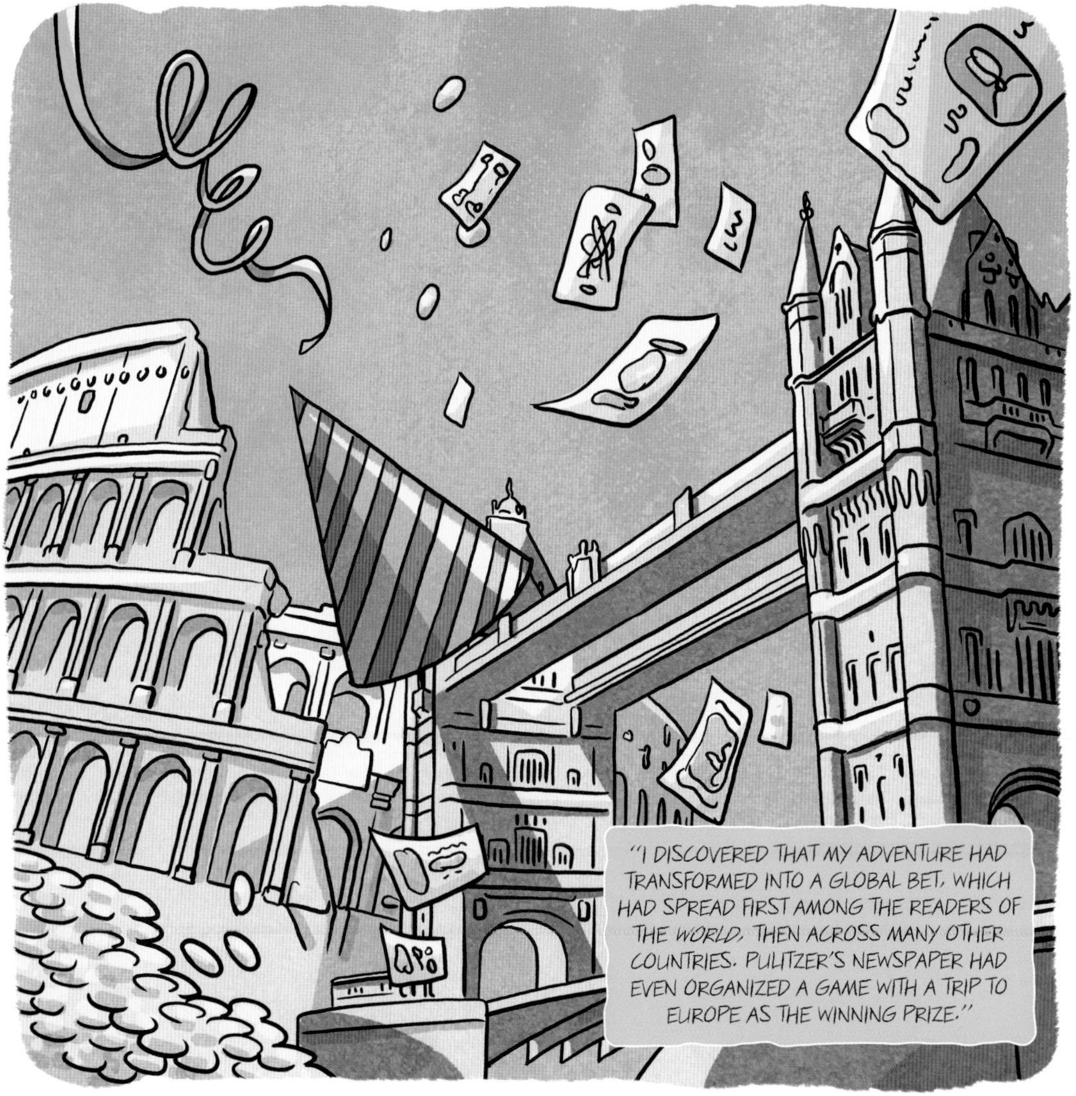
"I DISCOVERED THAT MY ADVENTURE HAD TRANSFORMED INTO A GLOBAL BET, WHICH HAD SPREAD FIRST AMONG THE READERS OF THE *WORLD*, THEN ACROSS MANY OTHER COUNTRIES. PULITZER'S NEWSPAPER HAD EVEN ORGANIZED A GAME WITH A TRIP TO EUROPE AS THE WINNING PRIZE."

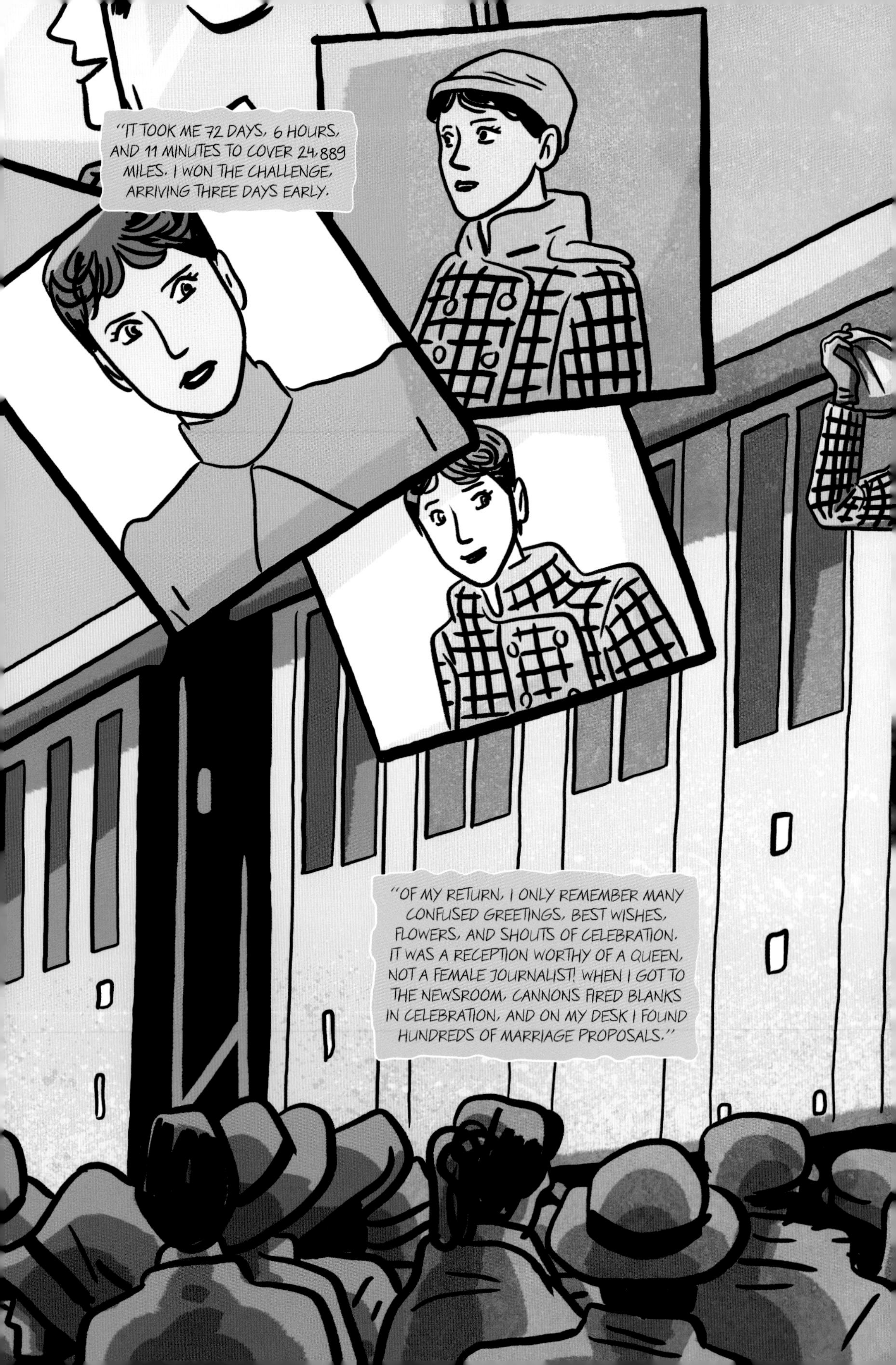
"IT TOOK ME 72 DAYS, 6 HOURS, AND 11 MINUTES TO COVER 24,889 MILES. I WON THE CHALLENGE, ARRIVING THREE DAYS EARLY.
"OF MY RETURN, I ONLY REMEMBER MANY CONFUSED GREETINGS, BEST WISHES, FLOWERS, AND SHOUTS OF CELEBRATION. IT WAS A RECEPTION WORTHY OF A QUEEN, NOT A FEMALE JOURNALIST! WHEN I GOT TO THE NEWSROOM, CANNONS FIRED BLANKS IN CELEBRATION, AND ON MY DESK I FOUND HUNDREDS OF MARRIAGE PROPOSALS."

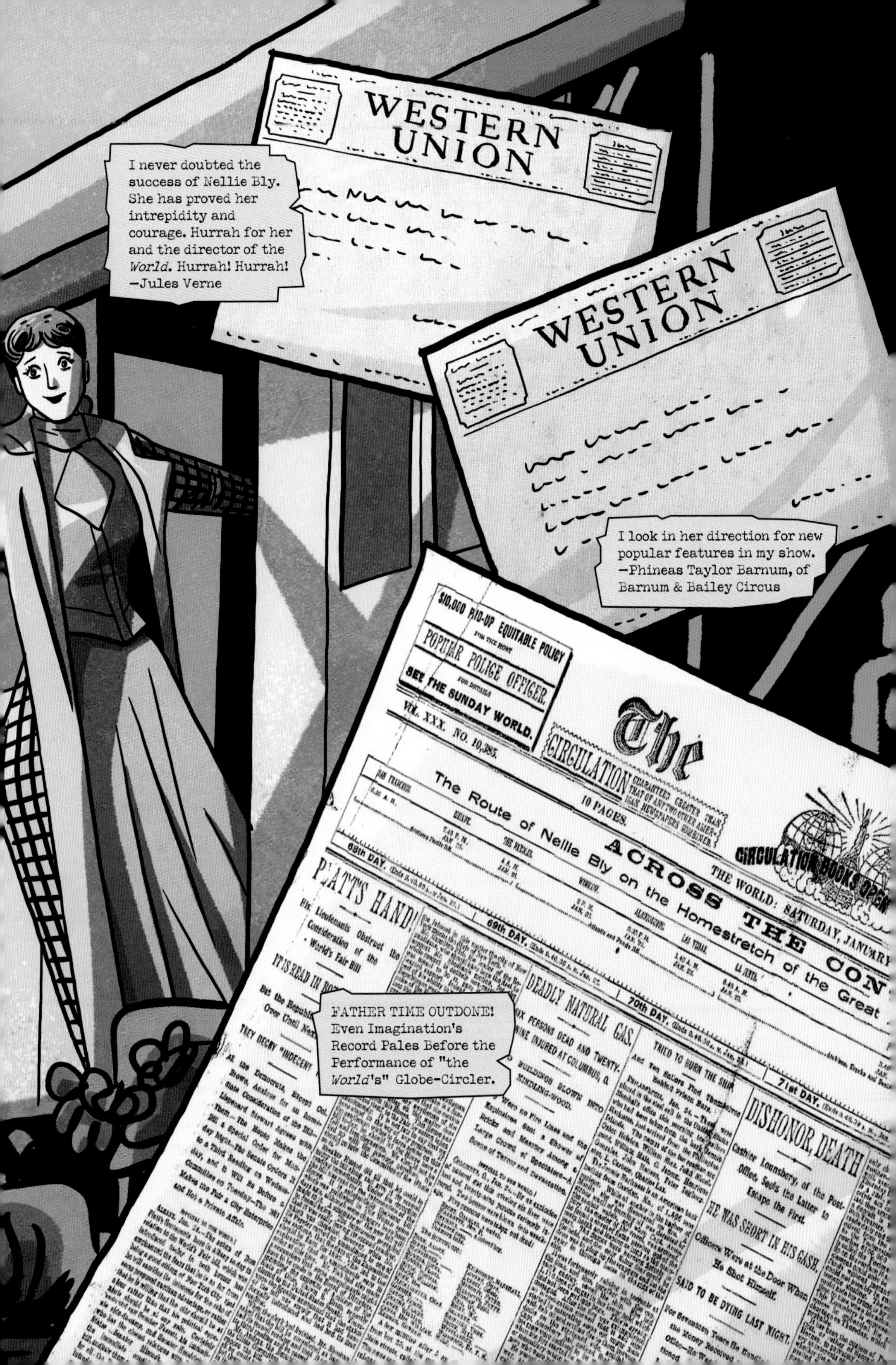

WESTERN UNION
I never doubted the success of Nellie Bly. She has proved her intrepidity and courage. Hurrah for her and the director of the *World*. Hurrah! Hurrah! —Jules Verne
WESTERN UNION
I look in her direction for new popular features in my show. —Phineas Taylor Barnum, of Barnum & Bailey Circus
$10,000 PAID-UP EQUITABLE POLICY
POPULAR POLICE OFFICER.
SEE THE SUNDAY WORLD.
VOL. XXX. NO. 10,385.
CIRCULATION
10 PAGES.
The Route of Nellie Bly on the Homestretch of the Great
ACROSS THE CON
THE WORLD: SATURDAY, JANUARY
68th DAY.
69th DAY.
70th DAY.
71st DAY.
PLATT'S HAND!
DEADLY NATURAL GAS.
DISHONOR, DEATH
HE WAS SHORT IN HIS CASH.
SAID TO BE DYING LAST NIGHT.
FATHER TIME OUTDONE! Even Imagination's Record Pales Before the Performance of "the *World*'s" Globe-Circler.

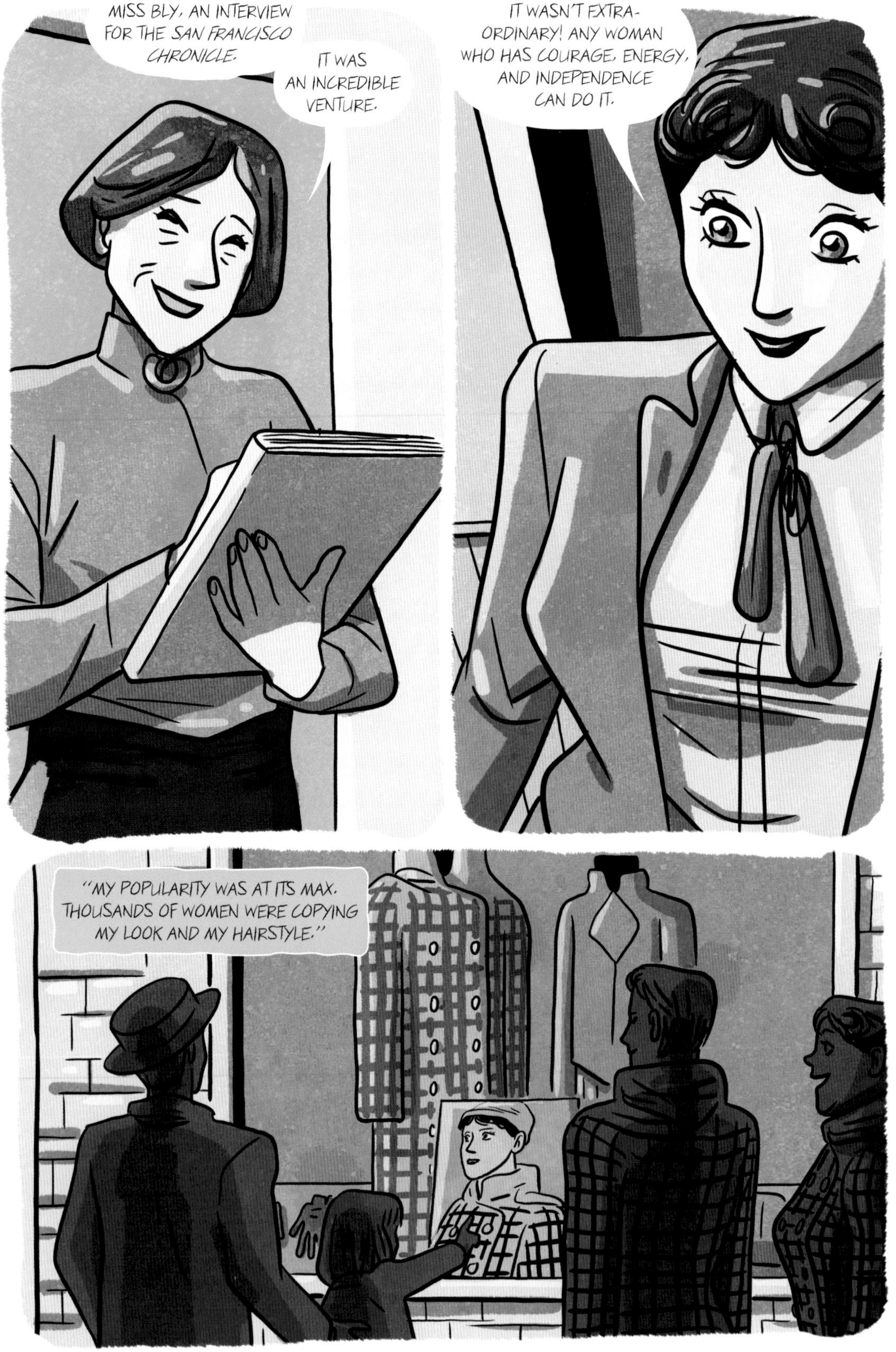
MISS BLY, AN INTERVIEW FOR THE SAN FRANCISCO CHRONICLE.
IT WAS AN INCREDIBLE VENTURE.
IT WASN'T EXTRA-ORDINARY! ANY WOMAN WHO HAS COURAGE, ENERGY, AND INDEPENDENCE CAN DO IT.
"MY POPULARITY WAS AT ITS MAX. THOUSANDS OF WOMEN WERE COPYING MY LOOK AND MY HAIRSTYLE."

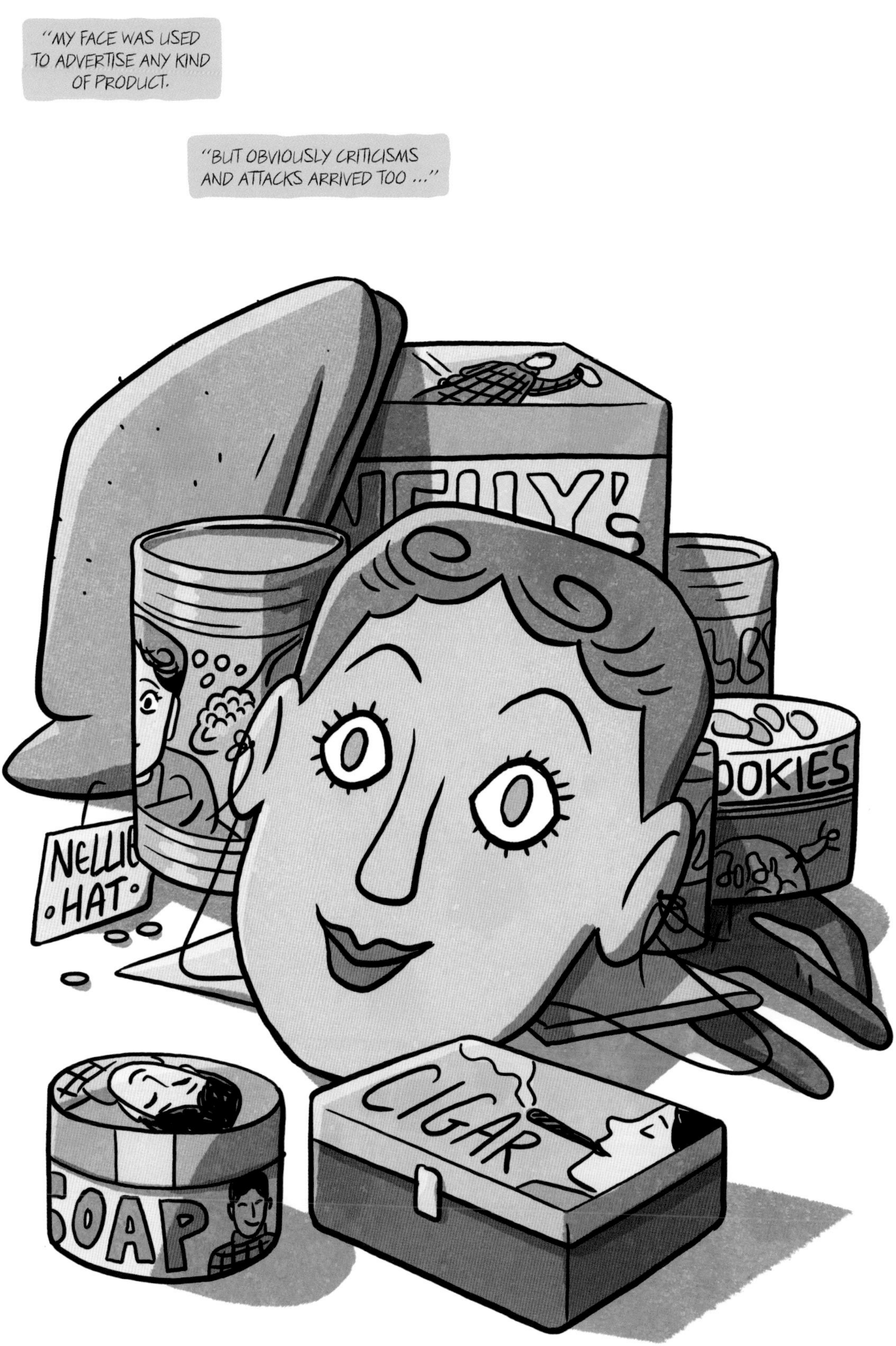
"MY FACE WAS USED TO ADVERTISE ANY KIND OF PRODUCT.
"BUT OBVIOUSLY CRITICISMS AND ATTACKS ARRIVED TOO ..."
HAT
CIGAR
SOAP

A lady an explorer? A traveller in skirts?
The notion's just a trifle too seraphic:
Let them stay and mind the babies,
or hem our ragged shirts;
But they mustn't, can't, and shan't be geographic...

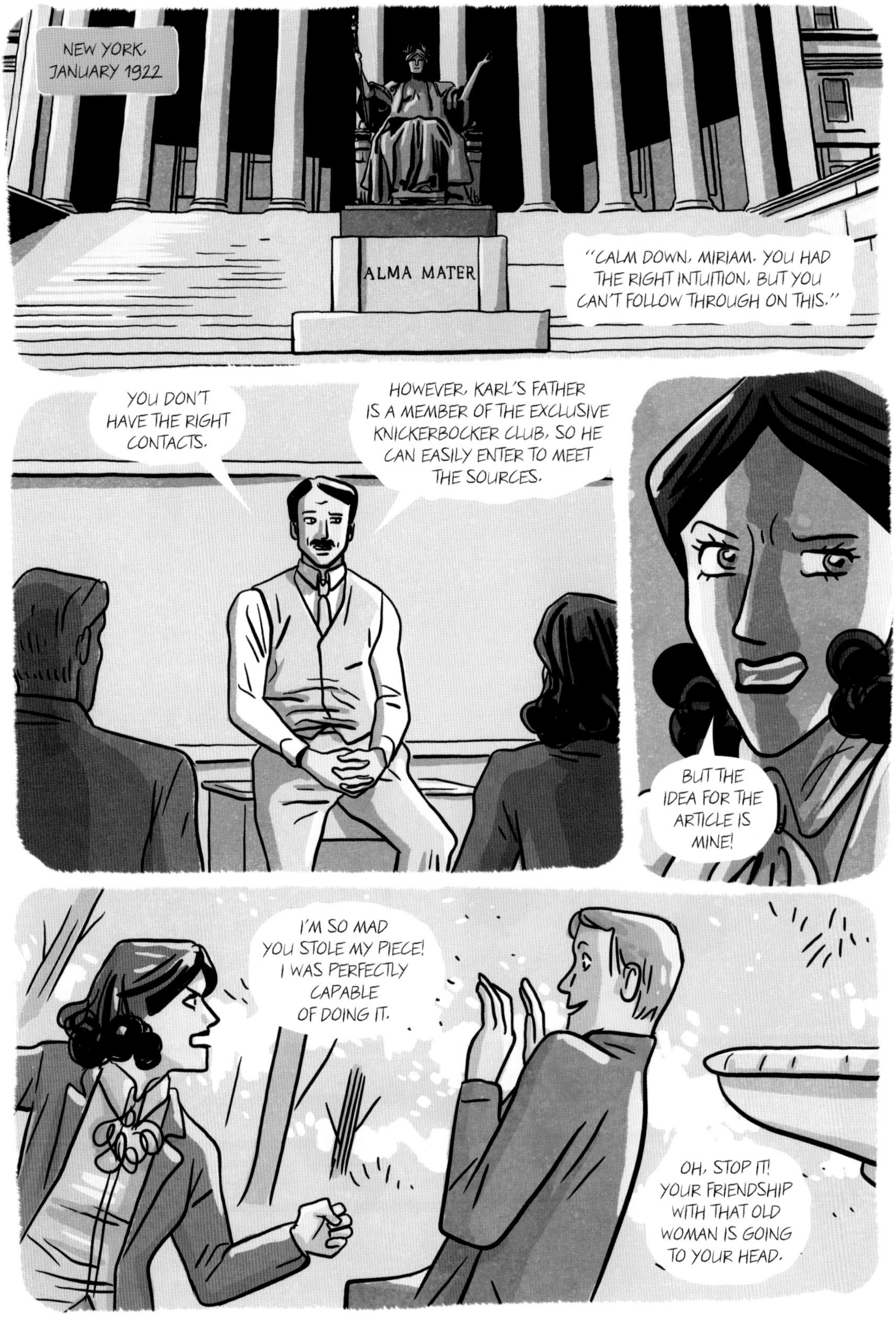
NEW YORK, JANUARY 1922
ALMA MATER
"CALM DOWN, MIRIAM. YOU HAD THE RIGHT INTUITION, BUT YOU CAN'T FOLLOW THROUGH ON THIS."
YOU DON'T HAVE THE RIGHT CONTACTS.
HOWEVER, KARL'S FATHER IS A MEMBER OF THE EXCLUSIVE KNICKERBOCKER CLUB, SO HE CAN EASILY ENTER TO MEET THE SOURCES.
BUT THE IDEA FOR THE ARTICLE IS MINE!
I'M SO MAD YOU STOLE MY PIECE! I WAS PERFECTLY CAPABLE OF DOING IT.
OH, STOP IT! YOUR FRIENDSHIP WITH THAT OLD WOMAN IS GOING TO YOUR HEAD.

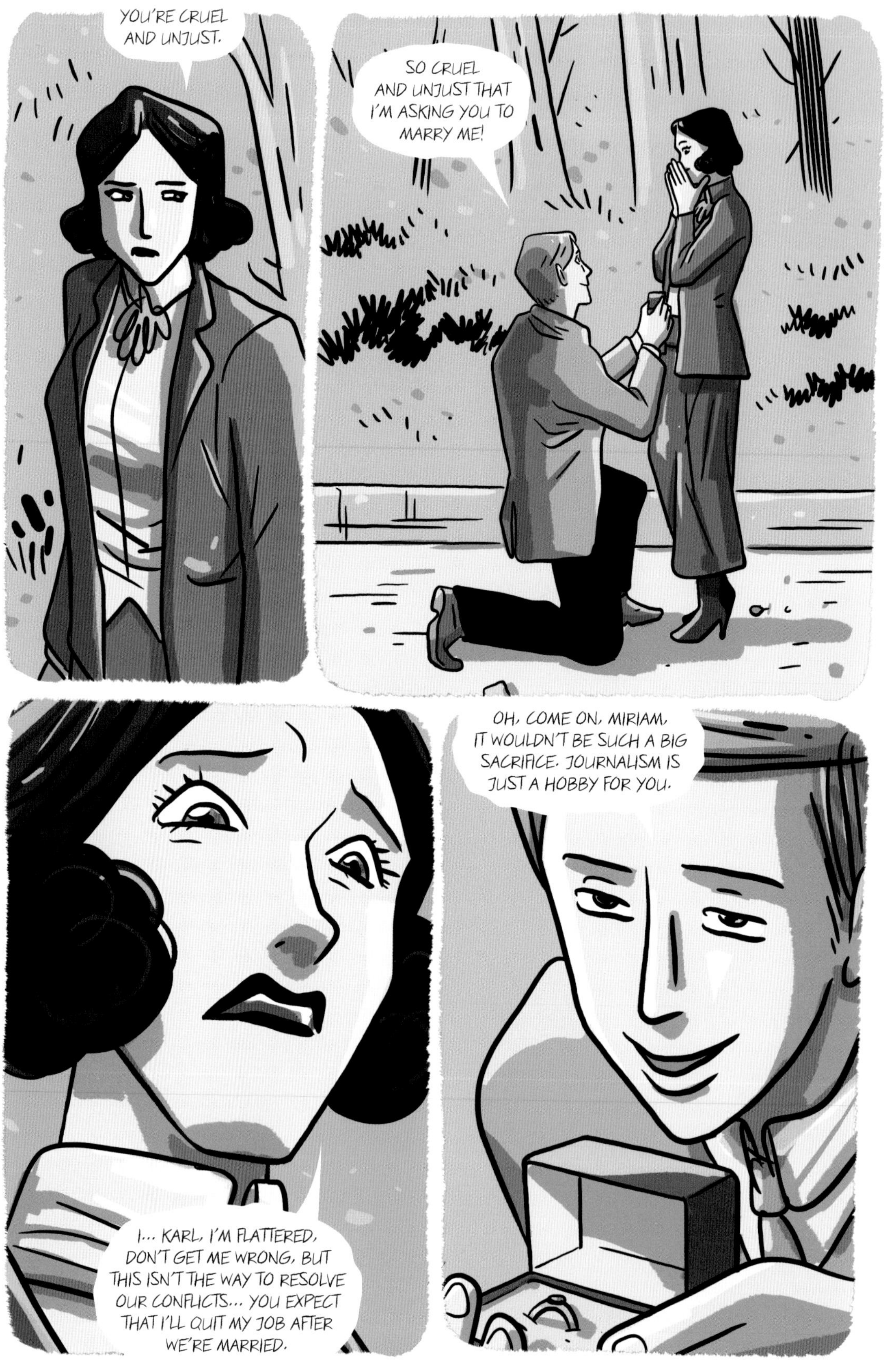
YOU'RE CRUEL AND UNJUST.
SO CRUEL AND UNJUST THAT I'M ASKING YOU TO MARRY ME!
I... KARL, I'M FLATTERED, DON'T GET ME WRONG, BUT THIS ISN'T THE WAY TO RESOLVE OUR CONFLICTS... YOU EXPECT THAT I'LL QUIT MY JOB AFTER WE'RE MARRIED.
OH, COME ON, MIRIAM, IT WOULDN'T BE SUCH A BIG SACRIFICE. JOURNALISM IS JUST A HOBBY FOR YOU.

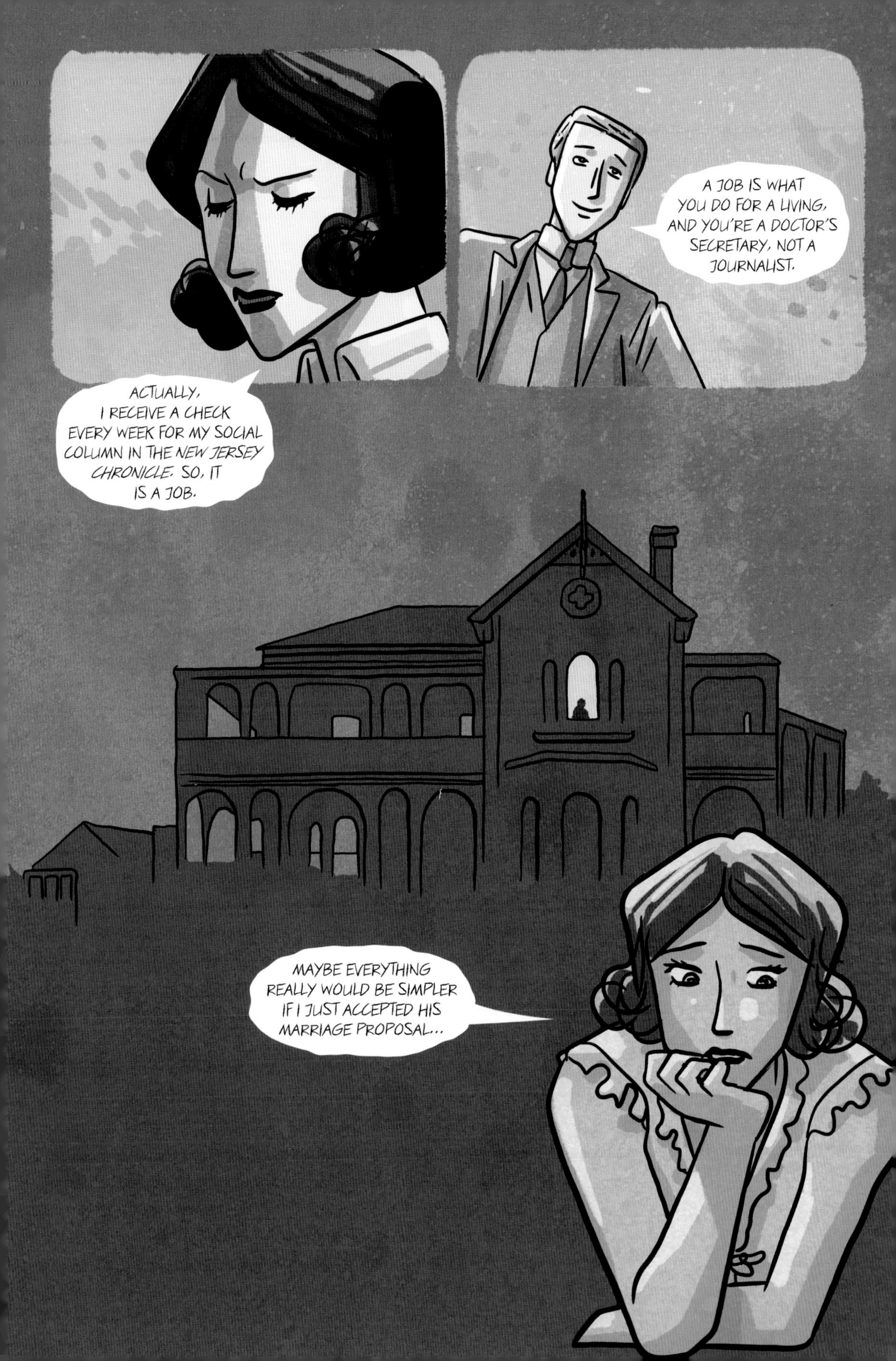
A JOB IS WHAT YOU DO FOR A LIVING, AND YOU'RE A DOCTOR'S SECRETARY, NOT A JOURNALIST.
ACTUALLY, I RECEIVE A CHECK EVERY WEEK FOR MY SOCIAL COLUMN IN THE *NEW JERSEY CHRONICLE*. SO, IT IS A JOB.
MAYBE EVERYTHING REALLY WOULD BE SIMPLER IF I JUST ACCEPTED HIS MARRIAGE PROPOSAL...

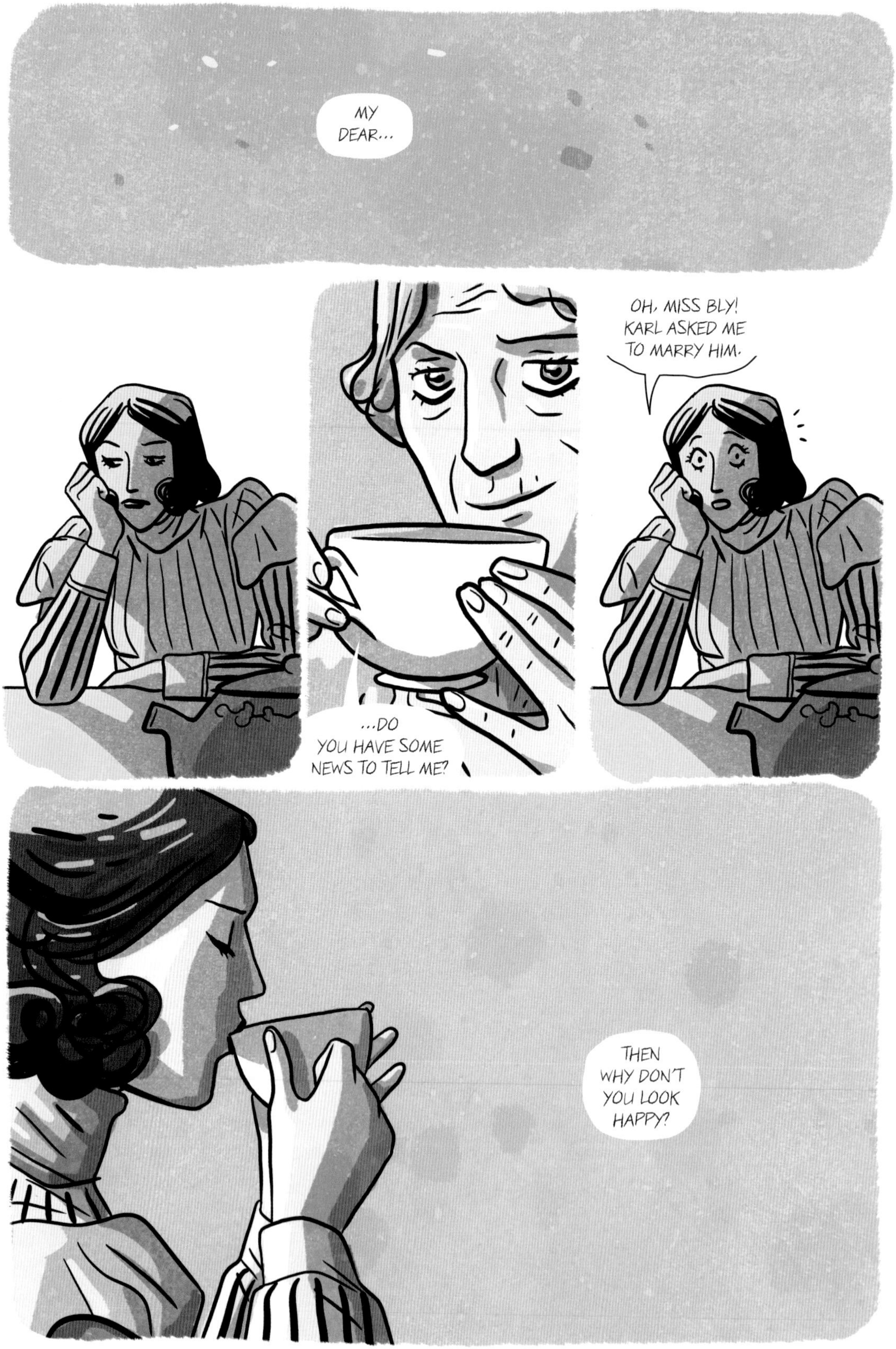
MY DEAR...
...DO YOU HAVE SOME NEWS TO TELL ME?
OH, MISS BLY! KARL ASKED ME TO MARRY HIM.
THEN WHY DON'T YOU LOOK HAPPY?

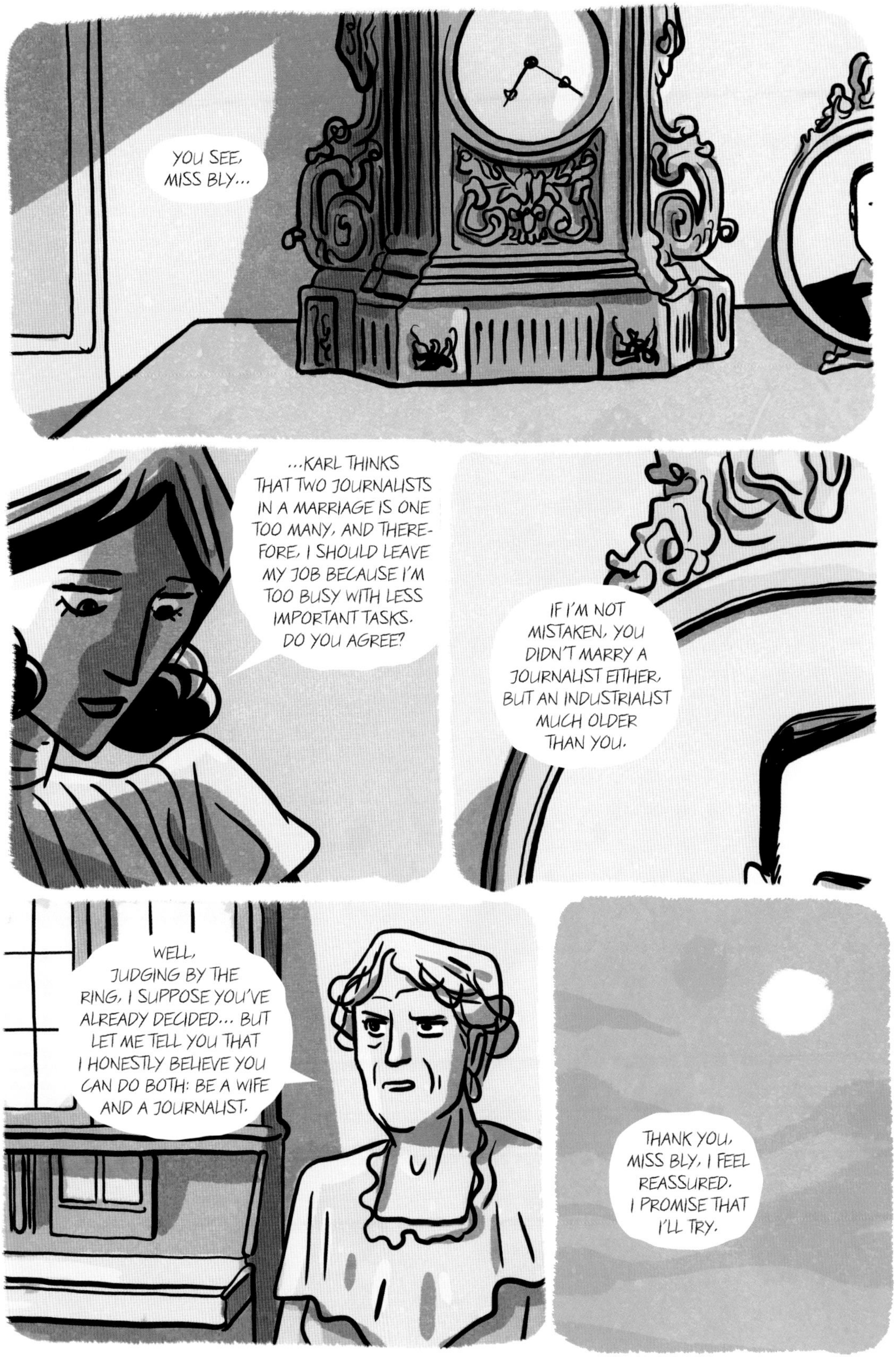
YOU SEE, MISS BLY...
...KARL THINKS THAT TWO JOURNALISTS IN A MARRIAGE IS ONE TOO MANY, AND THEREFORE, I SHOULD LEAVE MY JOB BECAUSE I'M TOO BUSY WITH LESS IMPORTANT TASKS. DO YOU AGREE?
IF I'M NOT MISTAKEN, YOU DIDN'T MARRY A JOURNALIST EITHER, BUT AN INDUSTRIALIST MUCH OLDER THAN YOU.
WELL, JUDGING BY THE RING, I SUPPOSE YOU'VE ALREADY DECIDED... BUT LET ME TELL YOU THAT I HONESTLY BELIEVE YOU CAN DO BOTH: BE A WIFE AND A JOURNALIST.
THANK YOU, MISS BLY, I FEEL REASSURED. I PROMISE THAT I'LL TRY.

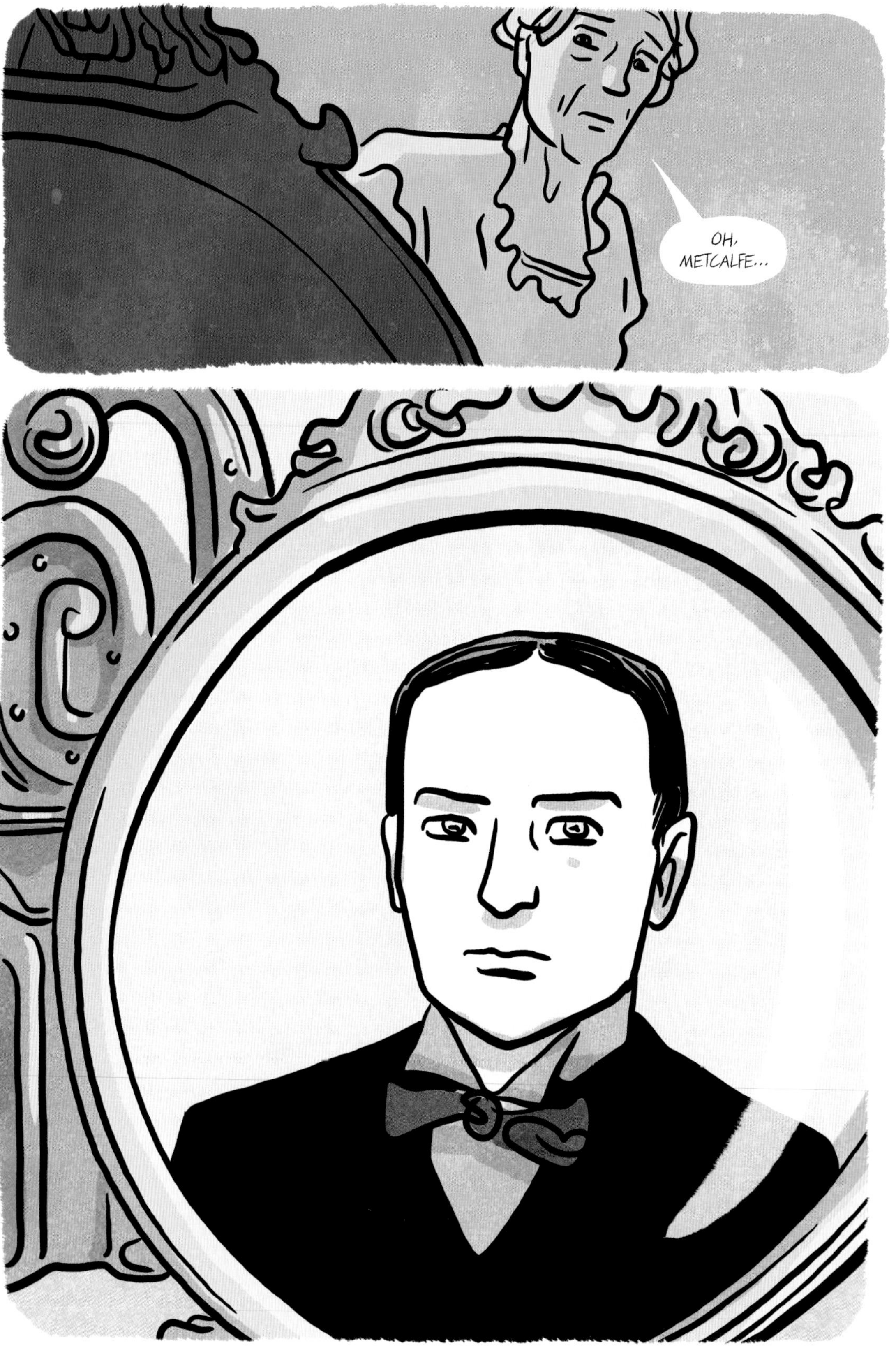
OH, METCALFE...

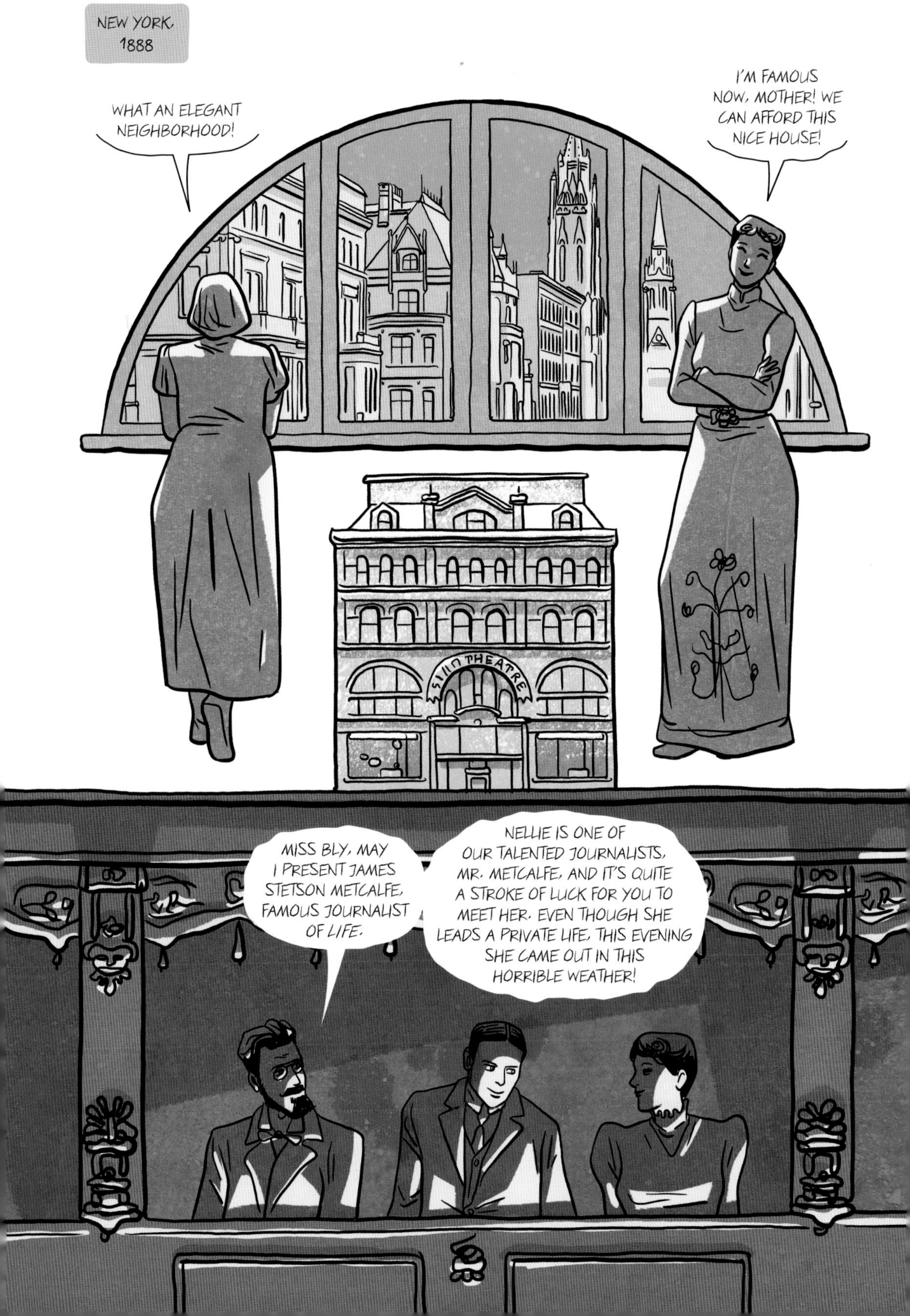
NEW YORK, 1888
WHAT AN ELEGANT NEIGHBORHOOD!
I'M FAMOUS NOW, MOTHER! WE CAN AFFORD THIS NICE HOUSE!
THEATRE
MISS BLY, MAY I PRESENT JAMES STETSON METCALFE, FAMOUS JOURNALIST OF LIFE.
NELLIE IS ONE OF OUR TALENTED JOURNALISTS, MR. METCALFE, AND IT'S QUITE A STROKE OF LUCK FOR YOU TO MEET HER. EVEN THOUGH SHE LEADS A PRIVATE LIFE, THIS EVENING SHE CAME OUT IN THIS HORRIBLE WEATHER!

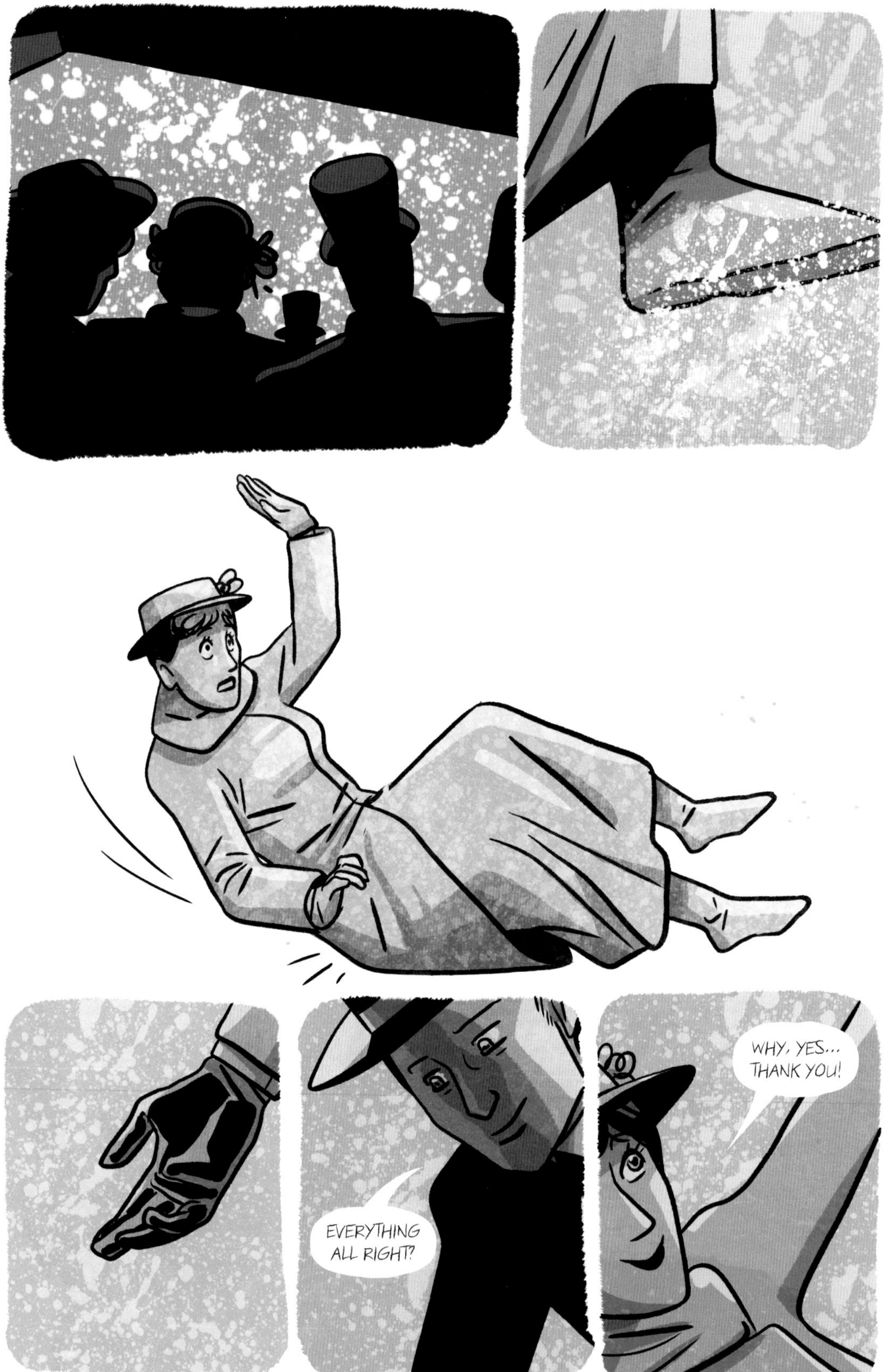
EVERYTHING ALL RIGHT?
WHY, YES... THANK YOU!

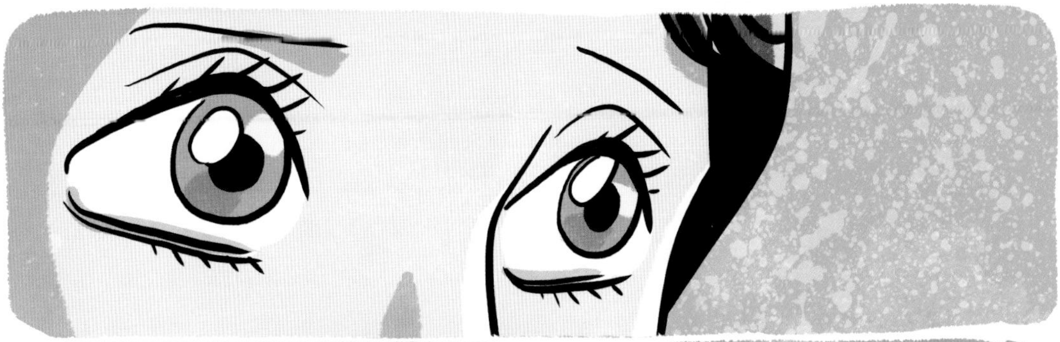

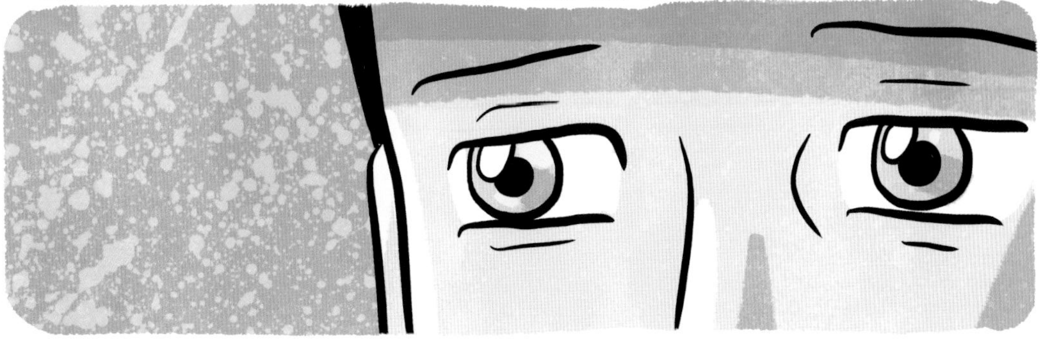

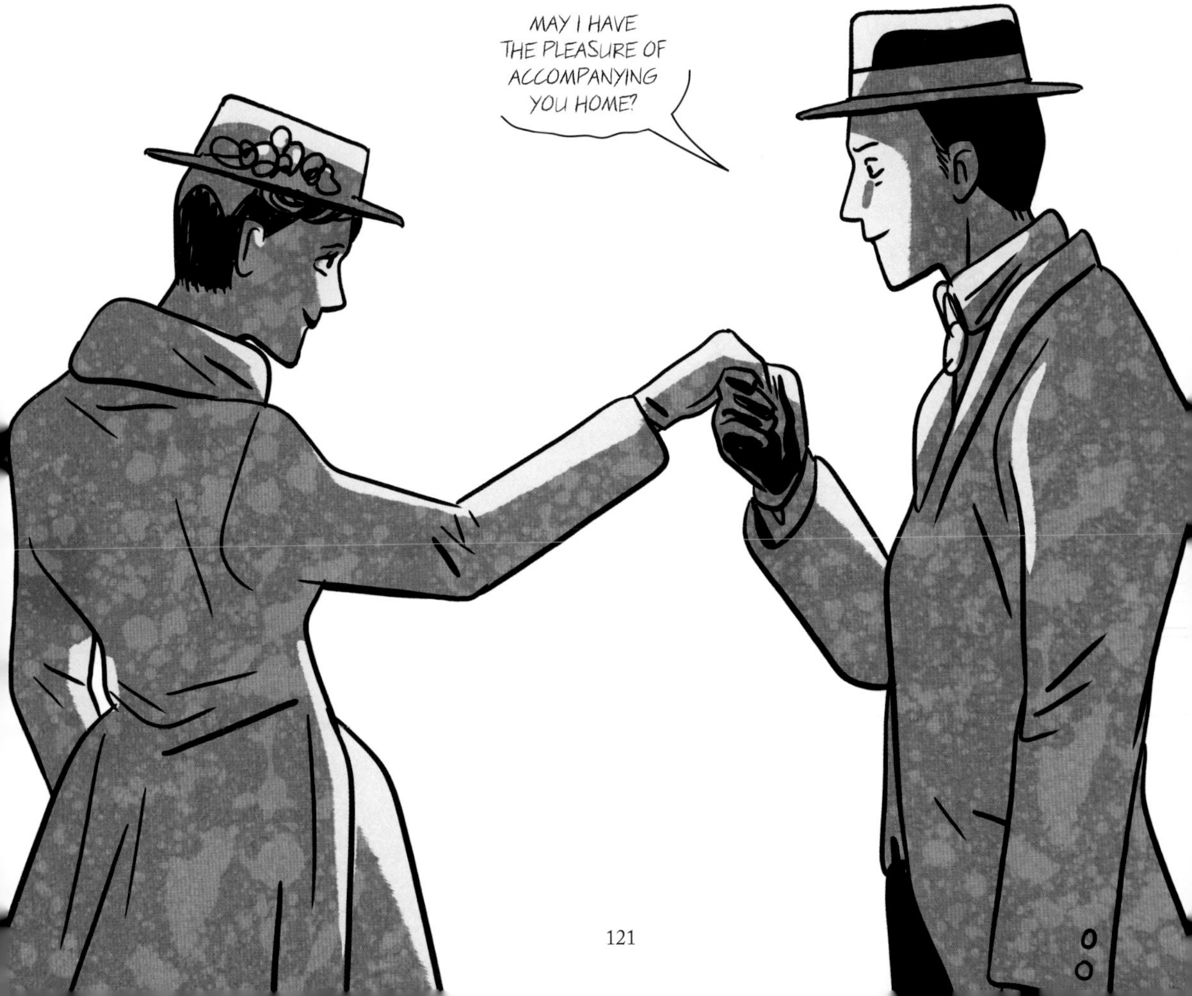
MAY I HAVE THE PLEASURE OF ACCOMPANYING YOU HOME?

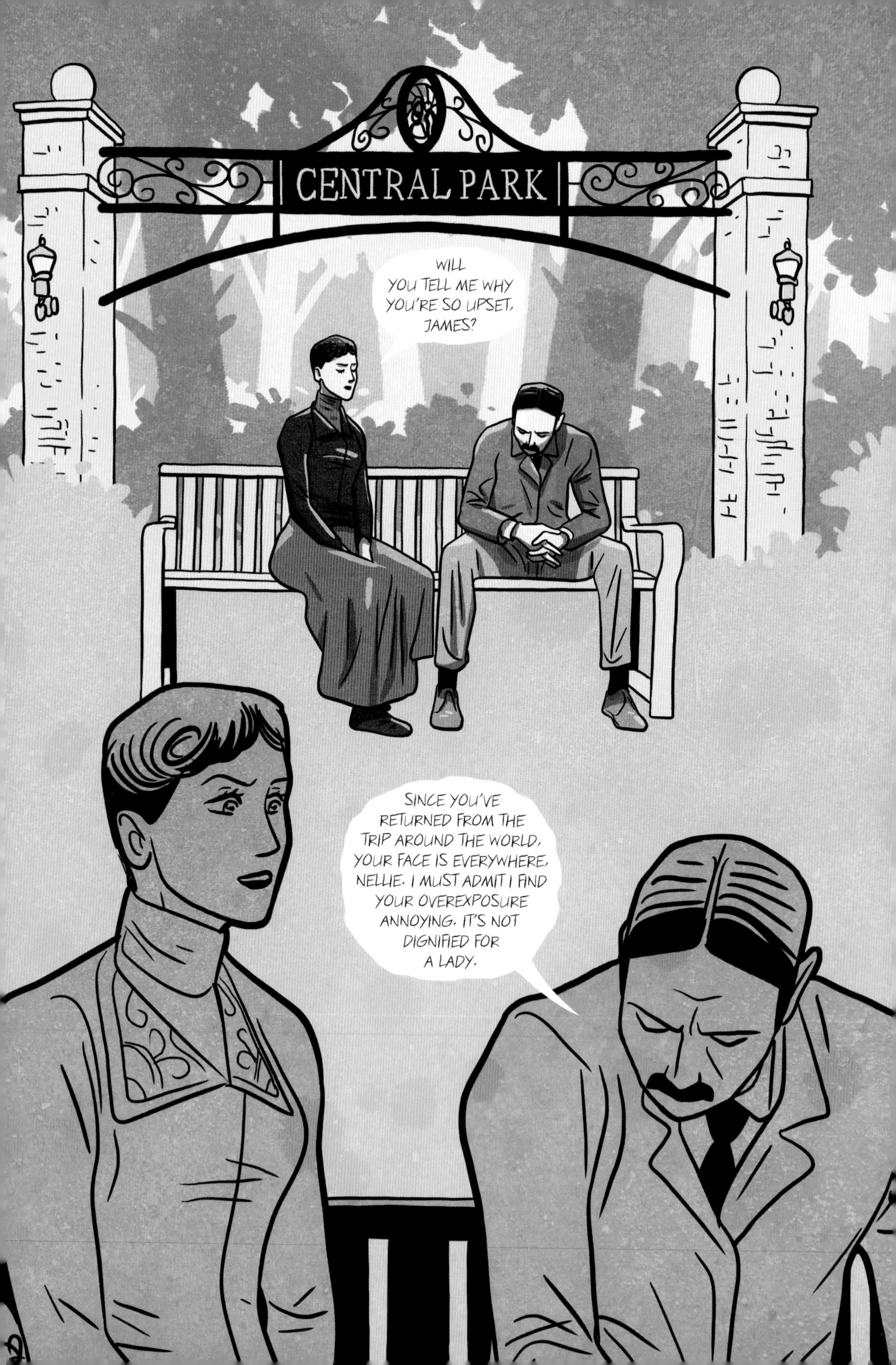
CENTRAL PARK
WILL YOU TELL ME WHY YOU'RE SO UPSET, JAMES?
SINCE YOU'VE RETURNED FROM THE TRIP AROUND THE WORLD, YOUR FACE IS EVERYWHERE, NELLIE. I MUST ADMIT I FIND YOUR OVEREXPOSURE ANNOYING. IT'S NOT DIGNIFIED FOR A LADY.

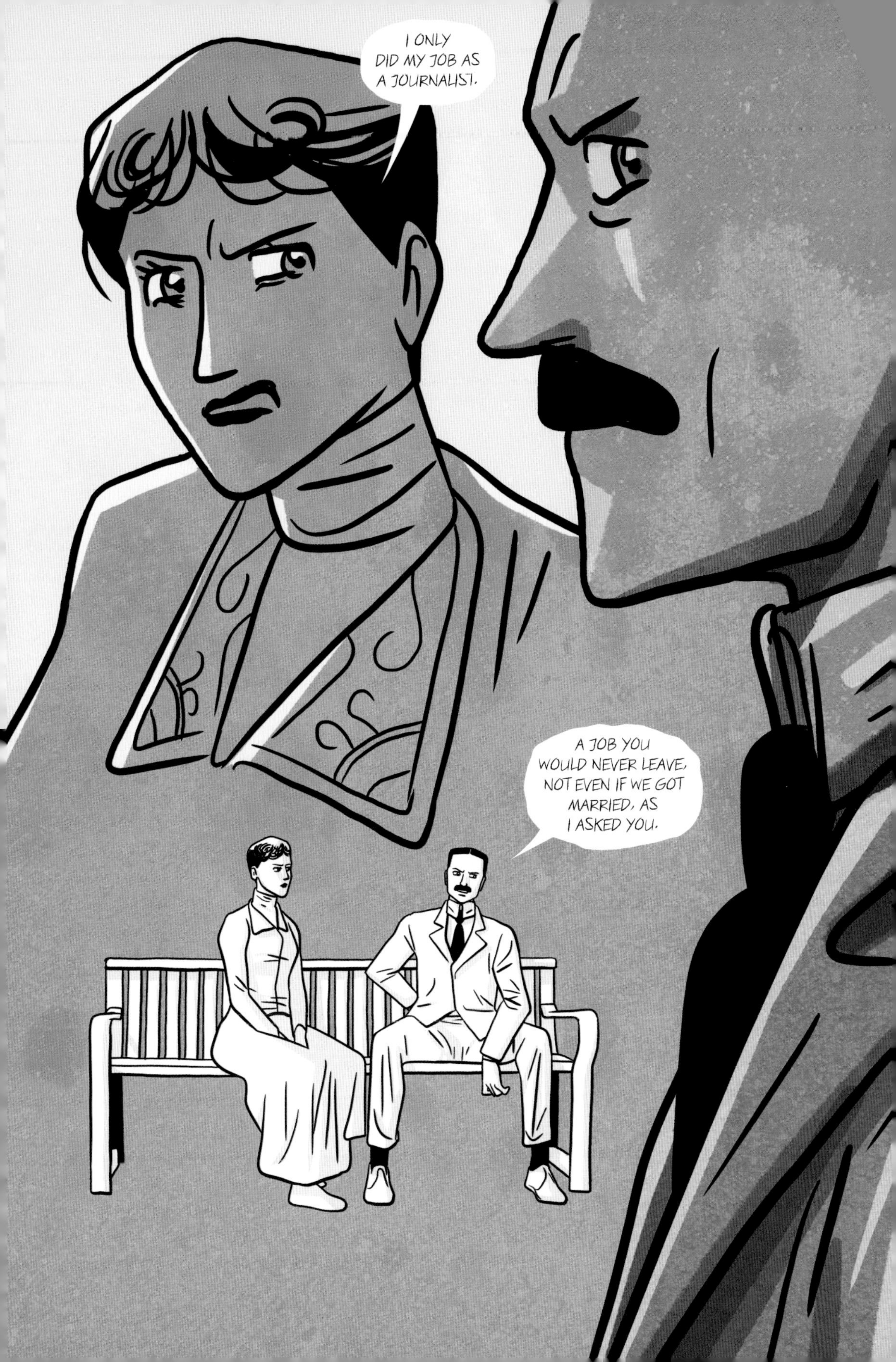
I ONLY DID MY JOB AS A JOURNALIST.
A JOB YOU WOULD NEVER LEAVE, NOT EVEN IF WE GOT MARRIED, AS I ASKED YOU.

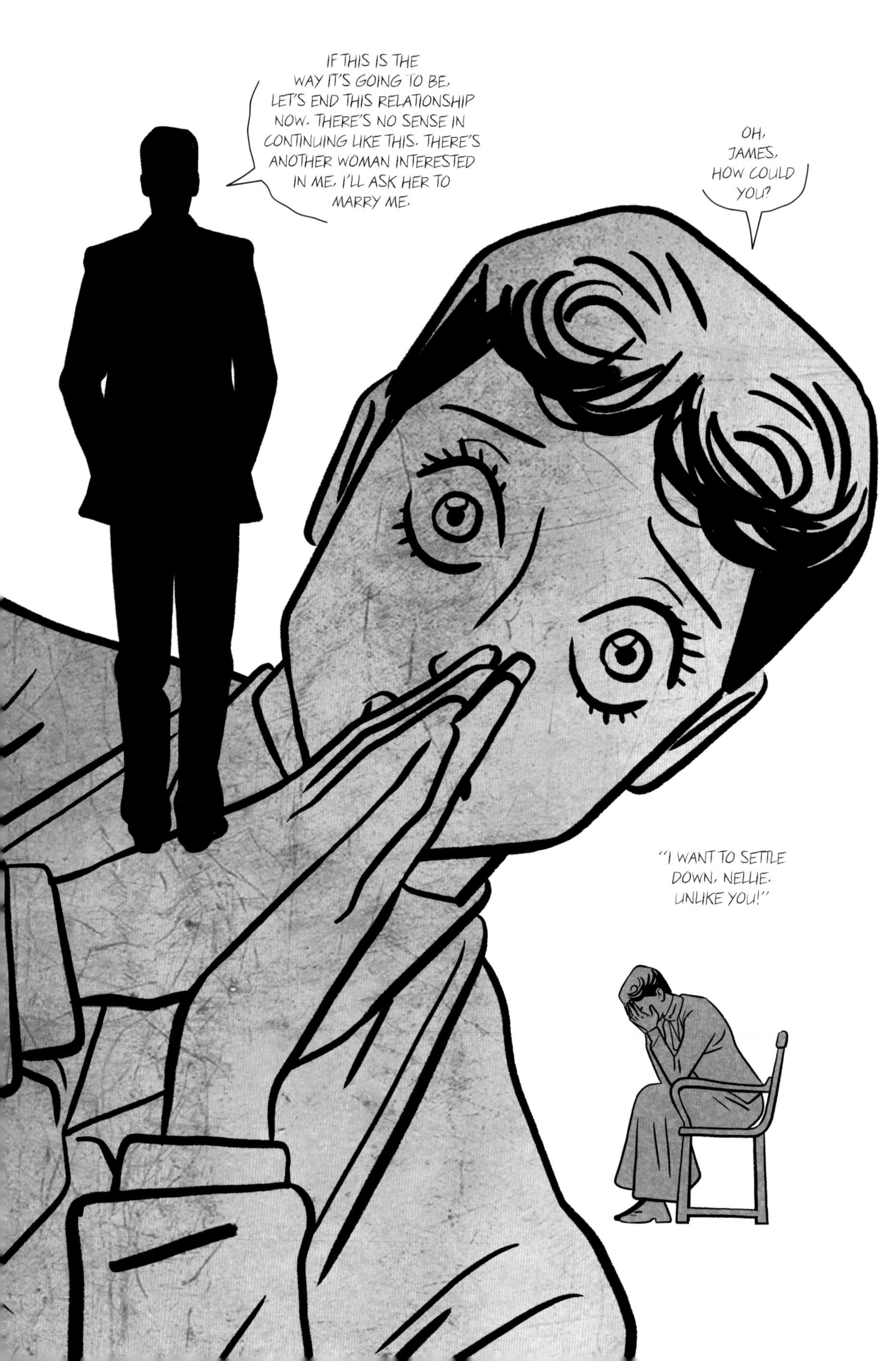
IF THIS IS THE WAY IT'S GOING TO BE, LET'S END THIS RELATIONSHIP NOW. THERE'S NO SENSE IN CONTINUING LIKE THIS. THERE'S ANOTHER WOMAN INTERESTED IN ME. I'LL ASK HER TO MARRY ME.
OH, JAMES, HOW COULD YOU?
"I WANT TO SETTLE DOWN, NELLIE. UNLIKE YOU!"

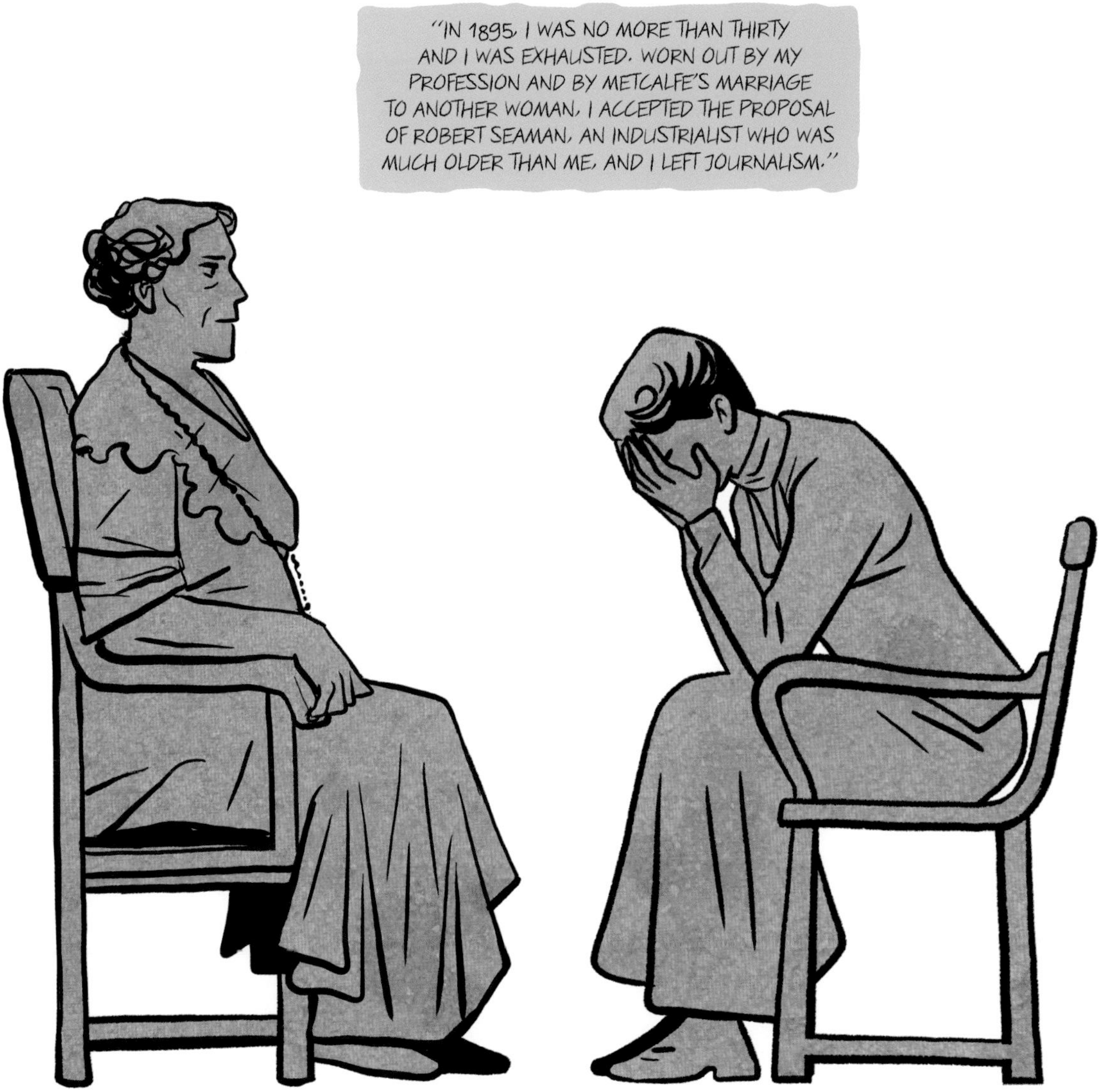
"IN 1895, I WAS NO MORE THAN THIRTY AND I WAS EXHAUSTED. WORN OUT BY MY PROFESSION AND BY METCALFE'S MARRIAGE TO ANOTHER WOMAN, I ACCEPTED THE PROPOSAL OF ROBERT SEAMAN, AN INDUSTRIALIST WHO WAS MUCH OLDER THAN ME, AND I LEFT JOURNALISM."

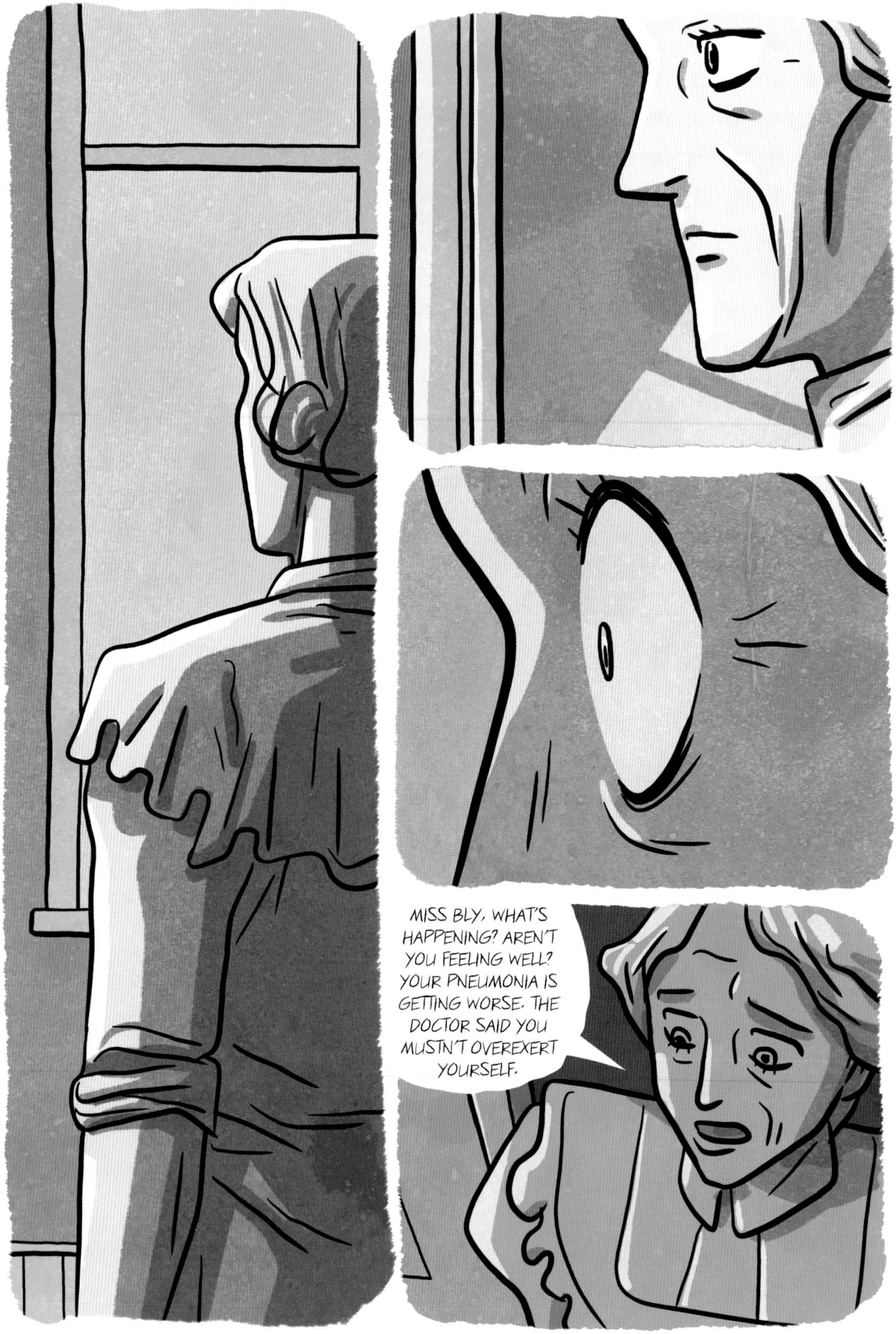
MISS BLY, WHAT'S HAPPENING? AREN'T YOU FEELING WELL? YOUR PNEUMONIA IS GETTING WORSE. THE DOCTOR SAID YOU MUSTN'T OVEREXERT YOURSELF.

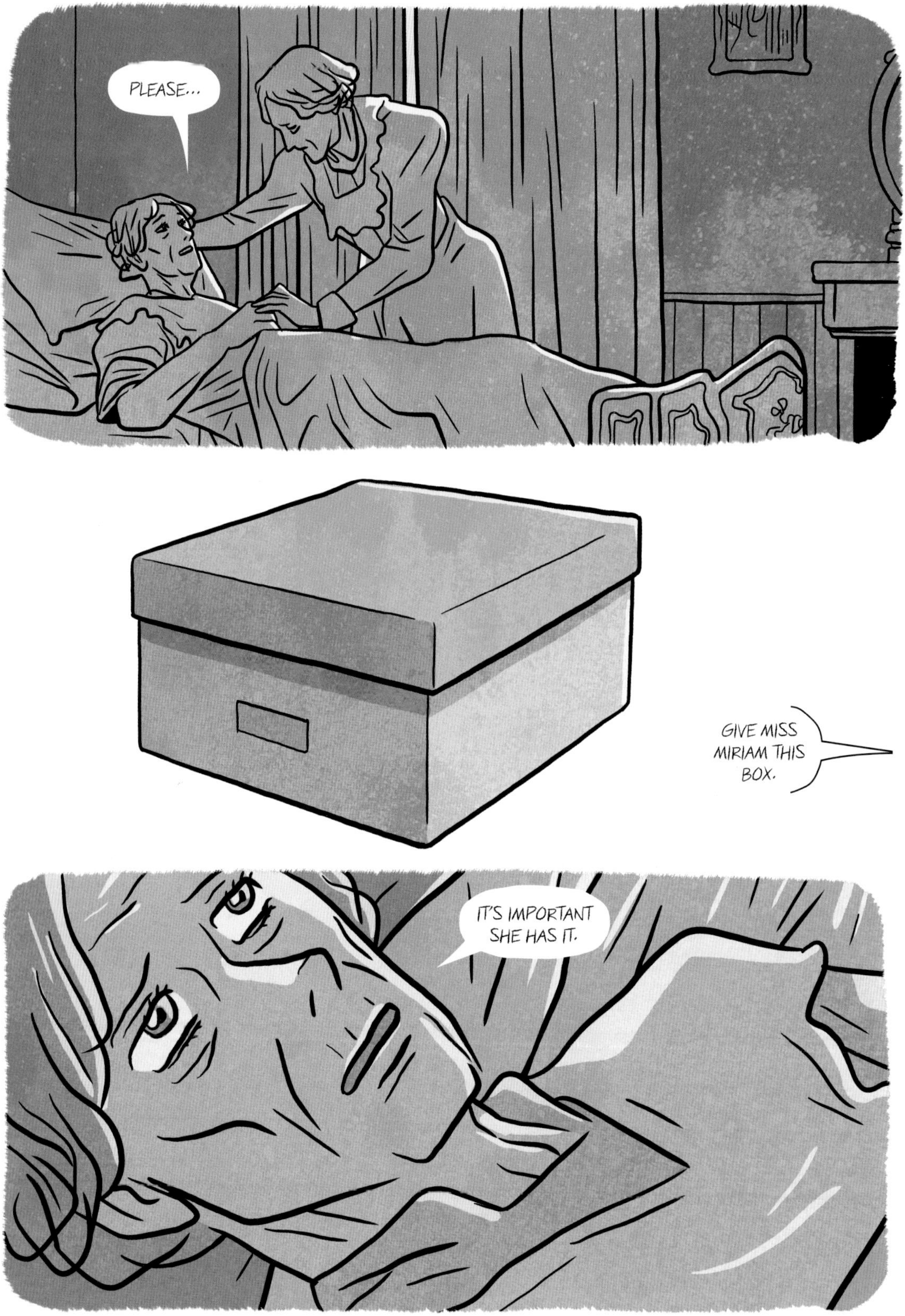
PLEASE...
GIVE MISS MIRIAM THIS BOX.
IT'S IMPORTANT SHE HAS IT.

"SO, DURING THE FIRST YEARS OF THE NEW CENTURY SHE GOT MARRIED... AND THEN WHAT DID SHE DO? WHAT DID SHE TELL YOU?"

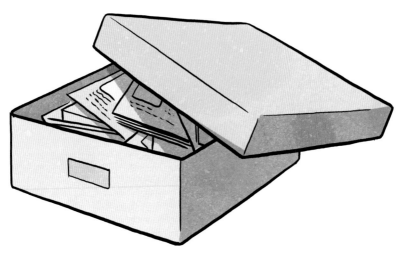

SHE WAS ALWAYS VERY EVASIVE ABOUT THE LAST YEARS. I KNOW WHEN HER HUSBAND DIED, SHE TOOK UP JOURNALISM AGAIN.

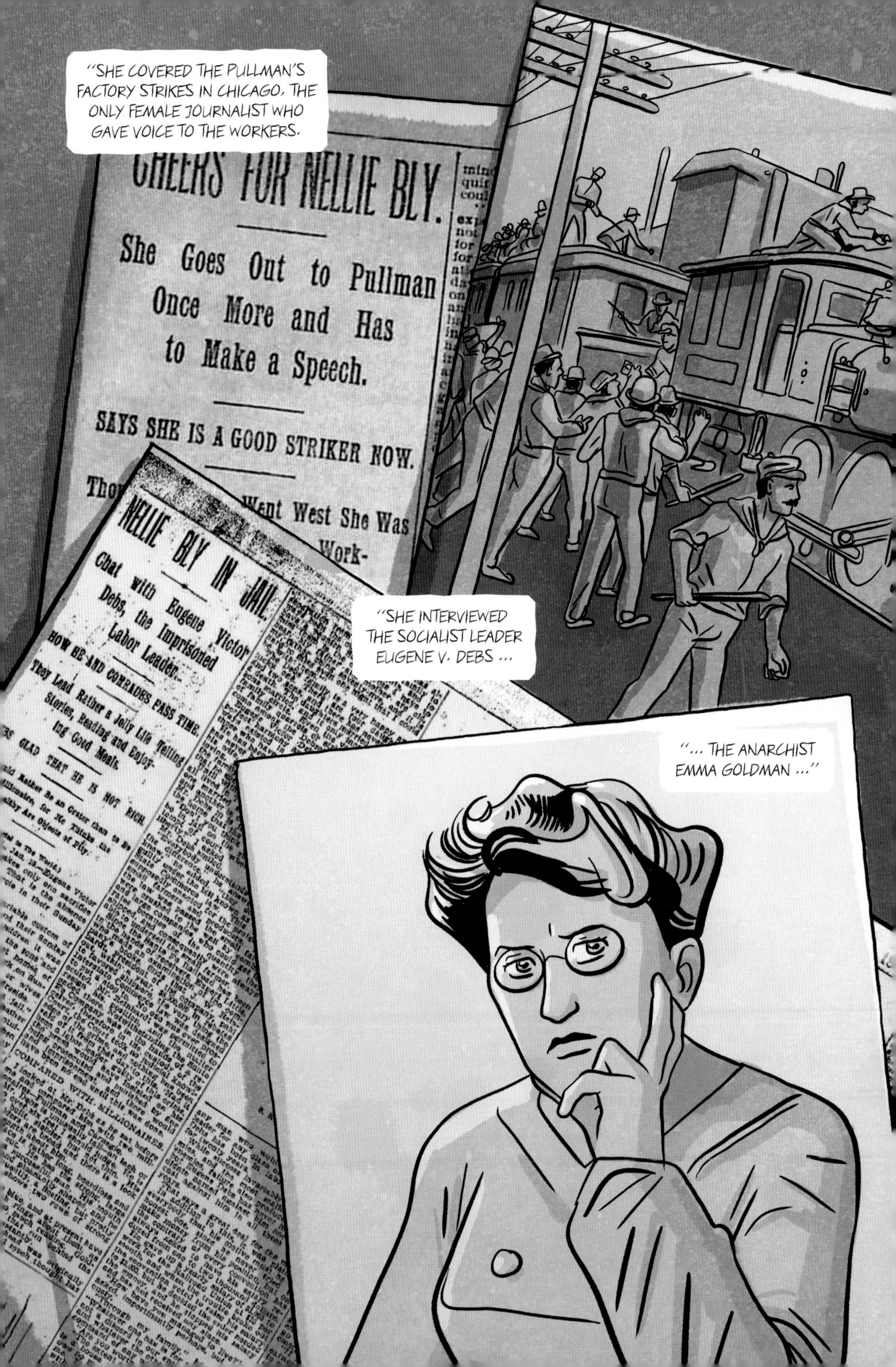
"SHE COVERED THE PULLMAN'S FACTORY STRIKES IN CHICAGO, THE ONLY FEMALE JOURNALIST WHO GAVE VOICE TO THE WORKERS.
CHEERS FOR NELLIE BLY.
She Goes Out to Pullman Once More and Has to Make a Speech.
SAYS SHE IS A GOOD STRIKER NOW.
NELLIE BLY IN JAIL.
Chat with Eugene Victor Debs, the Imprisoned Labor Leader.
HOW HE AND COMRADES PASS TIME.
They Lead Rather a Jolly Life Telling Stories, Reading and Enjoying Good Meals.
"SHE INTERVIEWED THE SOCIALIST LEADER EUGENE V. DEBS ...
"... THE ANARCHIST EMMA GOLDMAN ..."

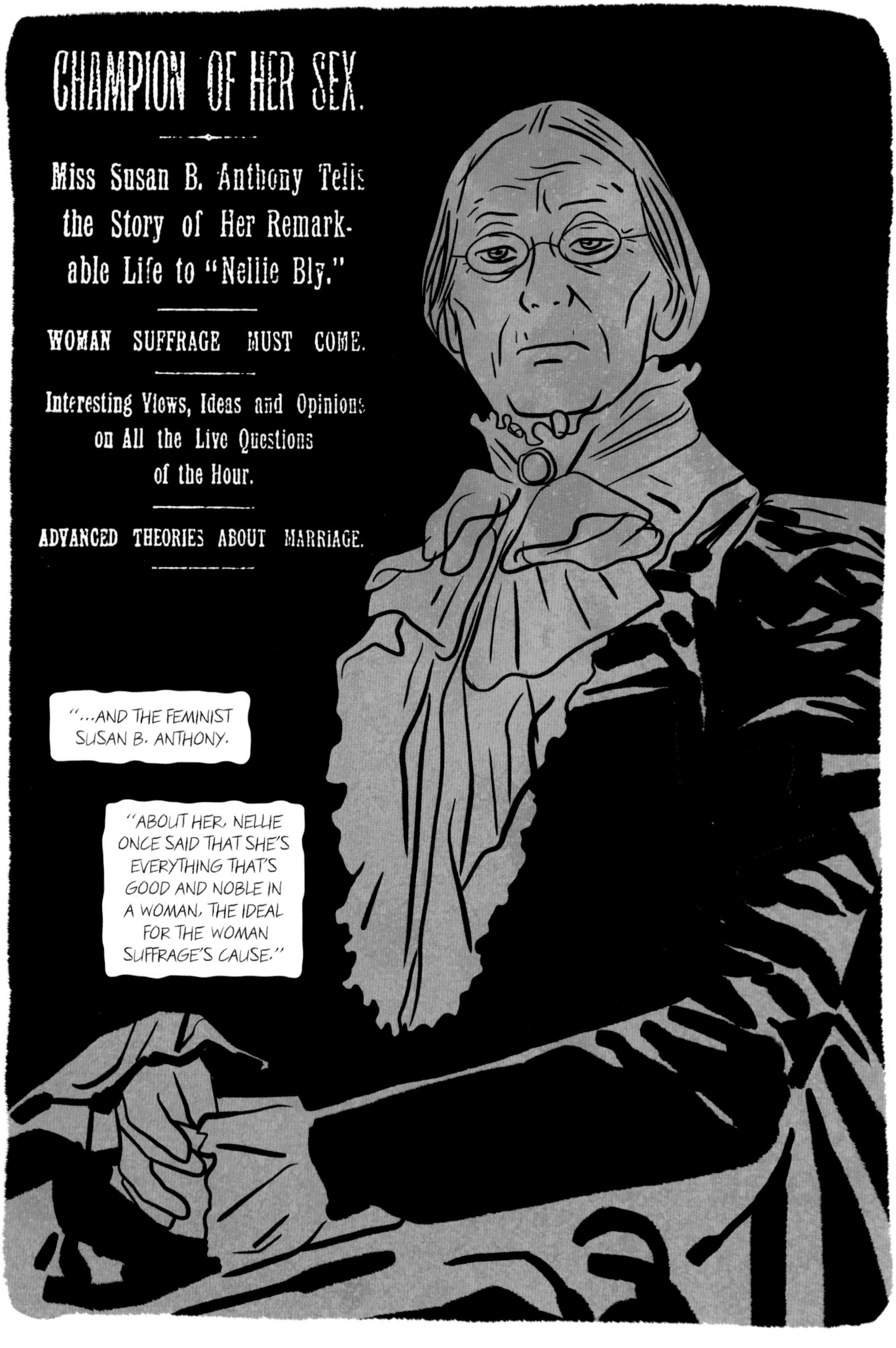
CHAMPION OF HER SEX.
Miss Susan B. Anthony Tells the Story of Her Remarkable Life to "Nellie Bly."
WOMAN SUFFRAGE MUST COME.
Interesting Views, Ideas and Opinions on All the Live Questions of the Hour.
ADVANCED THEORIES ABOUT MARRIAGE.
"...AND THE FEMINIST SUSAN B. ANTHONY.
"ABOUT HER, NELLIE ONCE SAID THAT SHE'S EVERYTHING THAT'S GOOD AND NOBLE IN A WOMAN, THE IDEAL FOR THE WOMAN SUFFRAGE'S CAUSE."

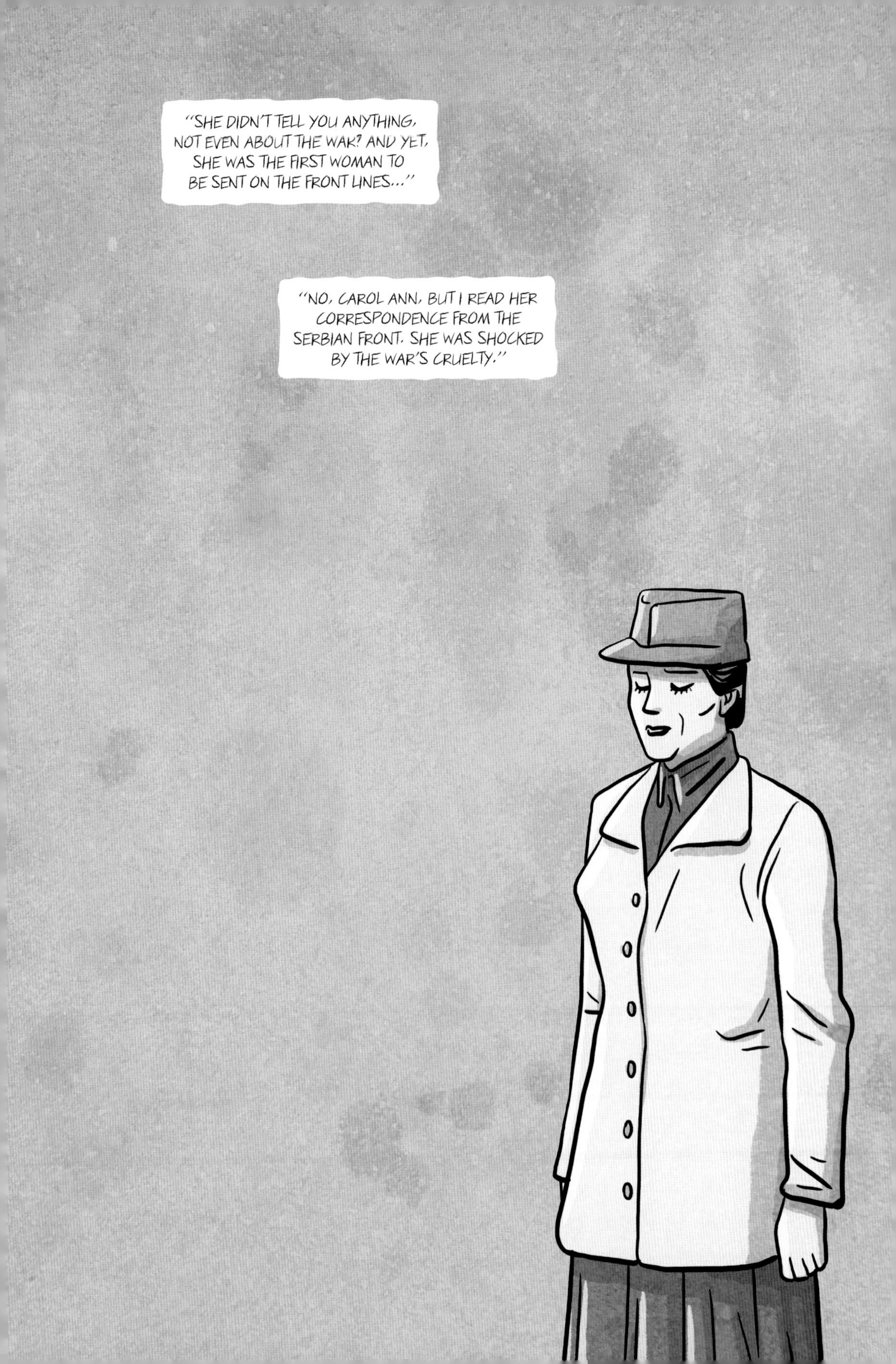
"SHE DIDN'T TELL YOU ANYTHING, NOT EVEN ABOUT THE WAR? AND YET, SHE WAS THE FIRST WOMAN TO BE SENT ON THE FRONT LINES..."
"NO, CAROL ANN, BUT I READ HER CORRESPONDENCE FROM THE SERBIAN FRONT. SHE WAS SHOCKED BY THE WAR'S CRUELTY."

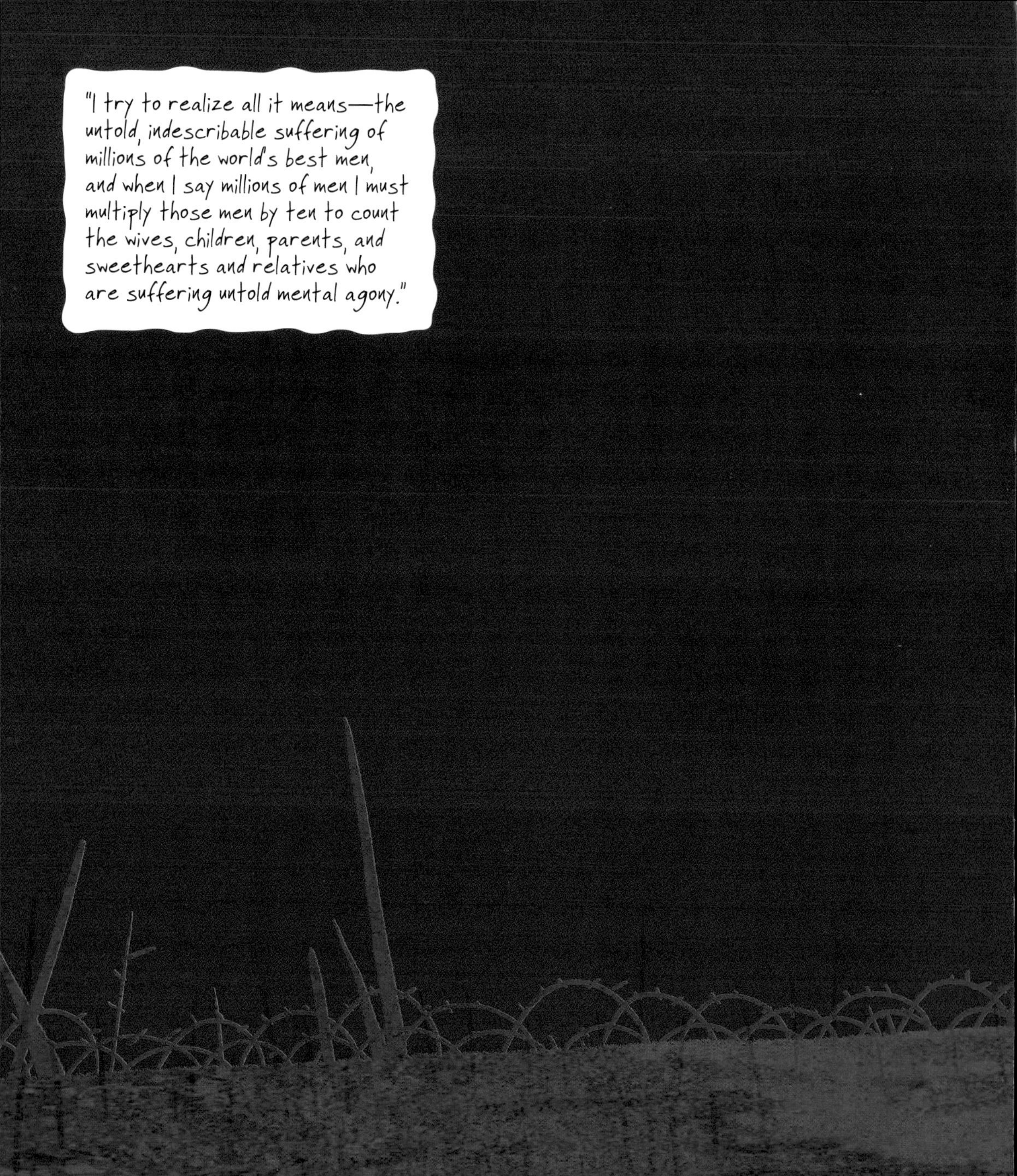
"I try to realize all it means—the untold, indescribable suffering of millions of the world's best men, and when I say millions of men I must multiply those men by ten to count the wives, children, parents, and sweethearts and relatives who are suffering untold mental agony."

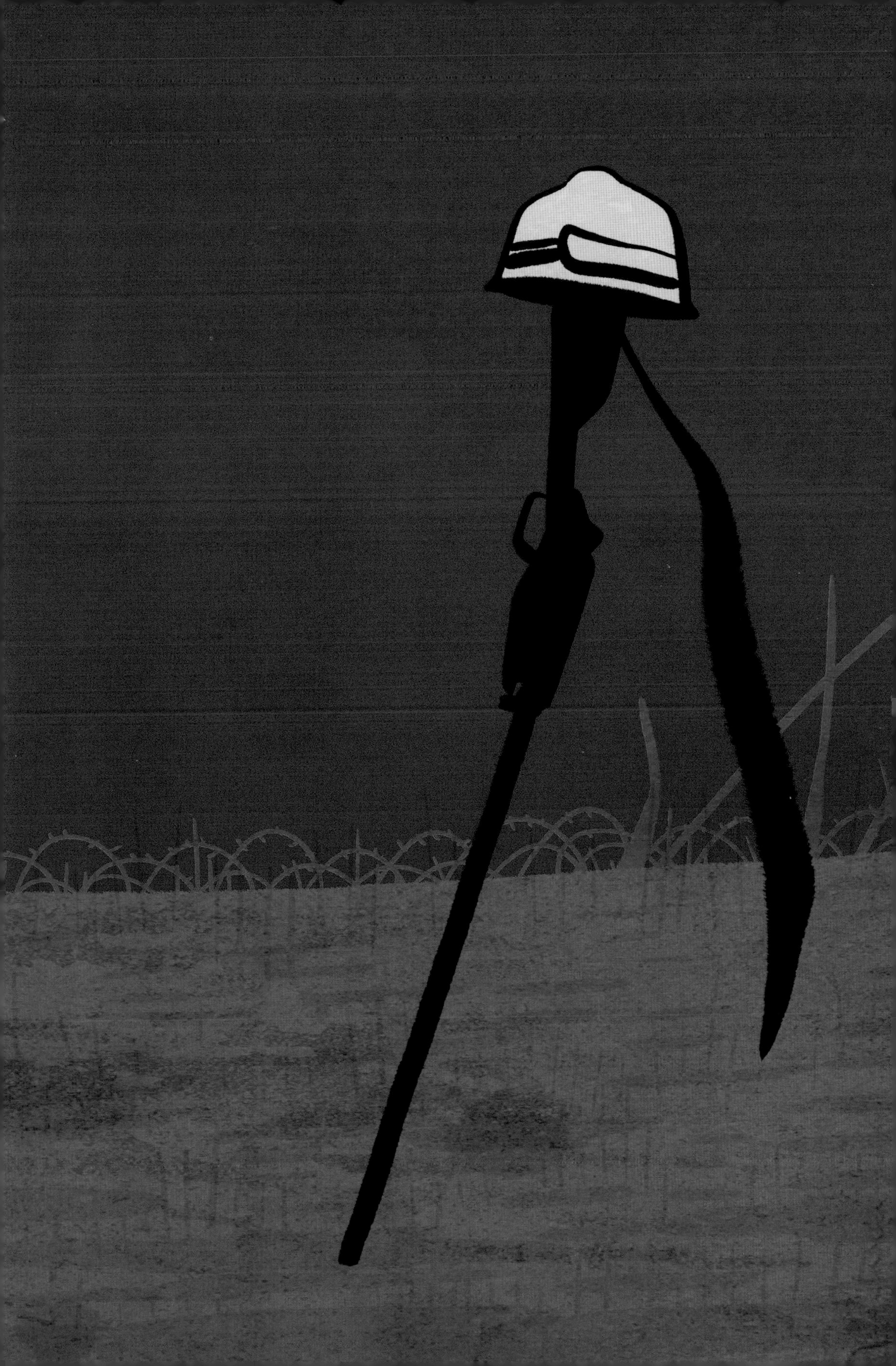

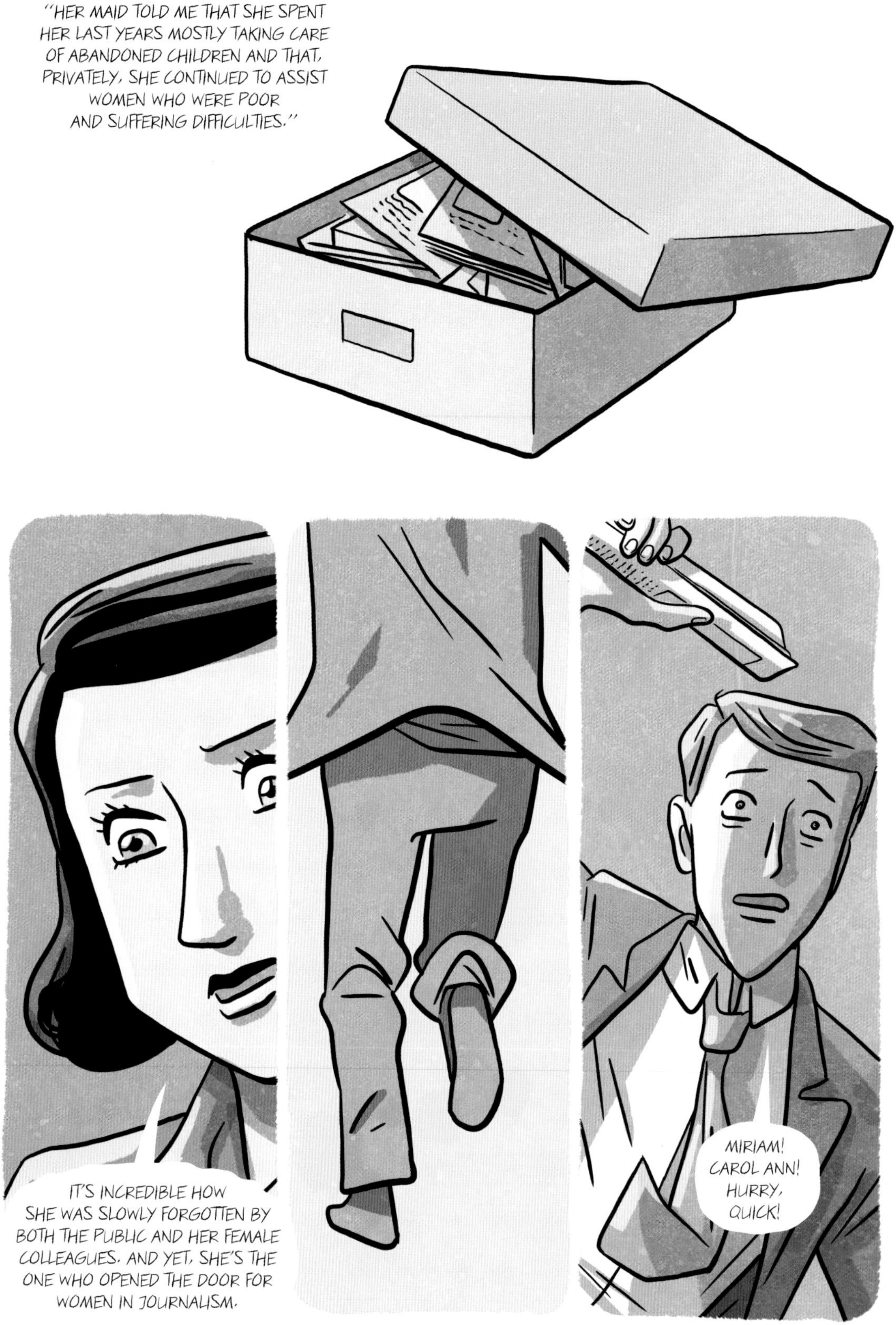
"HER MAID TOLD ME THAT SHE SPENT HER LAST YEARS MOSTLY TAKING CARE OF ABANDONED CHILDREN AND THAT, PRIVATELY, SHE CONTINUED TO ASSIST WOMEN WHO WERE POOR AND SUFFERING DIFFICULTIES."
IT'S INCREDIBLE HOW SHE WAS SLOWLY FORGOTTEN BY BOTH THE PUBLIC AND HER FEMALE COLLEAGUES. AND YET, SHE'S THE ONE WHO OPENED THE DOOR FOR WOMEN IN JOURNALISM.
MIRIAM! CAROL ANN! HURRY, QUICK!

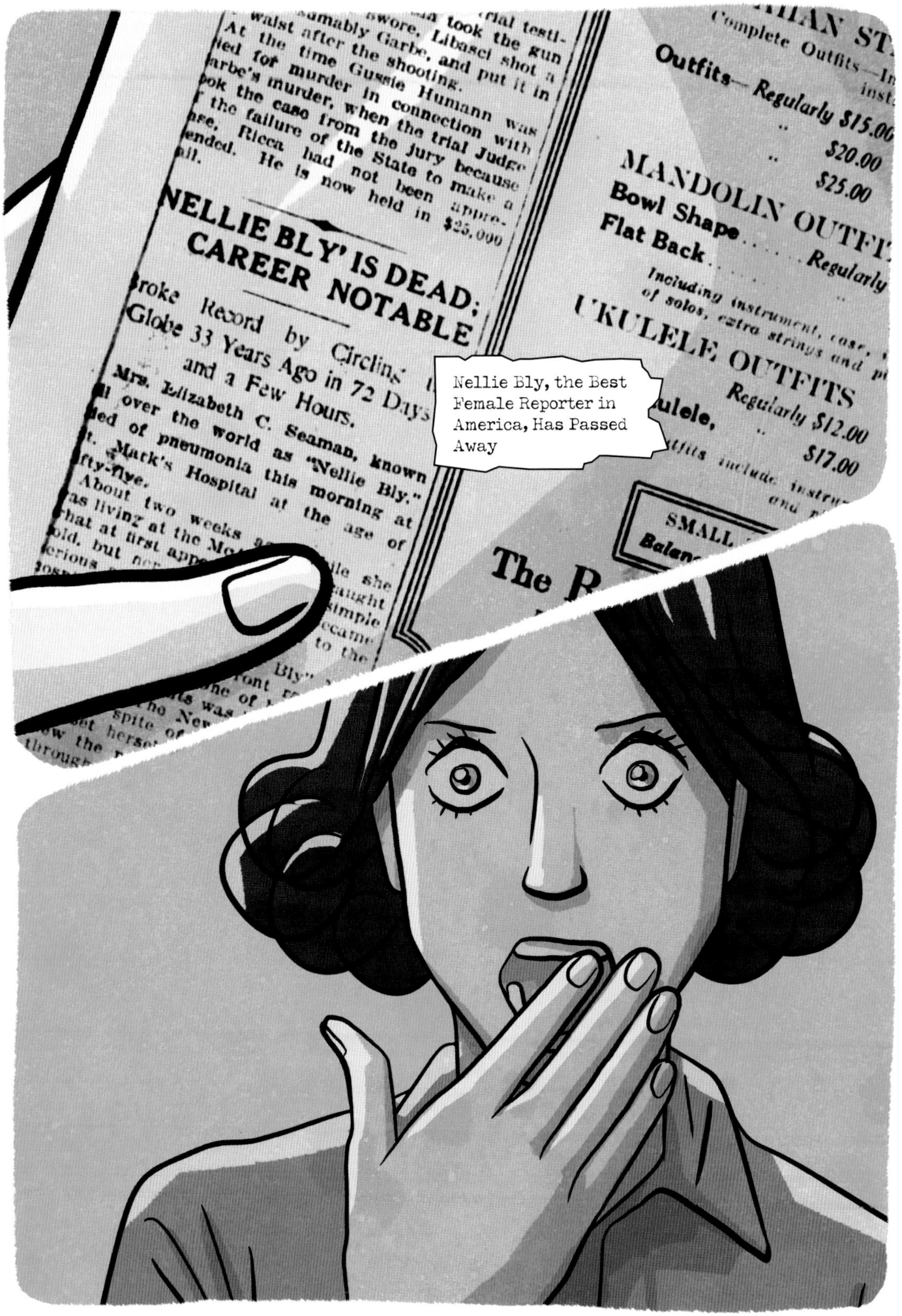
NELLIE BLY' IS DEAD:
CAREER NOTABLE
Nellie Bly, the Best Female Reporter in America, Has Passed Away

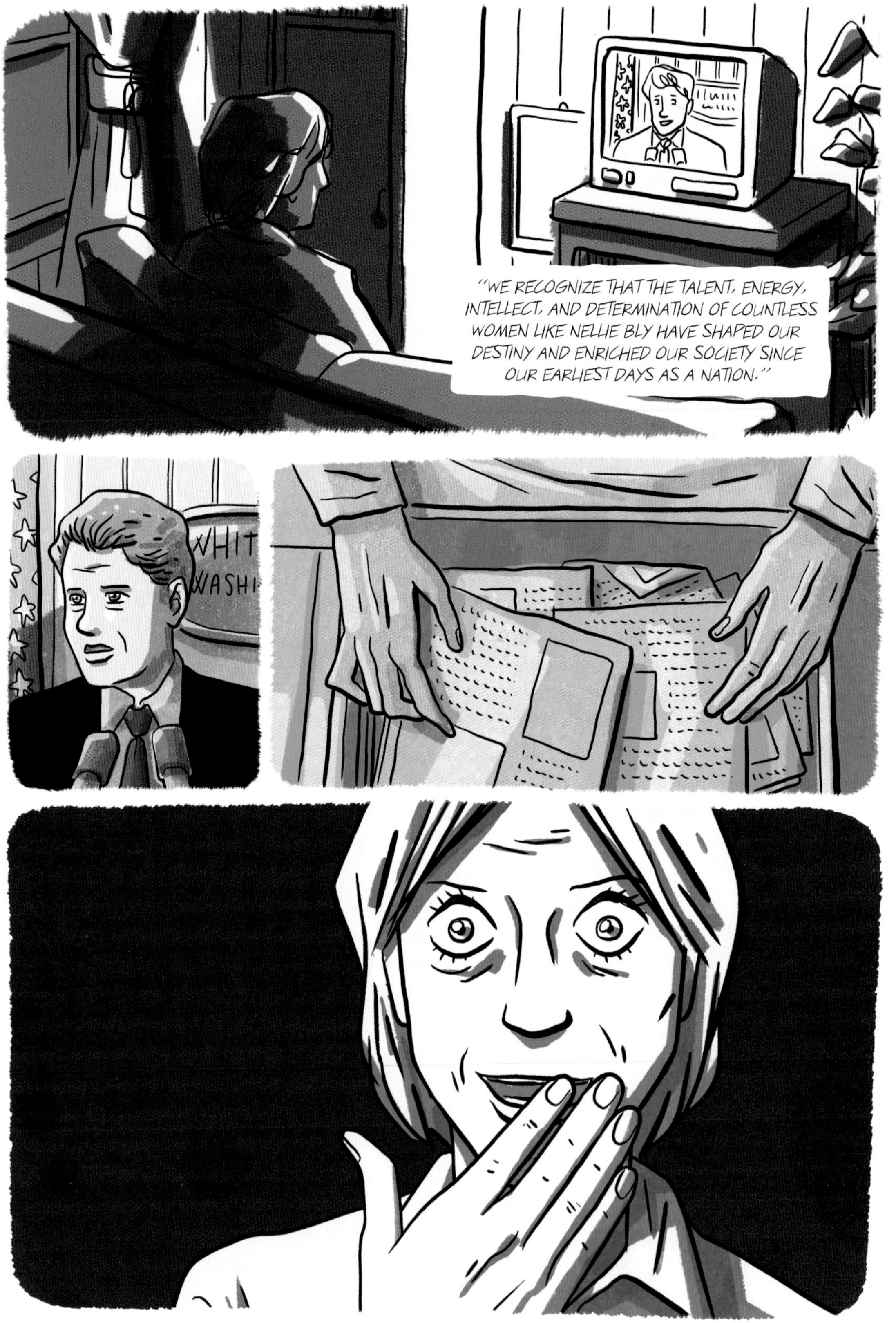
"WE RECOGNIZE THAT THE TALENT, ENERGY, INTELLECT, AND DETERMINATION OF COUNTLESS WOMEN LIKE NELLIE BLY HAVE SHAPED OUR DESTINY AND ENRICHED OUR SOCIETY SINCE OUR EARLIEST DAYS AS A NATION."
WHIT
WASHI

"YOU REALLY WON'T
TELL ME ANYTHING OF
YOUR LAST YEARS?"

"MY DEAR, I **CAN** TELL YOU THAT
I'VE NEVER WRITTEN AN ARTICLE THAT
DIDN'T COME FROM A DEEP FEELING...
ARE YOU SAD, MIRIAM?"

"I THINK THAT WOULD BE
A BEAUTIFUL EPIGRAPH."

"HA HA HA, YOU'RE RIGHT,
BUT I CAN'T MAKE IT MYSELF.
I'LL WRITE IT IN MY LAST PIECE!"

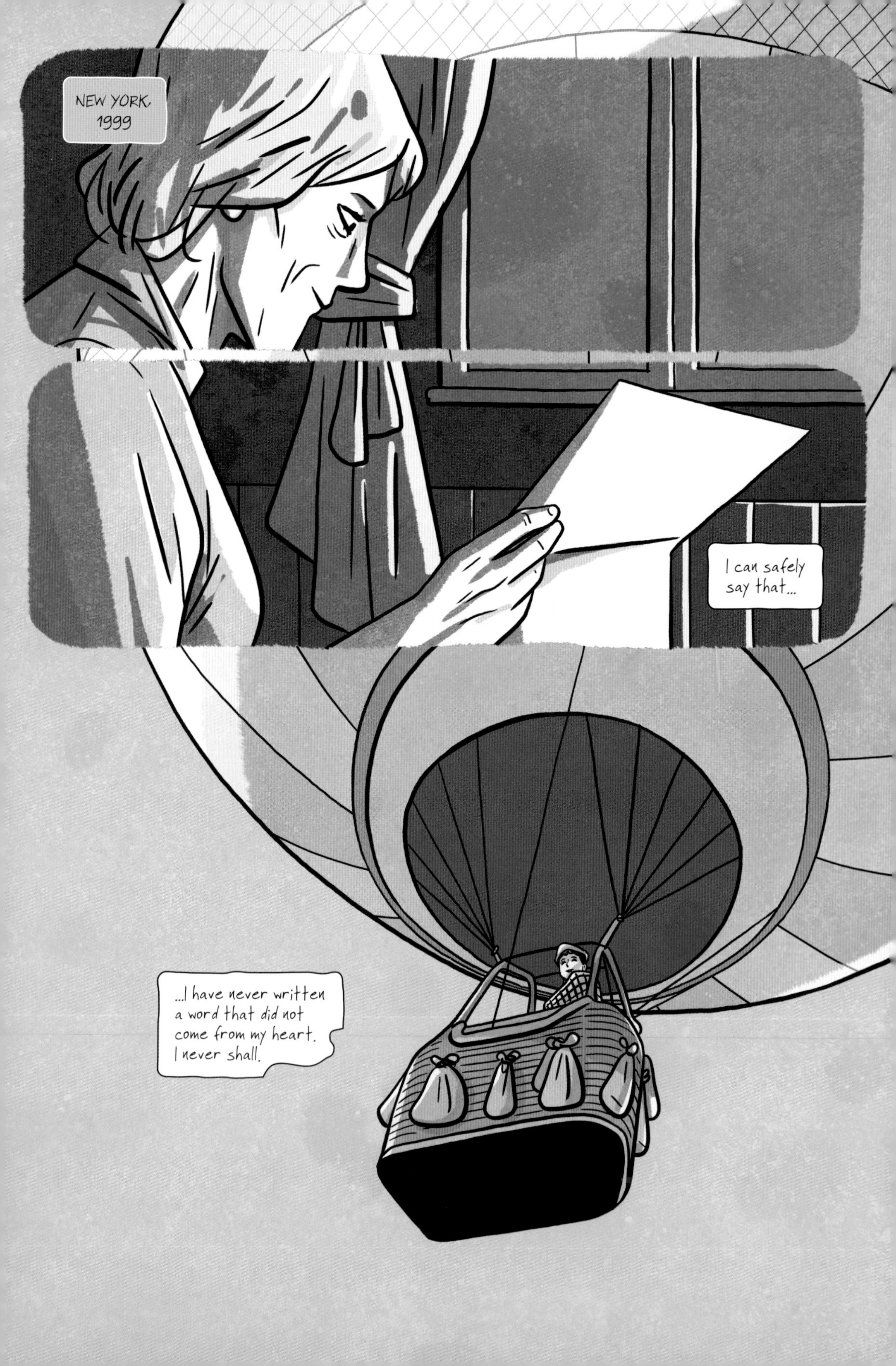
NEW YORK, 1999
I can safely say that...
...I have never written a word that did not come from my heart. I never shall.

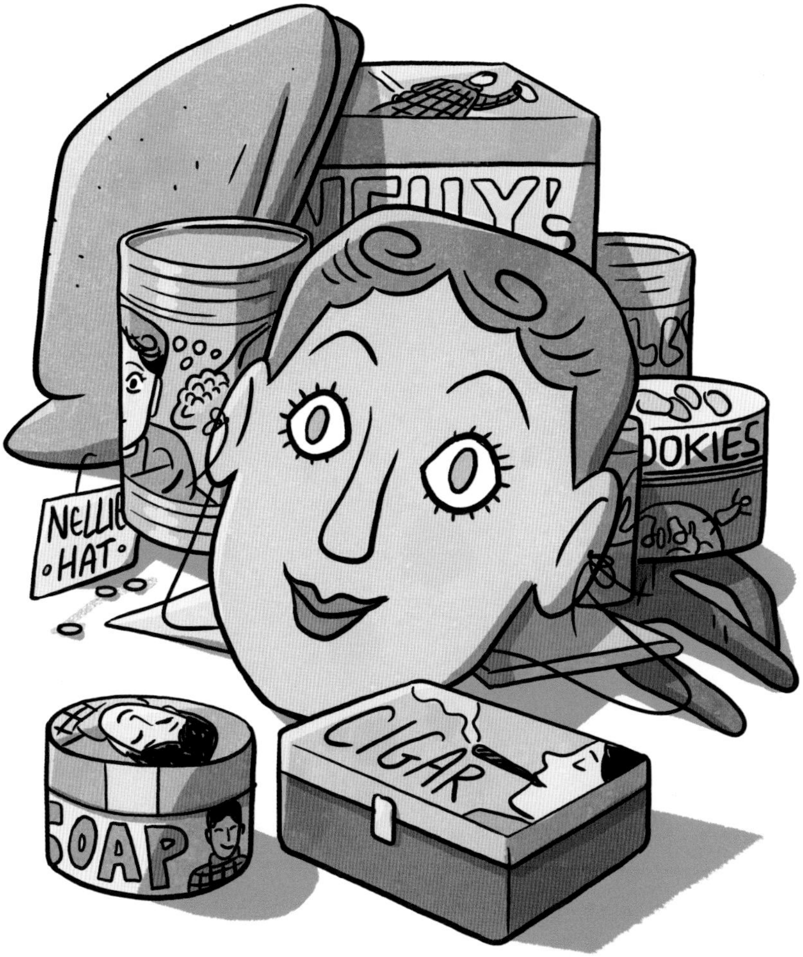
NELLIE
HAT
OOKIES
CIGAR
SOAP

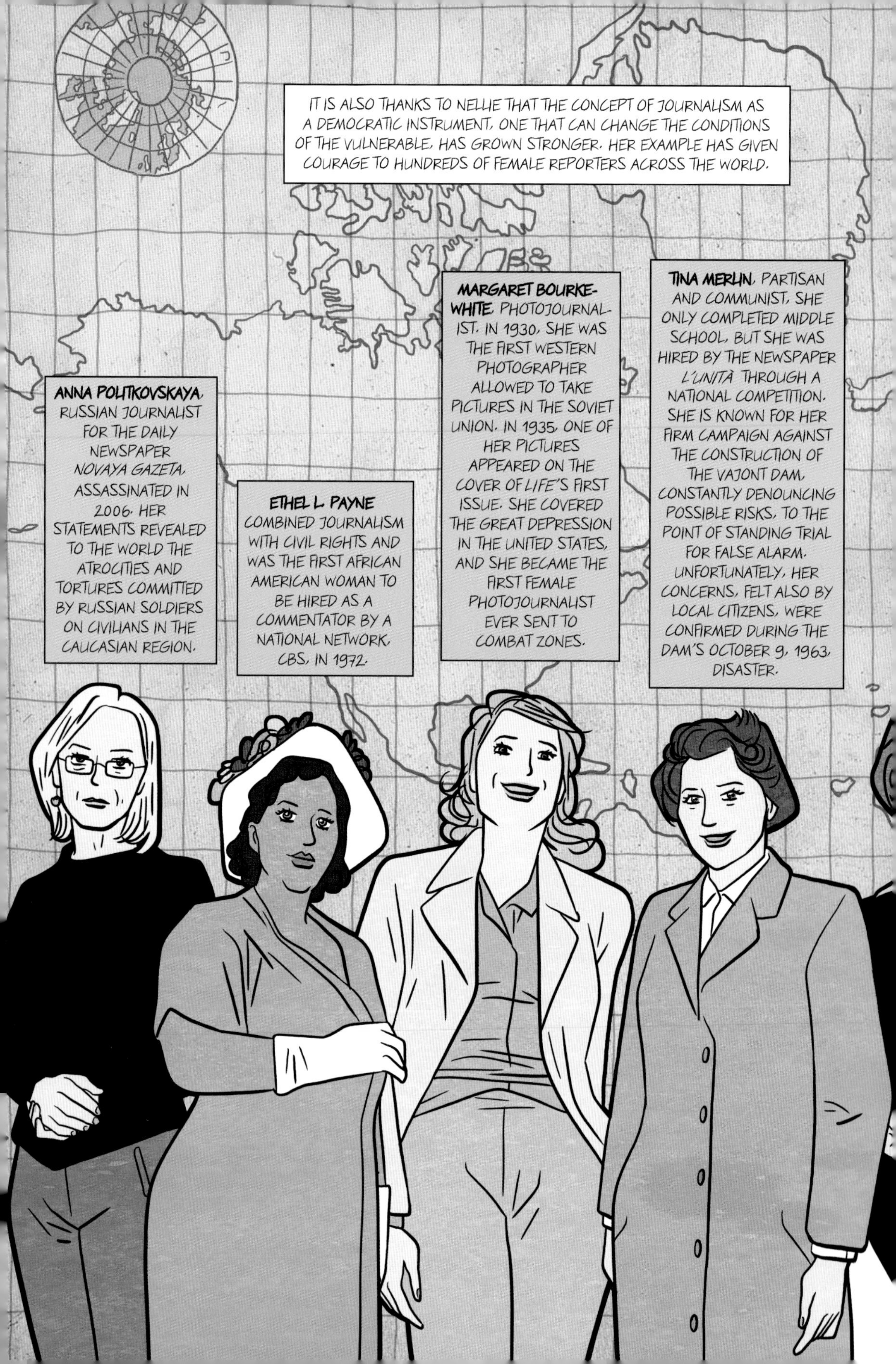
IT IS ALSO THANKS TO NELLIE THAT THE CONCEPT OF JOURNALISM AS A DEMOCRATIC INSTRUMENT, ONE THAT CAN CHANGE THE CONDITIONS OF THE VULNERABLE, HAS GROWN STRONGER. HER EXAMPLE HAS GIVEN COURAGE TO HUNDREDS OF FEMALE REPORTERS ACROSS THE WORLD.
ANNA POLITKOVSKAYA, RUSSIAN JOURNALIST FOR THE DAILY NEWSPAPER *NOVAYA GAZETA*, ASSASSINATED IN 2006. HER STATEMENTS REVEALED TO THE WORLD THE ATROCITIES AND TORTURES COMMITTED BY RUSSIAN SOLDIERS ON CIVILIANS IN THE CAUCASIAN REGION.
ETHEL L. PAYNE COMBINED JOURNALISM WITH CIVIL RIGHTS AND WAS THE FIRST AFRICAN AMERICAN WOMAN TO BE HIRED AS A COMMENTATOR BY A NATIONAL NETWORK, CBS, IN 1972.
MARGARET BOURKE-WHITE, PHOTOJOURNALIST. IN 1930, SHE WAS THE FIRST WESTERN PHOTOGRAPHER ALLOWED TO TAKE PICTURES IN THE SOVIET UNION. IN 1935, ONE OF HER PICTURES APPEARED ON THE COVER OF *LIFE*'S FIRST ISSUE. SHE COVERED THE GREAT DEPRESSION IN THE UNITED STATES, AND SHE BECAME THE FIRST FEMALE PHOTOJOURNALIST EVER SENT TO COMBAT ZONES.
TINA MERLIN, PARTISAN AND COMMUNIST, SHE ONLY COMPLETED MIDDLE SCHOOL, BUT SHE WAS HIRED BY THE NEWSPAPER *L'UNITÀ* THROUGH A NATIONAL COMPETITION. SHE IS KNOWN FOR HER FIRM CAMPAIGN AGAINST THE CONSTRUCTION OF THE VAJONT DAM, CONSTANTLY DENOUNCING POSSIBLE RISKS, TO THE POINT OF STANDING TRIAL FOR FALSE ALARM. UNFORTUNATELY, HER CONCERNS, FELT ALSO BY LOCAL CITIZENS, WERE CONFIRMED DURING THE DAM'S OCTOBER 9, 1963, DISASTER.

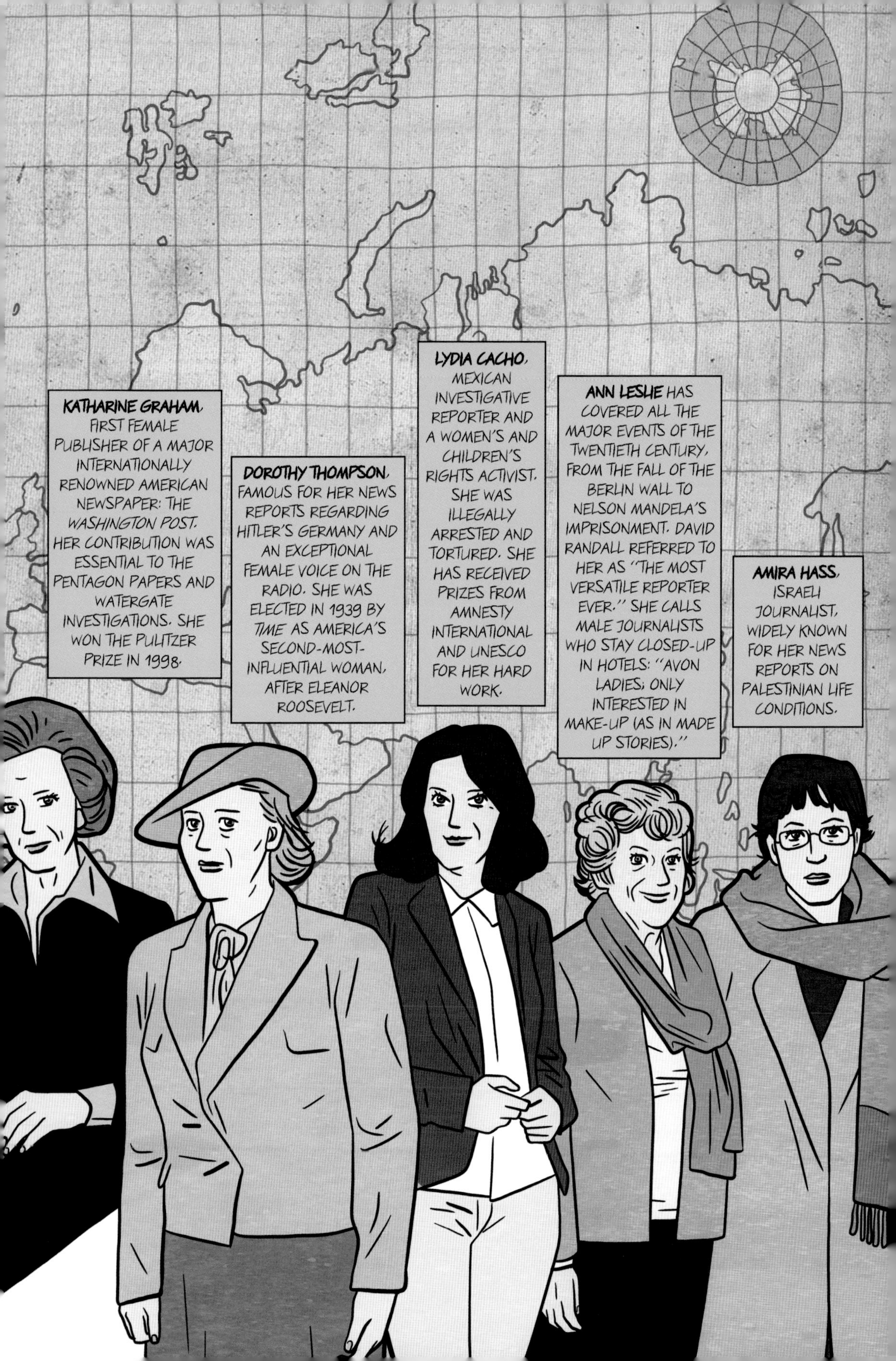
KATHARINE GRAHAM, FIRST FEMALE PUBLISHER OF A MAJOR INTERNATIONALLY RENOWNED AMERICAN NEWSPAPER: THE *WASHINGTON POST*. HER CONTRIBUTION WAS ESSENTIAL TO THE PENTAGON PAPERS AND WATERGATE INVESTIGATIONS. SHE WON THE PULITZER PRIZE IN 1998.
DOROTHY THOMPSON, FAMOUS FOR HER NEWS REPORTS REGARDING HITLER'S GERMANY AND AN EXCEPTIONAL FEMALE VOICE ON THE RADIO. SHE WAS ELECTED IN 1939 BY *TIME* AS AMERICA'S SECOND-MOST-INFLUENTIAL WOMAN, AFTER ELEANOR ROOSEVELT.
LYDIA CACHO, MEXICAN INVESTIGATIVE REPORTER AND A WOMEN'S AND CHILDREN'S RIGHTS ACTIVIST. SHE WAS ILLEGALLY ARRESTED AND TORTURED. SHE HAS RECEIVED PRIZES FROM AMNESTY INTERNATIONAL AND UNESCO FOR HER HARD WORK.
ANN LESLIE HAS COVERED ALL THE MAJOR EVENTS OF THE TWENTIETH CENTURY, FROM THE FALL OF THE BERLIN WALL TO NELSON MANDELA'S IMPRISONMENT. DAVID RANDALL REFERRED TO HER AS "THE MOST VERSATILE REPORTER EVER." SHE CALLS MALE JOURNALISTS WHO STAY CLOSED-UP IN HOTELS: "AVON LADIES; ONLY INTERESTED IN MAKE-UP (AS IN MADE UP STORIES)."
AMIRA HASS, ISRAELI JOURNALIST, WIDELY KNOWN FOR HER NEWS REPORTS ON PALESTINIAN LIFE CONDITIONS.

ABOUT THE
ARTIST

As with any book, I reflected at length on my drawing method. In my opinion, it's the story that's in charge, and every time I write one, I somehow start to create an idea during the drafting process. This time it went differently; the story was already written, thoughts could not emerge in that moment, so it took me a while, during which I did many trials to search for that "voice."

I consider the work on a comic book to be a mystical experience. I can't joke, I can't repeat myself, I can't rest on my laurels, I always need to do something different; I need to try to give something more to the work, but I can't go against the main rule: it's the story that's in charge.

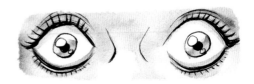

For many years now, I've been using a very thin and not so modulated line, but in this case, I wanted a full, important line, and I would have liked to have painted the panels with an imperfect, quick, instinctive water-color. Unfortunately, the search for a suitable tool for this kind of line was a continuous dead end. I think I tried all the existing pen-brushes on the market. I wanted one with a specific elasticity, which I found in a couple of mark-ers that weren't okay, though, for other reasons (the tip's thickness, the pigment's color, etc.). I didn't dislike the color, but the line was more important, so in the end I opted for a digital attempt. It worked.

This is my first graphic novel that was entirely digitally created. The colors have reached a shade which I couldn't have conceived with a brush, due to certain limits of mine, and I really do hope one can see that little step for-ward that I had promised myself to achieve.

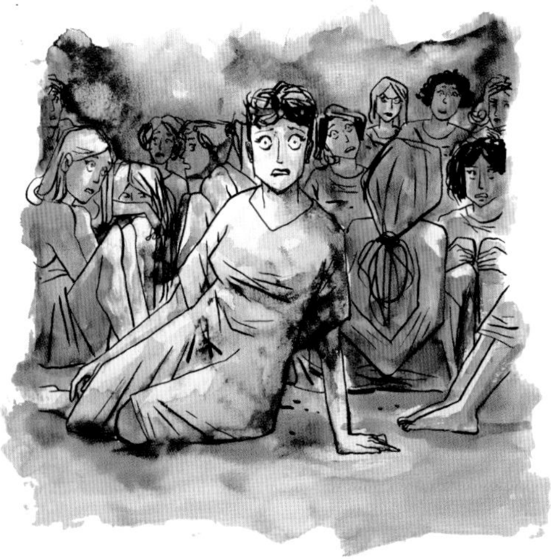

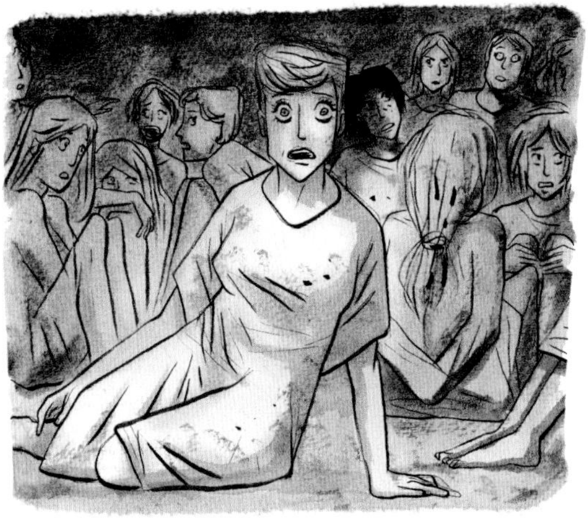

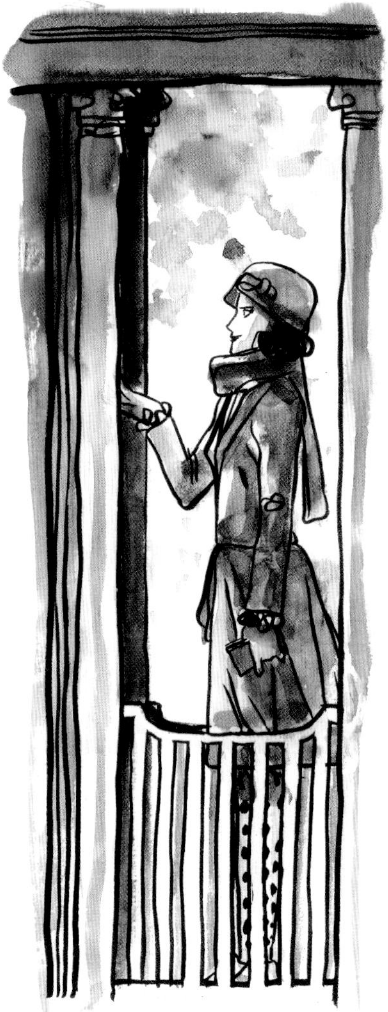

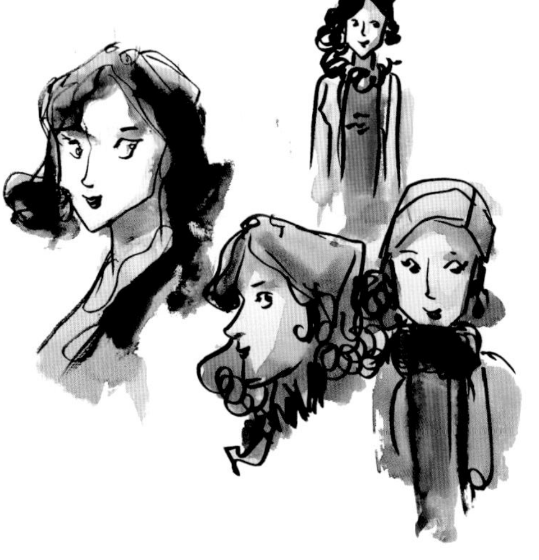

Luciana was fantastic because I let myself get carried away and I didn't limit myself to mechanically drawing what was written in the script. She never flinched; rather, she welcomed my notes and changes with great generosity. She made me feel like a complete author, even with a story that wasn't created and written by me, letting me actively participate in Nellie's tale.

These are just some of the attempts made during the reflective stage, where it's possible to notice changes in the atmosphere, in the shades, and above all in the thickness of the line.

Sergio

BIBLIOGRAPHY

Bly Nellie. 1887. "The Girls Who Make Boxes." *The New York World*, November 27, 1887.

Ibid. 1885. "Girl Puzzle." *The Pittsburgh Dispatch*, January 25,1885. https://efbbc0aa-141e-46c5-b161-0aa2d1550ca8.filesusr.com/ugd/d9c14a_1cb8374ac5f44fbab487816e111ef3e1.pdf.

Ibid. 1885. "Mad Marriage." *The Pittsburgh Dispatch*, February 1,1885. https://efbbc0aa-141e-46c5-b161-0aa2d1550ca8.filesusr.com/ugd/d9c14a_5fe8bff57798482d98a4dfd292a7fe0a.pdf.

Ibid. 1887. "Behind Asylum Bars." *The New York World*, October 8, 1887. https://thegrandarchive.wordpress.com/behind-asylum-bars/.

Ibid. 1888. "The King of the Lobby." *The New York World*, April 1, 1888. https://thegrandarchive.wordpress.com/the-king-of-the-lobby/.

Ibid. 1914. "Nellie Bly Describes War Horrors." *The New York Evening-Journal*, December 8, 1914. https://lccn.loc.gov/2004540423.

Ibid. *Around the World in 72 Days*. New York: The Pictorial Weeklies Company, 1890.

Ibid. *Six Months in Mexico*. New York: American Publishers Corporation, 1888.

Ibid. *The Collected Works of Nellie Bly* (Annotated). Golgotha Press, 2015

Erasmus, Wilson. 1885. "Quiet Observations." *The Pittsburgh Dispatch*, January 27,1885. https://efbbc0aa-141e-46c5-b161-0aa2d1550ca8.filesusr.com/ugd/d9c14a_f8078723fe7f45a8aa00af78aa1c918c.pdf.

Goodman, Matthew. *Eighty Days: Nellie Bly and Elizabeth Bisland's History–Making Race Around the World*. New York: Random House, 2013.

Graves, Lisa. *Trail Blazers: An Illustrated Guide to the Women Who Explored the World*. Irvine, CA: Xist Publishing, 2014.

Kroeger, Brooke *Nellie Bly: Daredevil, Reporter, Feminist*. Times Books. (1994).

New York World. 1887. Multiple articles. *The New York World*, October 9, 1887. http://sites.dlib.nyu.edu/undercover/sites/dlib.nyu.edu.undercover/files/documents/uploads/editors/The%20Nellie%20Brown%20Mystery_0.pdf.

New York World. 1890. "Father Time Outdone!" *The New York Word*, January 25, 1890.

Proclamation No. 7170, 73 Fed. Reg. vol. 64 no. 41 (March 3, 1999).

Scatamacchia, Caterina. *Nellie Bly: Un'avventurosa giornalista e viaggiatrice americana dell'Ottocento*. Italy: Morlacchi Editore, 2014.

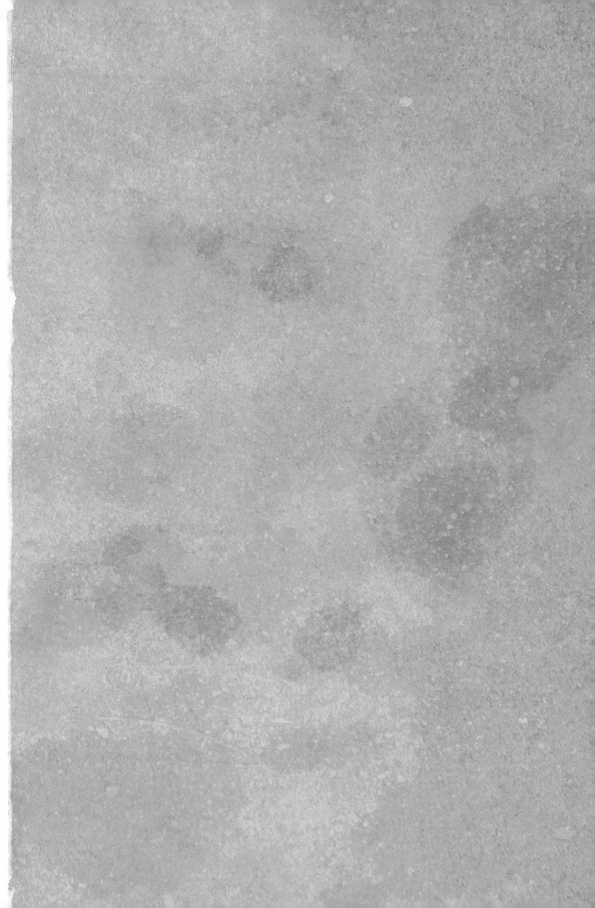

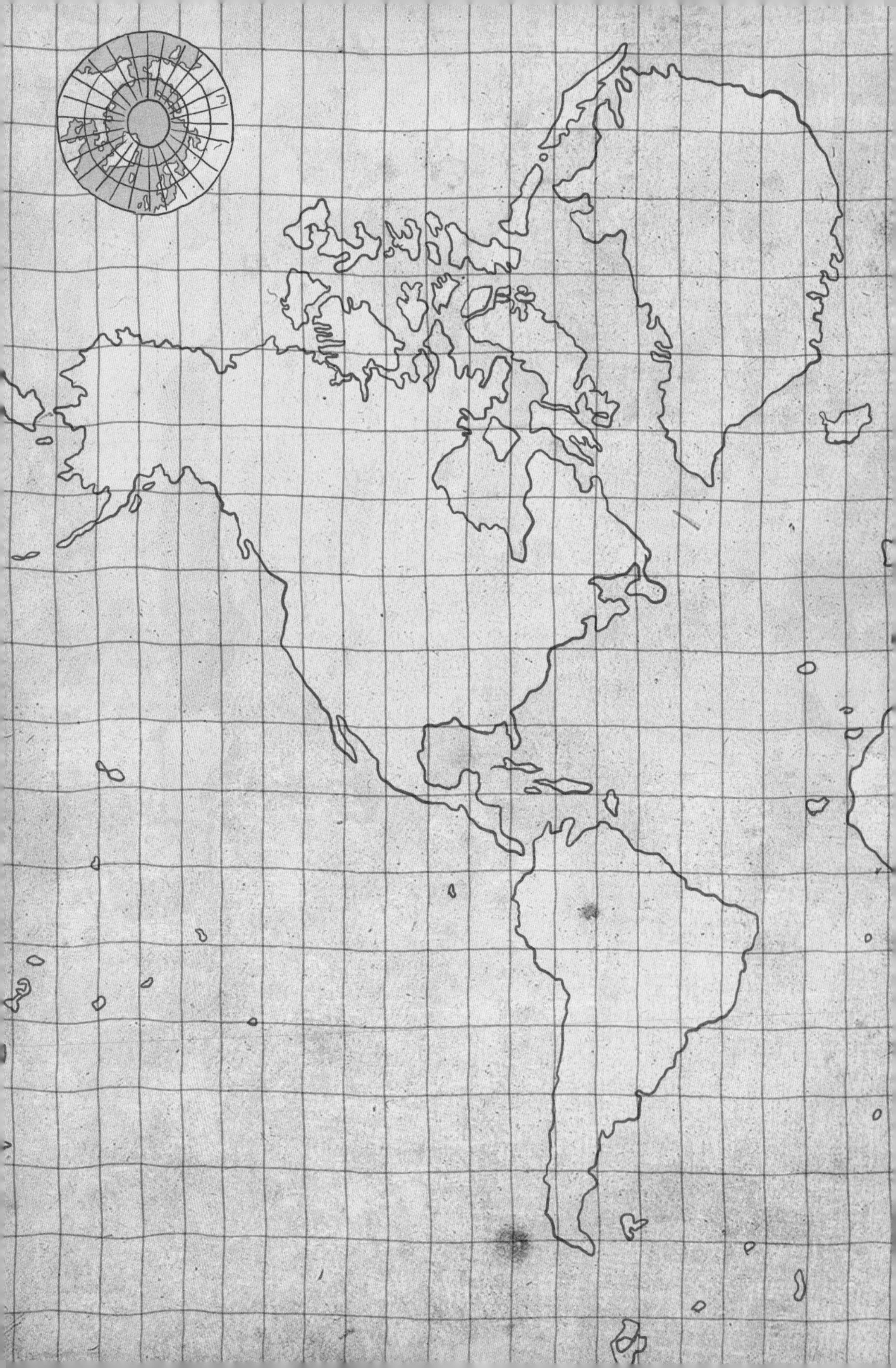